DATE DUE

Creativity and Madness

ALBERT ROTHENBERG, M.D.

CREATIVITY

◆ and

MADNESS

New Findings and Old Stereotypes

THE JOHNS HOPKINS UNIVERSITY PRESS
Baltimore and London

To the memory of my mother and father

© 1990   The Johns Hopkins University Press
All rights reserved
Printed in the United States of America

The Johns Hopkins University Press
701 West 40th Street, Baltimore, Maryland 21211
The Johns Hopkins Press Ltd., London

(∞) The paper used in this book meets the minimum
requirements of American National Standard for
Information Sciences—Permanence of Paper for
Printed Library Materials, ANSI Z39.48–1984.

Library of Congress Cataloging-in-Publication Data

Rothenberg, Albert, 1930–
    Creativity and madness : new findings and old stereotypes / Albert
Rothenberg
        p.   cm.
    Includes bibliographical references.
    ISBN 0–8018–4011–2
    1. Creative ability.   2. Mental illness.   I. Title.
BF408.R682   1990
153.3′5—dc20   90–30770   CIP

CONTENTS

ACKNOWLEDGMENTS

Portions of the material in this book have appeared in different versions in the following: *Saturday Review; American Poetry Review; College English; Psychology Today; American Journal of Social Psychiatry; Literature and Psychology; Sexual Behavior; Journal of the American Psychoanalytic Association; Psychiatry; Psychoanalysis, Creativity, and Literature* (Alan Roland, editor, Columbia University Press). I gratefully acknowledge my research subjects and my patients who provided the data, information, and experience used in this book and Austen Riggs Center (Daniel P. Schwartz, medical director), Yale University, National Institute of Mental Health, Gladys B. Ficke Estate, John Simon Guggenheim Foundation, Center for Advanced Study in the Behavioral Sciences, John D. and Catherine T. MacArthur Foundation, and Harvard University, who provided both occupational and financial support along the way.

For help with particular studies, I thank Donald Gallup and the Beinecke Rare Book Library of Yale University (O'Neill), Martha N. Noblick of the Jones Library of Amherst (Dickinson), Dr. Theodore Lidz (for first introducing me to the work and biography of August Strindberg), and Craig Daley (alcoholism). Special appreciation goes to Helen W. Linton, librarian of Austen Riggs Center, for her breadth of helpful knowledge, skilled reference work, and diligent procurement of bibliographic materials. Virginia Heaton helped with word processing of early drafts, but the major portion of the difficult and meticulous work of word processing this book into existence was carried out by Wendy Menatti. To her, I express warm appreciation. To my wife and love, Dr. Julia Rothenberg, whose heart and thoughts were with me through the writing of every word in this book, go my unstinting admiration and deep gratitude.

1 ◆◇ A Scientist Looks at Creativity

To start with, let me tell you some stories or, if you will, myths. You are walking near the park of a very large city. As you stroll, you become aware of a person walking toward you, half shaded by the streetlight, looking deep in thought, virtually rapt in concentration. He is medium tall, quite thin, and sensitive looking, with a slightly unkempt appearance. He is remarkably handsome, with hair that is long and full. As he approaches you, you are enormously surprised to see his expression change while his face suddenly lights up with excitement and pleasure. Without noticing your presence at all, he wheels around sharply, hurriedly retraces his steps in the opposite direction, and disappears in a doorway approximately half a block away.

Because of the strangeness of the experience, you follow him to the doorway through which he disappeared and, noticing a doorman standing there, you can't resist asking who this person was who so quickly entered in that door. The doorman, who, in this particular city would otherwise be quite surly to any passerby asking a question about one of the tenants of the building, cocks his head half in pride and half in amusement and says, "Oh, that's W. B. Y., the famous poet." Then he adds, as if to answer an unasked question, "A little strange, you know."

Recognizing the poet's name immediately as that of a winner of a Nobel Prize, you, too, are now transported. You begin to imagine the poet in his luxurious apartment upstairs, sitting down immediately at his desk and working on the inspiration he just had (for you now realize that *that* is exactly why he stopped suddenly on the street), feverishly engaged in writing his poem. As you walk on, you may think of him as staying up all night to continue working until he finishes the poem. Or, you may fantasize that he goes to bed for only a few hours and once again is aroused by an inner force that drives him back to the poem because he cannot stop, or sleep, until he completes it. When the poem is done, the next morning, you are sure it will be another one of his masterpieces, and you make a note of the date on which all of this occurred so that you can be sure to recognize the exact work when it is published.

Another story comes from another period of history, in ancient Greece, and another type of artistic medium—painting. At a large art exhibit in Athens, two artists named Zeuxis and Parrhasios are publicly discussing Zeuxis' painting in which he has depicted grapes that look so real that Parrhasios at first thinks they are actual grapes. They decide to take the painting outside for a test, and while several people look on, sparrows swoop down and attempt to peck at these painted grapes. Parrhasios is impressed and then says that he wants Zeuxis and the onlookers to come to his studio because he believes he can show Zeuxis a painting that also has a high degree of verisimilitude, or an uncanny resemblance to reality. When they arrive at the studio, Parrhasios points to a painting in the corner that demonstrates his own ability in this area. Zeuxis walks over and he turns to his colleague saying, "Would you please part the curtains on the painting so that I may see the subject." Parrhasios says that he cannot do so, unfortunately, because the curtains *are* the painting. Amazed, Zeuxis says, "You are better than I. I took in the sparrows, but you took me in."

The onlookers to all of this exchange between the two painters marvel at the events. They speak of Parrhasios as always having been a person of extraordinary talent. People whisper that they had heard that when he was a child, he could remember every single article of furniture in a room, every color, and every texture many months after having seen the room only once.

The final legend, myth, or story about a person of genius concerns the man or woman of science who slaves and slaves, attempting to solve a crucial problem until one day, while on vacation, or when sleeping at night, or when talking to a colleague—to cover several different legendary accounts—the solution bursts upon him or her ready-made as though welling up from the unconscious or coming as a stroke of lightning from a mysterious source.

In contrast to these stories, but related to them, are the mythic stories about the dreary homemaker or the driving business executive, the deteriorated schizophrenic, the enslaved drug addict, or merely every one of us ordinary persons who turns to so-called creative activities such as drawing and painting, or playing music, or acting in community theater, or learning to dance and use so-called creative movement, and who then experiences a sense of *transformation* in his life.

What do these stories have in common?

All are myths in the sense that they convey popular notions about creativity throughout history which have *not* been empirically assessed or substantiated.

Story 1, about the meeting in the park, is representative of the myth of the inspired poet who writes everything out of his head in one fell swoop. It is a time-honored myth, like the myth of Athena springing from the brow of Zeus, that is cherished by professionals as well as laity. It has been nurtured by creative people themselves. As in the story, such a miraculous faculty is often connected with strangeness as well as madness.

Story 2, about the painters, refers to the mythic idea of a very special talent—supposedly identifiable in the childhoods of all artists. Also, it includes the idea of unique special talent associated with what is called the *eidetic* faculty of being able to have perfect visual memory. There is, however, no evidence that eidetic memory, or synaesthesia (interchangeable sensory experience), or, for that matter, especially high intelligence has anything to do with creativity in general. There are exceptions to this, such as high intelligence in science or musical ability.

The scientist genius story is the myth that scientific creativity consists of ideas welling up from the unconscious. Many famous scientists such as Jules-Henri Poincaré and August Kekulé—the latter of whom was the initiator of the famous myth of the discovery of the benzene ring in a dream—have forwarded this. This myth is a variant of the dramatic inspiration idea.

The last story consists of a legendary type of focus on the idea that people have wellsprings of creativity which are released by participating in so-called creative activities. This idea is not completely false, as I shall clarify shortly.

Why have these myths developed? They have, partly because it has been difficult to get good data about the relatively small number of people throughout the history of the world who have been creative geniuses, partly because these creative geniuses have enjoyed perpetuating certain of these myths (the inspiration myth especially) for various reasons, but primarily because creativity is very, very positively valued. Because of this, it is cloaked in mystery and surmise, and everyone has very strong feelings and beliefs—right or wrong—about it. I venture to say that hardly anyone would disagree that creativity is positively valued. As a test, consider for a moment the idea of calling Adolf Hitler a creative person: some might call him a mad genius, perhaps, but a creative killer—not too likely.

The Definition of Creativity

As strong as this positive value is, however, there is little consistency or definite agreement about the meaning of the idea or of the specific term, *creativity.* In the dictionary, the word is defined merely as "bringing something into being." However, some would reserve the term to be used to describe only the most exalted types of bringing something into being, such as God's creation of the world, or the most glorified and prized achievements in the arts or in science; others would consider the term to be applied properly to virtually any type of producing or making, such as in the common linguistic use—for example, the phrase "creating a scene." This latter type of use might also be extended to such ideas as "creating a smoke ring," making a chair, or making an automobile on the assembly line. An irreverent student of mine once went so far as to state that he thought making a bowel movement was an instance of creating something. But, leaving irreverence and irony aside, production of something, or productiveness, is often labeled as creativity in our culture.

For the scientist, the matter of positive value is very important to consider because it is one of the reasons for trying to study and research the phenomenon. But things such as values produce special problems for scientists because it is very hard to deal with them objectively and, therefore, it is necessary to be clear about what is meant by them. Productivity—the mere turning out of large quantities of things—is not the same as creativity. Often, someone who writes a great many books or who constantly brings out lots of ideas or even makes copious drawings in a sketch pad is described as creative. However, as my irreverent and teasing student's comment points up, the result can be a large quantity of worthless material. There is a similar confusion regarding creativity and originality. Although the notion of originality is often used as though it were identical with creativity, originality in the sense of merely producing something unusual or out of the ordinary is not the same as creativity. We all know that many unusual and out-of-the-ordinary ideas are not at all worthy of attention and that some people go around being markedly different in the hope that somehow they will merit the honor of being called creative.

Creativity is, therefore, the production of something that is *both* new and truly valuable.

Creativity in Everyone

Is everyone potentially creative, or is the basic creativity in human beings generally unrecognized? This is the crux of the matter. One reason for studying creativity could be to find the answer to this question. Basically, I think it is a matter of definition. If we decide that creativity consists of being open-minded and flexible and arriving at useful or new solutions to work or living problems, then surely the potentiality for this type of creativity exists in everyone. If we decide that creativity consists of realizing and expressing the uniqueness of one's own personality, style, goals, and ways of interacting with other human beings, then this type of creativity is, theoretically at least, feasible for everyone. If we decide that creativity consists of the ability to grow and develop and change oneself in relation to inner aims and outer reality, then such creativity is widely possible, and quite important, to achieve. Or, taking our model for creativity from the arts, should we decide that its major component is an ability to carry out any type of task—be it cooking, or tennis, or everyday work—with a certain type of elegance and aesthetic grace, then we are justified in speculating, with a fairly high degree of security, that such creativity is possible for everyone despite the fact that such artistry is not a common experience. Finally, if we follow the position in the last myth I described and consider that creativity consists of working at some task in an artistic field such as drawing, playing a musical instrument, writing short stories or poems—regardless of how competently performed—then there is no doubt whatsoever that everybody can, with some degree of training and help, learn to carry out such acts and be gratified although not transformed by them.

To go on with this list of definitions of creativity and to discuss the implications and applications of each would be very interesting indeed and would take us deeply into questions about the enigma and meaning of life, philosophical and theological concerns as well as assessments of the goals of educational and psychiatric disciplines; it might even lead to issues of politics and the organization of society. But, a scientist's purpose in studying creativity, *my* purpose, cannot be as broad and far reaching as is implied by these types of definitions and questions. A scientist must look at specific issues and relate them to particular problems within the existing corpus of knowledge in his field. Consequently, the focus of my research in creativity—the project called "Studies in the Creative Process," of which I have been principal investigator for more than twenty-five years—has been on much more limited and specific questions, although these do have implications—as I shall specify later—for these broader matters.

Creativity and Psychosis

Among the many specific questions I have looked at regarding the psychological processes operating in creativity as well as normal functioning and psychotherapy, is the relationship of creativity to psychosis. Linking creativity to such a highly specific issue may seem a sharp shift from the very broad and all-encompassing areas I just mentioned, but let me explain what I mean. There seems little doubt that geniuses in every era of human history have been worthy of being designated as creative people. Their achievements in the arts, sciences, and other fields have almost invariably been *both* new and positively valuable, and the works of geniuses are essentially the models for every other interpretation or definition of creativity I have mentioned. In view of such high achievement and honor in connection with genius, I was at one time extraordinarily puzzled and piqued about the fact that so many outstanding persons also suffered from some form of psychosis. Although absolute proof of the matter is hard to establish, the presumptive list includes the artists Hieronymus Bosch, Vincent van Gogh, Wassily Kandinsky, and Albrecht Dürer; the scientists Michael Faraday, Isaac Newton, Johannes Kepler, and Tycho Brahe; the composers Robert Schumann, Hugo Wolf, and Camille Saint-Saëns; the writers Johann Hölderlin, August Strindberg, Arthur Rimbaud, Edgar Allan Poe, Charles Lamb, Guy deMaupassant, Theodore Roethke, Ezra Pound, T. S. Eliot, Virginia Woolf, Hart Crane, Sylvia Plath, Jonathan Swift, Lewis Carroll (Charles Dodgson), William Blake, Ernest Hemingway, and Charles Baudelaire; and the philosophers Arthur Schopenhauer and Friedrich Nietzsche.

Shakespeare had one of his characters say, "The lunatic, the lover, and the poet are of imagination all compact," and the idea of mad genius has long been popularly accepted in both our culture and our literature. Our project's interest from the beginning, however, has not been in either proving or disproving a connection between psychosis and genius—many have tried to do this and have failed; that is, they have failed to show any invariant connection between genius and psychosis—but we have been interested in how it is that two such seemingly opposite conditions ever could exist in a particular individual. The answer to such a puzzle surely sheds a good deal of light on both psychosis and genius. Thus, we have focused on studying high-level creativity, a study that has application to every type of creativity—of course.

The Method of Approach

We are not, I should emphasize, the first to attempt a *scientific* study of creativity. Not so long ago, we compiled and published a two-volume bibliography entitled *Index of Scientific Writings on Creativity;*[1] this bibliography listed 9,968 titles of books and articles. It was a comprehensive catalogue of studies in the field, and scientific approaches to creativity cited there consisted of psychological experiments; medical, psychiatric, and psychoanalytic case histories; anthropological and sociological field studies; genetic studies; psychohistorical and other types of theoretical analyses; and reports and assessments of clinical and educational interventions. Despite this rather voluminous prior literature on the topic, however, only bits and pieces of knowledge have heretofore been obtained.

Our research on creativity has been based on empirical data derived directly from creative people through very extensive and intensive psychiatric interviews, controlled psychological experiments with large numbers of subjects, and statistical and psychological analyses of literary manuscripts in conjunction with interviews of surviving families of outstanding creative persons. To date, I have personally carried out more than 2,000 hours of interviews with artists and scientists who have been winners of such honors as the Nobel Prize, Pulitzer Prize, National Gold Medal, the National and American Book Awards, and the Bollingen Poetry Prize; designated as Poet for the Library of Congress and Poet Laureate of the United States; elected to membership in the American Academy of Arts and Letters, the National Institute of Arts and Letters, the National Academy of Sciences, or the Royal Academy of London. I have worked with these persons as research subjects, *not as patients in therapy,* and they have collaborated in an intensive exploration of the psychological roots of their creative processes. The interviews, in other words, were focused on creative work in progress and were carried out at regular intervals until a particular creative work was completed. In the case of a novel, for example, interviews began when the author got his or her first idea for it and continued at regular weekly or biweekly intervals until the novel was published some two and a half or three years later. I also carried out extensive interviews with noncreative persons paid to engage in a literary or scientific project. Controlled psychological experiments were additionally carried out individually by me and in collaboration with my associates, both with these subjects and with large numbers of other subjects considered to have creative potential; these experiments consisted of special tasks designated to identify characteristic thinking processes.[2]

General Findings

From all of these researches, I can report a very clear conclusion that some factors underlie *all* types of creativity; there are common psychological factors operating in varying types of creative processes in art, science, and other productive fields. These common factors consist particularly of special types of thinking patterns used by creative persons during the process of creation itself.[3] But before touching on these important creative thought processes, I shall first report some generalizations about creative people derived primarily from my data. First, contrary to popular as well as professional belief, there is *no* specific personality type associated with outstanding creativity. Creative people are not necessarily childish and erratic in human relationships, as is often thought, nor are they necessarily extraordinarily egoistic or rebellious or eccentric. Second, I must emphasize that, surprising as it may seem, creative people are actually not all exceptionally intelligent, speaking of intelligence in the commonly accepted meaning of performance on verbal I.Q. tests. Many outstanding artists, writers, architects, and other types of creators are only slightly above average in intelligence. There is, moreover, no uniform personality style, if we speak of it in a technical psychological sense. Creators are neither generally compulsive nor impulsive, although many— even highly outstanding ones, interestingly—are somewhat rigid, meticulous, and perfectionistic rather than free and spontaneous. Some degree of introversion—inwardness and self-preoccupation—does predominate among creative people in many fields, but some are surprisingly extroverted. There is generally a good deal of idealism and striving for an ideal in their work, but there is neither a characteristic ideological position nor political affiliation. Authoritarianism tends generally to be despised, but there is inconsistency because some creators are rather authoritarian about matters of judgment and taste. Few of us—creative or not—tend really to like authoritarianism and are sometimes inconsistent, so there is no particular difference with this group. Only one characteristic of personality and orientation to life and work is absolutely, *across the board*, present in *all* creative people: motivation.

The Need to Create

Creative people are extraordinarily highly motivated, both to work and to produce, but, more than that, they are motivated to produce entities that are both new and valuable—creations. It is safe to say that *nothing* is ever created without the particular intention to produce a creation. Contrary to popular belief that great ideas often pop into certain people's minds spontaneously and without effort, the creative process always results from direct, intense, and intentional effort on the creator's part. Creative people, in other words, are always on the lookout for new and valuable ideas and thoughts and approaches and solutions. They want *specifically* to create and to be creative, not merely to be successful or effective or competent. Although important ideas do sometimes come spontaneously—and there always are rare but interesting and dramatic accounts of bolts from the blue which solve great problems or inspire great works of art—such inspirations do not become creations unless there has been a good deal of preparation for them or unless the person is able to elaborate and develop them after they appear. Painstaking work is involved in both the beforehand preparation and the elaboration after.[4]

I shall go into this matter in some detail in a chapter on inspiration, but what I am saying holds equally true for chance discoveries in science, the so-called factor of serendipity, or serendipitous discovery. Sir Alexander Fleming, for instance, was a creative scientist, not simply a lucky serendipitous observer. That is, once he noted the clear areas around an accidental growth of mold on his Petri dish, he was able to develop this observation into the eventual use of a mold product, penicillin, for general antibacterial use. There can be little doubt that such mold contamination and effect had already occurred in numerous laboratories, but it was either unobserved or undeveloped until Fleming had the vision to do so. Similarly, in the case of the discovery of the double-helical structure of DNA and the nature of the genetic code, many researchers were hot on the trail of finding it at the time, but only two—John Watson and Francis Crick—had the specific preparation and drive to make that creative leap. Creative people want very much—perhaps it may be correct to say they *need* very much—to create, partly because they have the talent to do so and partly because of strong environmental influences that instill such strong motivation. These strong environmental influences consist especially of the early family environment, a matter to which I will return shortly.

I shall come back to it because I know that now that I have mentioned this special need to create as well as the family environment of the creative person, you will immediately say, "Aha, he has neglected the most important issue; everyone knows that geniuses have special kinds of talent and that these talents are of such type and degree that it is very unlikely that they could have been produced by the environment. Even the word *genius*—pertaining to, or of the genes—suggests something one is born with, begotten, or inherited. Everybody knows that great geniuses like Wolfgang Amadeus Mozart and William Shakespeare were born, not made. The genius or creative person doesn't really learn how to carry out those sublime feats of thought or art and, even though he may dedicate himself to working and creating, the substantial material comes to him naturally and at moments when he isn't even absorbed or intensively working at the task. The genius is not constructed like ordinary people; his special innate talents allow him to wait for those special ideas or inspirations that start him on the way to a great masterpiece. We have been led astray."

Geniuses: Born or Made?

Some of this challenge is true, and some of it not. Many creative people do have an extraordinary capacity with crucial matters such as manual proficiency required for music, facility with language required for literature, or the use of abstract symbols in mathematics. But it is undeniably *not* true that learning is beside the point or that the creative person need only wait for inspiration that arrives naturally and spontaneously. Creative people are professionals just like any other professionals. They have undergone training and learning—virtually all go to college. Although their working habits vary and, in some cases, are more erratic than those followed by most of us—there is generally not a 9:00 to 5:00 (or 6:00, 7:00, or 8:00) working pattern—there are no real creators I know of who regularly only wait for inspiration from the muse. Also, there are none whose talent was not facilitated by upbringing and environment.

As an aside, I should tell you that no special working pattern characterizes creative people. Some are highly superstitious and carry out small rituals such as sharpening a certain number of pencils, counting the pages finished the previous day, sitting at a special desk, or using a special broken-down typewriter or souped-up word processor, but by and large they are all people who work at their profession on a daily basis. There is no clue to creative capacity and achievement in tracing their working patterns. They start at a regular hour that is best for them and stop at an appointed time. They are sometimes preoccupied with their work outside of working hours, just as many of us are, and sometimes, although not so commonly as is generally believed, they do get consumed with their task and work in a somewhat unbroken stream of time with a passion that approaches frenzy.

Major Findings and Their Implications

To return to your challenge, I will further specify my position only by saying that I do not know whether the talent for having creative thoughts, the special factor of creativity itself, is inherited. The major findings to come out of my research are that there are particular and specific thought processes used by creative people during the process of creation; this applies to the entire spectrum of disciplines, areas, and media. These special thought processes are the features that distinguish creative people from the rest of us. Although very complicated in structure and in psychological function, there is little doubt that these particular processes, or forms of creative cognition, are crucial to outstanding creative attainment. One of these processes is responsible for germinating creative ideas, another is responsible for producing metaphors and other unified structures in both artistic and scientific types of endeavor. Both of these are sequences and patterns of thinking that, when used by someone highly knowledgeable and sophisticated in a particular field or area or artistic endeavor, help to solve important problems and produce great forms and themes. I do not know if the capacity for these and other specifically creative types of thinking is inherited in creative people, but I have carried out experiments that suggest that use of at least one of these processes can be learned.[5] Also, although I do know of definite environmental influences, primarily from the family, that actually stimulate such types of thinking, I do not yet know whether there is an inherited potential for them which works in conjunction with the environmental influences.

Creativity and Psychosis: The Relationship

Now, to the heart of the matter I raised earlier: the question of the relationship between creativity and psychosis. The discovery of these processes answers that question quite conclusively. The creative thought processes I have discovered are used by the creator when he is in a perfectly rational and conscious frame of mind; he or she is not undergoing what some have called an altered or transformed state of consciousness. Involved, however, are unusual types of conceptualizing, and I think it is precise to say that the processes transcend the usual modes of ordinary logical thought. Therefore, I refer to them as translogical types of thinking. As a corollary to the firm connection of these processes with both logic and consciousness, there is an important conclusion: nothing is pathological about them, nor do they arise from pathological motivations; on the contrary, their roots are instead highly adaptive and healthy in their psychological nature and function.

What does this mean in relation to creativity and psychosis? It means that key aspects of creative thinking have nothing really to do with psychosis. They consist of healthy thought processes that generally arise from healthy minds. In those cases in which a creative person is suffering from a psychosis, it is still correct to say that while he is using these specific processes and engaged in the creative process, he is at those moments or periods of time thinking healthily. You see, there are some superficial similarities and connections between these creative cognitions and psychotic modes of thinking. Both types of thinking are quite unusual in superficially similar ways. There is thus a thin *but definite* borderline between the most advanced and healthy type of thinking—creative thinking—and the most impoverished and pathological types of thinking—psychotic processes. The great creative person who is also psychotic can, and does, shift back and forth between these pathological and creative processes. Jealousy, hatred, revenge, and other preoccupations of a psychotic artist often play a role in determining some of the themes and contents of a work of art, but the processes that mold and structure such preoccupations and themes into great creations are healthy, not pathological. This fact has many implications both for the therapy of psychotic people and for the goal of nurturing and developing creativity in children. For one thing, justifying avoidance of treatment on the basis that psychotic suffering is necessary for creativity is unwarranted. Also, fostering children's withdrawn or egocentric or other types of disturbed behavior with the hope that it is necessary for original and creative thinking is ill advised. On the other hand, acceptance by parents and teachers of tendencies to what I call and shall further describe as translogical modes of thinking can nurture and facilitate creative capacity.

Family Background and Creativity

With respect to family environment, there is also a thin but definite borderline between the type of family interaction which nurtures psychosis and nurtures creativity. Both types of family emphasize unusual modes of thinking, and in both there are often remarkable discrepancies between what family members say they feel and what they actually feel, thereby forcing a child within such an environment to become unusually sensitive to implicit messages. But, whereas in the case of a psychotic person both parents are commonly disturbed, the creative person almost invariably has *at least one parent* who is rather healthy psychologically. Furthermore—and this is the cardinal feature of the family environment of the creative person—there is almost always one parent who has in some way been interested, or has tried and not succeeded, in a particular creative field. Thus, Mozart's father was a musician but not a great composer like his son; Eugene O'Neill's father was an actor but not a playwright; Picasso's father was an art teacher; Einstein's father did not pursue an early interest in mathematics and was largely unsuccessful in the electrochemical field; and all my writer and scientist subjects had one parent who, although a business executive or a homemaker or other, told stories, wrote poetry or diaries, or else were interested in tinkering with puzzles or problems and pursuing scientific activities. The creative person, in other words, strives to fulfill a parent's *implicit, unrealized* yearnings.

"Madness"

These are some of the general issues emerging from my research on creativity. In the pages to follow, more specific matters concerning art, science, psychosis, psychotherapy, and other matters pertaining to "madness" will be considered. With the study of any human attribute, focusing on a particular feature leads to questions about interrelationships with other factors. My deliberations about the connection between creativity and psychosis have therefore naturally led to wider considerations about connections between creativity and other forms of psychopathology or deviation such as alcoholism, drug dependence, and depression. Although technically none of these conditions (including homosexuality) should be designated by the popular term *madness,* I have (perhaps perversely) chosen to bring them together in this book. Popular and literary allusions to aberrations in creative people tend to lump all under *madness,* or a similar pejorative designation, and even philosophical treatises on creativity treat madness as a unitary force or factor. Furthermore, even when not used pejoratively, the word *madness* conjures up an image of a certain type of passion often associated with creativity. To meet the challenge raised by such usage, therefore, I attempt to consider separately in this book many of the *madness* issues that have been raised about creativity, including the functioning of the unconscious, the perplexing phenomenon of inspiration, and the role of alcohol and homosexuality as well as connections between creativity and specific types of psychopathology. *Madness,* as used here, then, refers to all the designations of aberration, deviance, and malfunction that Western civilization has managed to connect to its hallowed faculties of genius and creativity.[6]

2 ◆◇ The Creative Process in Art and Science

W*hile working* on an essay for the *Yearbook of Radioactivity and Electronics* in 1907, Albert Einstein had what he called "the happiest thought of my life." Einstein's happy thought was the key to the most far-reaching scientific breakthrough of the twentieth century: the general theory of relativity. The unusual circumstances surrounding it were revealed for the first time in another essay, unpublished and discovered only recently, entitled "Fundamental Ideas and Methods of Relativity Theory, Presented in Their Development."[1]

Einstein had already developed the special theory of relativity, which holds that since the speed of light is constant for all frames of reference, perceptions of time and motion depend upon the relative position of the observer. He had been forced to postulate the theory, he said, to explain the seeming contradictions in electromagnetic phenomena; that "one is dealing here with two fundamentally different cases was, for me, unbearable." Einstein was trying to modify Isaac Newton's classical theory of gravitation so that it could be encompassed within a broad relativity principle. He struggled for many years because he lacked a specific physical basis for bringing together Newton's theory and his own special theory.

Pondering those seemingly irreconcilable constructs, Einstein all at once reached a startling conception: "For an observer in free fall from the roof of a house," he realized, "there exists, during his fall, no gravitational field . . . in his immediate vicinity. If the observer releases any objects, they will remain, relative to him, in a state of rest.

The [falling] observer is therefore justified in considering his state as one of 'rest.'"

The general theory itself is highly complex, and the points of connection to Einstein's "happiest thought" are not simple to explicate or trace. But the specific structure of the key step is clear: Einstein had consciously concluded that a person falling from the roof of a house was both in motion and at rest at the same time. The hypothesis was illogical and contradictory in structure, but it possessed a superior logic and salience that brought Newtonian physics and his own into the same overall conceptual scheme.

The Janusian Process

I have described this creative cognitive sequence as the *janusian process*, after Janus, the Roman god of doorways and beginnings, whose faces (he is variously portrayed as having two, four, and even six of them) look in opposite directions at the same time. The janusian process lies at the heart of the most striking creative breakthroughs. Contrary to the romantic notion that creativity grows largely out of inspiration, the thinking of dreams, or some unconscious source, I have found the janusian process—a major element of the creative process—to be a conscious, rational process.

In the janusian process, multiple opposites or antitheses are conceived simultaneously, either as existing side by side or as equally operative, valid, or true. In an apparent defiance of logic or of physical possibility, the creative person consciously formulates the simultaneous operation of antithetical elements or factors and develops those formulations into integrated entities and creations. It is, as I said, a leap that transcends ordinary logic. What emerges is no mere combination or blending of elements: the conception contains not only different entities, but also opposing and antagonistic elements that are experienced and understood as coexistent. As a self-contradictory structure, the janusian formulation is surprising when seriously posited. Although it usually appears modified and transformed in the final product, it leaves the mark of implicit unexpectedness and paradox on the work.

The janusian process seldom appears in the final artistic product, but it occurs at crucial points in the generation and development of the work. In the initial phases of interviews with some of the writer subjects with whom I worked, the subjects reported using numerous opposite ideas, images, and concepts, but there were usually no clues at that point as to the importance of those ideas. Their plays, novels, and poems showed elements of conflict, irony, tragic tension, and aesthetic ambiguity as major elements, but there was no reason to believe that those elements derived from a factor like the janusian process or that such thinking played any major role in key creative conceptions. It was generally only after weeks or months of interviewing and the development of some confidence and rapport that the research subjects revealed the precise—and self-contradictory—nature of the critical ideas in their creations.

For instance, a Pulitzer Prize-winning novelist told me, after we had discussed for some months the novel he was working on, that he had developed the key idea as he sat in a lawn chair reading Erik Erikson's book on Martin Luther's rebellion. He thought of constructing a novel about another rebel, a revolutionary hero who, he said, "was responsible for the deaths of hundreds of people, but he himself would kill only one person with his own hand—and this was the one person who had been very kind to him and the one person he loved." Playwright Arthur Miller told me he had come up with the specific idea for the play *Incident at Vichy* while traveling through Germany. "Driving on the autobahn, I suddenly felt amazed and overwhelmed at how beautiful Germany had become." He then thought of writing a play that would simultaneously depict both the beauty of modern Germany and Hitler's destructiveness. "And then, I remembered a story I'd been told[2] about a sacrifice made by an Austrian nobleman for a Jew in a Nazi official's waiting room." Later, Miller incorporated that sacrifice into his play.

Two poets described initial conceptions that were only implicitly present in their finished poems. Because I had been conducting regular interviews with them during the writing of their poems, I knew that their recall of circumstances and thoughts was quite exact. Richard Wilbur[3] said that he had been walking on a beach and became interested in the quality of some rocks along the sand. As he touched the surface of the rocks, he noted that they seemed to feel like human skin, but they were also hard and heavy—violent weapons. The idea that the rocks were at once sensual objects as well as weapons led to a conception of the simultaneous operation of sex and violence in the world, and Wilbur elaborated those aspects separately in the final version of this poem.

On another occasion, he was sitting at his desk and thought of a poetic line connoting rest and movement as operating simultaneously in the action of long-distance running. The thought led him to write a poignant poem, entitled *Running*, about marathon racing and the ravages of time and age, which elaborated on, and modified, the initial line.

The other poet, also a major American writer, had been home thinking about a past incident in which a horse had appeared at a lonely desert site, when it occurred to him that horses are animals who, he said, "renounce their own kind in order to live our lives." The idea that horses live human lives, that they are both beast and not-beast and human and not-human simultaneously, generated a vibrant poem with a central image and theme of a happy and intense relationship between a young person and a horse, followed by a sad, resigned separation.

When, after a year's interviewing, I focused with novelist John Hersey on the earliest idea for his book *Too Far to Walk,* he referred to a line in it indicating that love and hate were the same. The phrase had also guided the novel's whole construction. Similarly, another poet subject said her first idea for a certain poem was the line, "Cream of celery soup has a soul of its own." She had been thinking, she recalled, about the simultaneously formed and unformed qualities of both souls and soup. Another playwright said that the earliest formulations in one of his works grew out of ideas and phrases that came to him while imagining that the white knight in a television commercial was a black man.

Poet and novelist Robert Penn Warren told me that he was doing his morning exercises when he thought of a series of poetic lines that, as he described them, would use the last word of each line as the first word of the next—a juxtaposition that sets one word to opposite functions, both ending and beginning a poetic thought. In the end, his poem implicitly retained that structure.

Janusian processes appeared and reappeared throughout the interviews and studies of creative people. Comparisons were carried out with a group of subjects matched for success, age, and sex with the creative group but confidentially rated as noncreative by bosses and peers, and who embarked on a writing project for a fee. This latter comparison group never displayed the janusian process in their thoughts or in any aspect of the writing assignment they were asked to do. Instead, they approached the writing in various ways: constructing a story outline, trying to think of a good ending, or merely trying to write out every thought that came to them. As with the creative group, I discussed with them the general themes and detailed revisions they made during the course of writing from week to seek. Some persevered to complete an imaginative work, but many gave up. Although some occasionally wrote interesting lines and found fairly interesting themes, their earliest conceptions, and those along the way, were devoid of simultaneous antitheses. And no creative results appeared from their labors.

Because creative achievement is generally defined as something that "stands the test of time," I used another empirical method to study creativity in outstanding works of the past. This involved doing statistical assessments of patterns of revisions in manuscripts by playwrights Eugene O'Neill and Maxwell Anderson, developing specific hypotheses and predictions about their behavior in the course of writing the works, and then interviewing surviving family members, wife Carlotta Monterrey O'Neill and son Quentin Anderson, respectively, to assess the predictions.

In these studies, I first found elements of the janusian process through reconstructing aspects of O'Neill's creation of the play *The Iceman Cometh*. As I describe in detail in Chapter 11, I discovered evidence for the author's construction of a simultaneous antithesis and the development of insight regarding an event many years after it happened: a friend and roommate of his youth committed suicide because he was distressed over his wife's infidelity—but also because he had unconsciously wanted her to be unfaithful to him. The insight produced the focus on infidelity, both religious and sexual, in the substance and title of the play.

Similarly, Maxwell Anderson created the prizewinning play *High Tor* with the idea of presenting characters who were both alive and dead at the same time. The characters were not merely ghosts but lost persons struggling to survive and to understand what had happened to them. The play is both humorous and poignant, and much of the action turns on the conflicting dual nature of these long-dead survivors of a Dutch explorer's ship who interact with modern inhabitants of the Hudson River Palisades.

Conceiving the novel *Nostromo*, Joseph Conrad followed a janusian sequence that he described in the preface. Struck by a story he had heard about an "unmitigated rascal" who had stolen a large quantity of silver somewhere on the seaboard of South America during a revolution, he wrote, "I did not see anything at first in the mere story." Then, he said, "It dawned upon me that the purloiner of the treasure need not necessarily be a confirmed rogue, that he could even be a man of character." This key idea of the criminal as both rogue and man of character was elaborated in the story of a land that was both good and evil simultaneously. As Conrad reported, "It was only then that I had the first vision of a twilight country . . . with . . . its high, shadowy sierra and its misty campo for mute witnesses of events flowing from the passions of men short-sighted in good and evil. Such are in very truth the obscure origins of *Nostromo*—the book. From that moment, I suppose, it had to be."[4]

I have found evidence of the janusian process in some of the most profound creations in music and the visual arts as well. Successive sketches for Pablo Picasso's mural *Guernica,* for instance, reveal that the painter's first construction consisted of a female figure oriented spatially in diametrically opposite directions. In the first sketch, Picasso represented the figure (who is holding a torch in the completed mural) as both looking into a room and looking out onto a courtyard at the same time (see Figure 2.1). In successive sketches, he made this feature of the figure less obvious. The completed mural, however, portrays human carnage both inside a room and outside at the same time (see Figure 2.2). This can be appreciated especially in the representation of the source of the light at the top center portion of the mural—it is both the sun and an incandescent light bulb at once.[5]

Other artists, among them Leonardo da Vinci, Vincent van Gogh, and John Constable, as well as members of the modern schools, have provided descriptions of similar formulations. The celebrated British sculptor Henry Moore said, "To know one thing, you must know the opposite . . . just as much, else you don't know that one thing. So that, quite often, one does the opposite as an expression of the positive."[6] Josef Albers, the influential painter of the "hard edge" school, described his own approach. "I start from experiences and read . . . always between polarities . . . loud and not-loud . . . young and old . . . spring and winter. . . . If I can make black and white behave together instead of shooting at each other only, I feel proud."[7]

In a series of Harvard lectures on music, Leonard Bernstein described the simultaneous operation of the antithetical factors of diatonicism (the tonal relationships among the notes within the traditional scales) and chromaticism (the relationship among the various keys) in the construction of virtually all types of music. Using a Mozart piece to make his point, Bernstein demonstrated such conceptualization in Mozart's creative process and left little doubt that it is an important aspect of his own work.[8]

To return to science, Nobel laureate Edwin McMillan's formulation of "critical phase stability" directly leading to his development of the synchrocyclotron (later called the synchrotron) was derived from a sudden realization involving simultaneous opposition. The synchrotron is a high-energy particle accelerator that has allowed for the discovery of a number of new particles and other nuclear effects. McMillan described the sequence of events to me in the following way.

"It was in the month of July. I think it was the month of July. I didn't put down the date—I should record these things. It was night. I was lying awake in bed and thinking of a way of getting high energy and I was thinking of the cyclotron and the particle going around and encountering the accelerator field—the right phase each time

Figure 2.1. Composition study (first sketch for the *Guernica* mural), Pablo Picasso, 1937. Pencil on blue paper, 8¼ × 10⅝". Collection, Museo Nacional del Prado, Madrid.

Figure 2.2. Guernica, Pablo Picasso, 1937. Oil on canvas, 11′5½″ × 25′5¾″. Collection, Museo Nacional del Prado, Madrid.

around." Then, he focused on the idea that certain of the particles would be out of phase and would fall out of step. *"It gets behind and it gets the opposite sense,"* he said. *"It gets pushed back again, so it will oscillate. It's going to oscillate back and forth, be going at too high and too low energy.* Once I realized that, then the rest was easy. . . . The very next day I called it phase stability. Stability implies that it clings to a certain value. It may oscillate about, but it clings to a certain fixed value."

In developing the key idea leading to the synchrotron accelerator, McMillan had conceived the simultaneously opposite states of too high and too low energy. Out-of-step particles would fall back in the accelerator field and would be forced to accelerate. They would be lower in energy because they were heavier and out of phase and would be also higher in energy because they would overshoot. The simultaneous opposition would manifest itself physically through oscillation and, consequently, they would be stable overall with respect to the field. As he elaborated further, "Once you have an oscillation, you have the element of stability. The things will stay put. They will wiggle around but they won't get away from you. . . . You can then push this thing anywhere you want." He concluded, "That all happened one night and the next day I started to write down the equations for that and proved that it would work."

The Janusian Process and Mental Illness

To make his discovery of critical phase stability, McMillan had to conceive of opposites operating simultaneously, a conception none of his colleagues was able to do at the time. Like Einstein, he was fully conscious, aware, and logical at the moment—but in that creative leap, he was able to transcend the bounds of ordinary logic and cognition. Because such thinking is unusual and seemingly illogical on the surface, it has been confused with the thinking in psychosis or in what is called primary process cognition. The primary process was originally described by Sigmund Freud in connection with his landmark work on dreams. One of its characteristics is an absence of contradictions and, hence, that opposites may be substituted for each other. Freud also believed that the primary process was characteristic of an early childhood period before the development of logical or so-called secondary process cognition. And others, as well as he, have consistently described its appearance in the delusions and hallucinations of persons suffering from psychosis. An example of this is when a schizophrenic patient says to a doctor, "I am a human like yourself, but I am not a human." This delusional statement is similar to the janusian formulations I have described so far but, unlike those, it is truly illogical. Psychotic patients do not appear to be aware of the contradiction when making such an assertion, and they therefore manifest the primitive primary process mode of thinking rather than a creative one.

To assess scientifically the validity of the distinction I have just made, I carried out an experiment with Nobel laureates in the physical sciences, psychiatric patients, and talented undergraduates from Yale University. Twelve Nobel laureates participated, including Allan Cormack, developer of the principle of the computerized axial tomography (CAT) scan type of X-ray; Arthur Kornberg, first to synthesize the genetic substance DNA; and other highly creative figures. The experiment consisted of asking each subject to give the first word that came to mind when hearing each of ninety-nine stimulus words—a standard word-association test. These tests were all individually administered, and responses were electronically recorded, with speed of responding measured in the time span of 0.001 second. The purpose of the experiment was to find out whether the Nobel laureates showed a tendency to the janusian process—manifested by giving extremely fast opposite-word responses to the stimuli—and whether that tendency was also present in the different types of other subject groups. These control subject groups consisted of 18 hospitalized psychiatric patients, with a wide range of types of psychiatric diagnoses, and 113 Yale students, divided further into two subgroups assessed as either potentially creative or noncreative. The clear-cut result was that both the Nobel laureate and the potentially creative Yale subgroup showed tendencies to using the janusian process type of thinking, but neither the psychiatric patients nor the lower creative potential ("noncreative") students did. Although only 16% of the patient group had a history of psychosis, many of the other patients were quite seriously ill, and the experiment overall *sharply distinguished between mental illness and tendencies to creative thinking through the janusian process.*

Janusian Cognition and the Creative Process

Characteristically, as specified in the Einstein, McMillan, Miller, Wilbur, Hersey, Warren, Picasso, and Conrad examples, janusian concepts occur early in the creative process. Although they do not, of course, account for the entire creation, they are key steps that are later elaborated and transformed. Einstein's enormous intellect and capacity for both inductive and deductive logic certainly played a role in the development of his theory. So did his ability to articulate symbols, his intense concentration, and his profound understanding of the categories of science and mathematics. McMillan has some of those capacities as well. Conrad's facility with language, his personal experience with sailing and exotic lands, and his dual identity as an Englishman and the son of Polish intellectual gentry all entered into the elaboration of the initial janusian construct and the arduous creation of *Nostromo.*

Commonly, in the final product or creation—the scientific theory or crucial experiment, the poem, play, musical composition, or work of architecture, philosophy, or religion—there is little overt sign of the janusian constructs that have occurred along the way. In several of the world's religions, however, there are integrations that retain a clear simultaneity, and tension, between opposite and antithetical factors. In Taoism, the yin and the yang are two opposite and universal moral principles operating together as a single force. Opposed and unified in Buddhism are nirvana, the end of the cycle of rebirth, and samsara, the endless series of incarnations and reincarnations of living things. And nirvana itself is both nonlife and nondeath. Some Western theologies postulate a similar tension in the opposing powers of God and the devil.

In philosophy, simultaneous oppositions and antitheses are manifest in the pre-Socratic conceptions of being and becoming, Nietzsche's Dionysian and Apollonian principles, Søren Kierkegaard's belief by virtue of the absurd, and Jean-Paul Sartre's representation of being and nothingness. In psychology, there are Freud's formulation of the conscious operating together with the unconscious, the theory of the dually functioning but opposed instincts of sex and aggression, and Carl Jung's opposed but concomitant animus and anima.[9]

The janusian process differs from the types of creative cognition that other investigators have hypothesized. In the Einstein instance, that scientist could not have come to his theory merely by associating two incompatible elements, as Arthur Koestler has proposed.[10] It was by consciously formulating the given in a different way, by conceiving the inconceivable—attributing the possibility of rest to the state of falling—that Einstein was able to see the larger context of relativity. That is not merely association, in which any number of alternatives could fit the definition. In the janusian process, the creative person, as is evident in the Einstein, McMillan, and other descriptions, is fully rational and purposeful at the time he chooses particular opposites and juxtaposes them.

Clearly, in using this form of thinking, bringing together any opposites at all won't do. It matters very much which opposites are selected and how the janusian formulation is elaborated in a particular work. In artistic fields, the creator chooses and develops those opposites and antitheses that most meaningfully crystallize and express personal as well as universal values, experiences, and feelings. The scientist also selects and elaborates the context to some extent, but he has the specific task of determining which opposites derived from the world of natural events are significant at a particular point in the evolution and growth of theory and knowledge.

The action of the janusian process in creative activities helps to explain, among other things, some of the earlier mentioned sense of surprise and even disbelief when creations first appear. Always surprising is the discovery that the opposite of a previously held idea, concept, or belief is operative or true. Even more surprising is this: not only is the opposite true, but both the opposite and the previously held idea are operative or true.

The Homospatial Process

Whereas the janusian process operates frequently in early idea-generating phases of the creative process, other types of creative thinking function later to extend, develop, and unify janusian formulations as well as to generate other creative structures and ideas. One of these later functioning types I have described as *homospatial process*. The term derives from the Greek meaning of *homoios*, that is, the same. The homospatial process consists of *conceiving two or more discrete entities occupying the same space, a conception leading to the articulation of new identities*. In this process, concrete entities such as rivers, houses, human faces, as well as sound patterns and written words are superimposed, fused, or otherwise brought together in the mind and totally fill its perceptual space—the subjective or imaginary space experienced in consciousness. We generally describe this space as that in the *mind's eye*, but to describe the process accurately, we should include unusual terms such as the *mind's ear, mind's touch* because entities perceived in any of the sensory spheres may be involved: visual, auditory, tactile, kinesthetic, olfactory, and gustatory.

The homospatial conception of discrete entities occupying the same space is always a rapid, fleeting one. Discrete elements cannot remain unified for very long, even in the mind, and the diffuse initial conception soon leads to a separating out of various components. But, the important thing is that the components separated out of a homospatial conception are new ones, they are not simply aspects of the original discrete entities presented or considered in some stepwise fashion.

Take, for instance, the poetic metaphor, *the branches were handles of stars*. Most people, when asked how they think this particular metaphor was conceived, will say—I know, I have asked the question many times—that the poet was walking in the country at night or he was thinking of such a walk, and when he looked up at the trees, he *noticed* that the branches of the trees looked like they connected with the stars shining through them; or else they say that the poet was walking in a park at night or thinking about it, and he *felt* like he could lift the branches of the trees to the stars; or they speculate about some experience combining the two types of circumstances; or they vary the details.

Now, the homospatial conception does not occur in that way, and the homospatial process is a prime factor in the production of poetic metaphors. The common view of metaphor creation is based on people's experience of the impact of a metaphor when heard or read. When hearing or reading *the branches were handles of stars*, one tends to think of the ways that branches look like handles topped by fiery stars, and one also becomes suddenly aware of previously unnoticed similarities and connections, an experience that is part of the aesthetic reaction. But the poet did not create this metaphor in just that way; he did not merely notice similarities between different or disassociated elements which were previously unnoticed. Nor did he have unusual associations or undertake searches for comparisons and analogies to something he perceived. He actively produced this metaphor through the homospatial process as follows. Attracted to the words *handle* and *branch* because of their shared sound qualities—the assonance or shared *an* sound in the center—as well as the shared shape of the wooden objects themselves, the poet superimposed and fused them in his mind's eye; he brought them together because he felt they *ought* to be together. Then, in the next fleeting moments, he said to himself, "When in reality are they the same?" while also fleetingly experiencing a vivid mental impression of the letter *a* overlapping in the two words. Only then was the idea of stars generated, not before. The idea of the country (or park) at night did not generate this metaphor; it was derived from the homospatial conception and provided both the real scene and sound qualities that unified the words and their meanings.

Also, consider another type of metaphor, *the tarantula rays of the lamp spread across the conference room*. In this case, a poet was sitting at a desk thinking about a vacation in the tropics and, among the various thoughts and words that came to mind, he too became interested in sound similarities—the central *a* assonance between the two words *tarantula* and *lamp*—and was also fleetingly intrigued by a sense of contrast. He actively superimposed images of the spider and a light source together, along with images of the letters in the words, because he wanted to create a metaphor of both together. Then, after mentally visualizing spidery light radiating out from a central source in the superimposed images, he thought of *tarantula rays of the lamp.* Deciding to elaborate that fragment with a suggestive context, he tried some alternatives until he conceived of *conference room.* Once the entire construction was created, he thought of overtones such as wars in the tropics, the idea of the slow crawl of a tarantula in contrast with the dazzling speed of light, and, experiencing an awesome type of beauty, he was pleased. In both these cases, the authors mentally visualized a vague scene as well as found the answer in words. And later, they visualized more fully developed and vivid scenes similar to the ones experienced by a reader or audience. But the fully visualized scenes did not produce the metaphors; they mainly added to each poet's feeling of the aptness of his creation.

Discrete elements may be brought together for many other reasons besides, or in addition to, similarities in their shape or in the sound of words. Rhythmic connections, verbal overtones and associations, emotional relationships, aesthetic feeling, and conceptual formulations may stimulate the homospatial process. For example, in the earlier mentioned instance of the poet whose initial idea for a poem was the janusian formulation of a horse as both human and beast simultaneously, that formulation was subsequently integrated into a central poetic metaphor (a "poetic image") by a homospatial conception. A horse and human being were conceived as occupying the same space; that led to the construction of the following image in which a horse and a rider were virtually fused:

> One spring twilight, during a lull in the war,
> At Shoup's farm south of Troy, I last rode horseback.
> Stillnesses were swarming inward from the evening star
> Or outward from the buoyant sorrel mare
> Who moved as if not displeased by the weight upon her.
> Meadows received us, heady with unseen lilac.
> Brief, polyphonic lives abounded everywhere.
> With one accord we circled the small lake.[11]

Notice that the resulting image was neither a centaur, a mythical entity that is part human and part horse, nor was it some other combination of horse and man. The homospatial conception leads to an integration in which the components interact and contribute to the whole and are not simply blended or combined. This integration is an essential feature of effective metaphors.

Metaphorization is a prime element in poetic creation, and it is also a crucial aspect of other types of creation as well—both artistic and scientific. Metaphors occupy a central place in the creations of painters, novelists, composers, sculptors, architects, and scientific theorists. For an example in science, the productive metaphor *black holes in space* has been important in modern astrophysics. Such metaphors are characteristically produced by the homospatial process.

Additionally, the process produces other types of creative unifications. In literature, it is a major factor in the creation and development of literary characters. Novelists, playwrights, and poets actively fuse and superimpose images of persons they have known, images of themselves, and the developing image of the character they are creating. They do not, as is commonly supposed, simply add together or combine various characteristics of themselves and others, either consciously or unconsciously. Also, the homospatial process leads to effective literary double meanings and directly produces poetic rhymes, assonances, and alliterations.

For the painter, sculptor, and composer, the process brings foreground and background elements in a visual or auditory image or experience into the same spatial plane, superimposed or fused with one another. This leads to integrations and unifications of visual and musical patterns, respectively. For example, Henry Moore emphasized the crucial role of what is clearly a homospatial process in the creation of sculptural works of art as follows:

> This is what the sculptor must do. He must strive continually to think of, and use, form in its full spatial completeness. He gets the solid shape, as it were, inside his head—he thinks of it, whatever its size, as if he were holding it completely enclosed in the hollow of his hand. He mentally visualizes a complex form from all round itself; he knows while he looks at one side what the other side is like.[12]

In music, auditory metaphors and new musical patterns and themes develop from a homospatial process, as in the following description by Ludwig van Beethoven: "the underlying idea [of a musical work] . . . rises . . . grows, I hear and see the image in front of me from every angle, as if it had been cast." Robert Schumann described this in his musical creative process as "certain outlines amid all the sounds and tones, . . . form and condense into clear shapes."

For other manifestations of the homospatial process in science and mathematics, we must look again at Einstein's account of the construction of the general theory of relativity. Because, even though his "happiest thought" was a janusian formulation, it too was conceived in the spatial terms of a man falling from a roof, and we know, also from his own testimony, that Einstein was given to think in terms of mental images.[13] One is reminded, when thinking of Einstein's image of a man falling from a roof—a person both falling and at rest—of

*Figure 2.3.
Le Saint
Voiturier* (the
holy carter),
Marc Chagall,
1911. Private
collection,
Kreseld,
Westphalia,
Germany.

the painting *Le Saint Voiturier* by Marc Chagall (see Figure 2.3). There, the falling man's head and chest are upright and curved away from his vertically plummeting waist and legs; in effect, two distinct bodies are perfectly integrated into a single form that appears to be both falling and at rest. The painting seems to be an extraordinarily apt representation of Einstein's thought. An even more detailed instance of a homospatial conception leading to the achievement by Jacques Hadamard of an important mathematical discovery was given by him in the following way:

> When I think of the example . . . [of the thought leading to the discovery of the valuation of a determinant] I see a schematic diagram: a square of whose sides only the verticals are drawn and, *inside of it*, [italics mine] four points being the vertices of a rectangle and joined by (hardly apparent) diagonals—a diagram the symbolic meaning of which will be clear for technicians. It even seems to me that such was

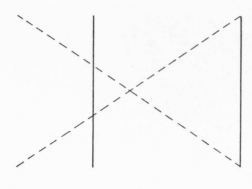

Figure 2.4. Representation of Hadamard's conception leading to the creation of the valuation of a determinant. (The diagonals are drawn to suggest an image that is impossible to present physically. The rectangle is superimposed upon the square; therefore, the mental image consists of diagonals within the area of the square, not, as drawn here, ending in an extrapolated spatial location.)

my visualization of the question in 1892, [when I made the discovery] as far as I can recollect.[14]

A rectangle inside a square! Although the symbolic meaning of this diagram can now be interpreted by technicians, as Hadamard states, it is clear that his initial conception, the creative thought leading to the solution, was of two discrete entities occupying the same space (see Figure 2.4).

And there is also the great mathematician Poincaré's description of the thoughts leading to the discovery of a crucial aspect of his famous Fuchsian functions, a description that specifies a homospatial conception:

> For a fortnight I had been attempting to prove that there could not be any function analogous to what I have since called Fuchsian functions. I was at that time very ignorant. Every day I sat down at my table and spent an hour or two trying a great number of combinations, and I arrived at no result. One night I took some black coffee, contrary to my custom, and was unable to sleep. A host of ideas kept surging in my head; I could almost feel them jostling one another, *until two of them coalesced*, so to speak, to form a stable combination. When morning came, I had established the existence of one class of Fuchsian geometric series. I had only to verify the results, which only took a few hours.[15] [italics mine]

Outside of mathematics, scientist subjects have spontaneously reported similar experiences to me. A Nobel laureate microbiologist, for instance, described arriving at an important new idea after consciously visualizing himself superimposed upon a living cell. In addition, the noted Fuller Albright reportedly arrived at innovative formulations of cellular mechanisms "by thinking of himself as a cell."[16]

To test experimentally the connection between the homospatial process and creativity, a colleague and I constructed a special set of visual stimuli to be used for instigating creative production. Reasoning that the mental representation of multiple elements occupying the same space involved superimposition of these elements upon each other, we constructed superimposed visual images by transilluminating photographic slides upon a screen. These externalized representations of homospatial conceptions were drawn from a wide range of visual subject matter such as war, sex, youth, old age, flowers, landscape, seascape, and cityscape. For example, in one pair of superimposed images, a slide photograph of a group of soldiers crouching behind a tank was transilluminated on a screen together with a slide of an empty French four-poster bed (see Figure 2.5).

Our subjects in these experiments were writers and artists, including a special group of young artists chosen from a national competition by faculty members of the Yale School of Art. Writer subjects were asked to create metaphors stimulated by the images and artists were asked to draw pastel sketches. Four different experiments, two with writers and two with artists, were carried out in which half of each group saw different types of variations of the superimposed images and served as experimental controls. For example, one half of a group created metaphors after seeing a superimposed slide image, and the other half created them in a different room after seeing the same images separated and side by side. Another control variation in a separate experiment consisted of cutting out a major feature of one slide image and constructing a picture in which one image blocked out features of the other instead of being displayed as superimposed and appearing to occupy the same spatial location (see Figure 2.6). In all these experimental variations, and with all groups, significantly more creative products resulted after subjects saw the superimposed visual images than with any other type of image presentation. Consequently, the homospatial process, as represented by the superimposed image displays in these experiments, was shown to be responsible for enhanced creative production.

The Homospatial and Janusian Processes in Creativity

What, then, are the operations in creativity of these processes, janusian and homospatial, and what is their interrelationship? In the arts, the operations and relationships are broadly as follows. The janusian process serves to bring together specific interrelated elements out of

the relatively diffuse substratum of experience and knowledge; elements that are opposite or antithetical, rather than only divergent or unrelated, are crystallized and juxtaposed. *Black*, for instance, is opposite and highly related to *white* as a designation of color. Once juxtaposed and brought together as, let's say, *black whiteness*, these opposites and antitheses continue to be in conflict to some degree and will generate a sense of tension. The homospatial process, when operating in conjunction with the janusian one, serves at first to blur and change the contours of the specific interrelated elements such as *black whiteness* in the janusian formulation by placing them in the same space. Out of this diffused and changed conception a new and unified product is composed. The resulting creation is an integrated unity in which the discrete elements are still discernible and still generate some degree of tension.

A final example of a product of janusian and homospatial processes operating together in art, from the study described in Chapter 11, should help make the point clear. The memorable and penetrating title of O'Neill's play *The Iceman Cometh* is the central metaphor representing that drama's many levels—intellectual and emotional. This title integrates several different simultaneous oppositions: (1) the sexual "coming" of an iceman and the coming of the biblical bridegroom, Christ; (2) the striking verbal opposition between the sacred biblical word *cometh* and the mundane, or actually coarse and profane sounding *iceman*; (3) the coming of bleak death, as specifically cited in the play, and the coming of Christ the savior; (4) a bridegroom and an adulterer; (5) sexual potency and death; (6) Christian morality and illicit sexuality; (7) fidelity and infidelity. Hearing or reading the title itself produces an immediate and unified impact and, at the same time, the tension between the discrete conflicting elements of *iceman* and *cometh* are also experienced. And once the play is seen, an overall sense of fusion between the myriad opposing elements is both enriched and enhanced.

In science, where tension between opposing elements is not as important as in art, the janusian process serves to crystallize and specify symmetries in the form of polarities and opposites; it also serves to encapsulate an area of knowledge by bringing together its

---

Figure 2.5. Superimposed image produced from individual slides. *Top,* superimposed images of crouching soldiers and tank scene with French four-poster bed. *Bottom (left),* the French four-poster bed; *(right),* the soldiers and tank scene.

polar extremes or boundaries. The homospatial process serves to uni-fy abstract elements in spatial terms, as in the Einstein example, and it serves to produce specific metaphors that are important factors in creative scientific thinking.

The Creative Process and Mental Illness

Both the janusian and homospatial processes are unusual types of thinking, and both play a major role in creativity. Because they differ a good deal from everyday types of conceiving, particularly logical stepwise ones, they may be mistaken for psychotic ways of thinking and behavior. That something is both true and not true at the same time is highly illogical and, on the surface, quite irrational. That two or more elements can occupy the same space is beyond the dictates of our experience, and it seems a formulation of the incredible, bi-zarre, and fantastic. Persons in the throes of psychosis do indeed have such conceptions as these, believe literally in them, and allow them to guide their behavior. Creative persons who have been psychotic, such as those I listed in Chapter 1, have surely also believed literally in such conceptions and have been unable to use them in a creative way.

   While the demarcation between psychotic thinking and cre-ative thinking is superficially thin, the underlying psychological dyna-misms are worlds apart. Both homospatial and janusian processes are active, intentional operations that are employed for purposes of pro-ducing creations. They therefore appear during the course of a cre-ative process after the person has developed a particular creative goal such as writing a novel, constructing a sculpture, or developing a scientific theory. At this point, the truly creative person is oriented toward producing something outside of himself, is rational, and is completely aware of logical distinctions. His emotional energy is not directed toward himself, as in psychosis, and he knowingly formulates unusual conceptions in order to improve on reality and to create. He is able to take mental risks and formulate the seemingly illogical and incredible because he is relatively free of anxiety and can assess reality

---

Figure 2.6 (*opposite page*). Blocking (*foreground* and *background*) and superimposed images produced from individual slides. *Top* (*left*), superimposed images of tulip and gambling scenes; (*right*), same images with tulip scene in the foreground. *Bottom* (*left*), tulip scene; (*right*), gambling scene.

well. At those moments, his thinking is unhampered by emotional interference. Unlike psychotic episodes, in which bizarre thinking develops because of the person's inability to tolerate extreme anxiety and that thinking also seems to serve a defensive function, the creative process requires an ability to tolerate high levels of anxiety and a relative lack of defensiveness in order to proceed. In sum, although creative people may be psychotic at various periods of their lives, or even at various times during a day or week, they cannot be psychotic *at the time they are engaged in a creative process*, or it will not be successful. Homospatial and janusian processes are healthy ones.

Although these processes are healthy, they are, however, trying and difficult to employ. Holding janusian and homospatial conceptions in consciousness generates both intellectual and emotional strain. Think of attempting it yourself. Can you conceive of something lying horizontally and vertically at the same time? Or of dry rain? Or of the sun rising and setting simultaneously? All of these have in some way been used as janusian formulations in creative processes or are potentially usable as such. Trying to think these thoughts in a serious way does, I am sure you will agree, produce a feeling of tension and mental strain. As for homospatial conceptions, try to visualize a face and a tree occupying exactly the same space. Or a piranha fish and the moon. Or a nun and racehorse jockey. Again, these conceptions have been, or potentially can be, used in creative processes, and again, there is some mental strain in contemplating them seriously. To be more precise, in the case of the physical visual images in the homospatial conception, there is mental strain involved in just keeping the superimposed entities together.

This mental, and often accompanying emotional, strain is usually a limited one for creative people, because it occurs during creative activities and not necessarily at other times. In other words, mental and emotional strain may arise in creative activities but not in other aspects of a creative person's life. But this is, by no means, a hard and fast rule. Although this strain can usually be confined to periods of creative activity, it may often spill over into other activities and interpersonal relationships, and the tension associated with creative thinking may directly and indirectly affect them.

For these and other reasons—pertaining to factors of social recognition and appreciation which I shall discuss in Chapter 12—creative people who are not otherwise psychiatrically ill may show emotional and mental strain to a greater degree than healthy noncreative persons. They may even behave in unusual ways and seem highly eccentric, or even mad, at times. Or, they may succumb to the constant tension of their work and suffer frank illness. This is not to say that creative people do not become psychiatrically ill for reasons other than their work. Psychosis does exist side by side with creativity. I do mean to say, however, that creative work can be risky. Although janusian, homospatial, and other creative operations derive from healthy functions, they generate mental conflict and tension. While causing difficulties for their users, they lead to the gratifying achievement of lasting works of art, novels, poems, and scientific theories.

3 ◆◇ Inspiration and the Creative Process

*A*mong *the* mythical fallacies connecting mental illness with creativity is the idea of the creator's frenzy and transport in the experience of inspiration. This dramatic inspiration, it is usually assumed, is the starting point of the creative process. Quite persistent is that popular image I presented earlier of a brooding and silent figure whose face suddenly becomes transfigured and illuminated by a thought or idea that is quickly converted into scribbled notes, musical phrases, artistic patterns, mathematical formulas, or even full-blown scientific discoveries. More than a romantic popular misconception, this image is also an implicit influence on some of the most learned analyses of the creative process. The philosophers Plato, Aristotle, Longinus, Denis Diderot, Benedetto Croce, Henri-Louis Bergson, Jacques Maritain, Samuel Alexander, and Friedrich Nietzsche have all emphasized intense inspiration as a major factor in creativity. Outside of philosophy, Ernst Kris, the influential psychoanalytic theorist of the creative process, also devoted much of his attention to inspiration. His term *regression in the service of the ego* was meant to explain the psychological basis of the entire creative process, but it applies and is most clearly worked out in relation to inspiration.[1]

Creative people have done little to correct or disavow this emphasis. In fact, they have generally appeared hell-bent on perpetrating it and enlarging it, in public statements at any rate. William Blake and Samuel Coleridge are prominent examples of writers who published accounts of poems written in altered inspired states. Blake asserted that an entire poem came to him word for word in a dream, and Coleridge's account of the dramatic genesis of the poem *Kubla Khan* in a drugged fantasy state is well known.[2] Although few creative people claim this degree of automatism, the published remarks of many tend to emphasize the crucial importance of inspiratory experiences. The list includes artists Wassily Kandinsky and Max Ernst; writers George Chapman, Robert Herrick, John Milton, Sir Philip Sidney, John Keats, Percy Bysshe Shelley, George William Russell (A.E.), Stephen Harold Spender, Karl Jay Shapiro, and Allen Ginsberg; composers Ludwig van Beethoven, Robert Schumann, and Paul Hindemith; scientists Jules Henri Poincaré, Carl Friedrich Gauss, and Hermann von Helmholtz. The writer Edgar Allan Poe is a notable exception, but he went to the opposite extreme: he described a highly rationalistic, plodding approach to the creation of the poem *The Raven*. Actually, his account makes that poem seem so contrived and uninspired that most serious critics and poets doubt the description's honesty. Many modern creators have begun to take a middle ground on inspiration, indicating that it occurs, but they deemphasize its importance. But the impact of testimonials by earlier giants still exerts considerable influence.

There is good reason to believe—public testimonials to the contrary notwithstanding—that the emphasis on inspiration is fallacious. Inspiration is neither the invariant starting point of the creative process, nor is it necessarily the most critical aspect. It has become important to assert this not only for scientific reasons, but because erroneous notions about inspiration have in modern times led to an almost dangerous situation. Many young people have at various times resorted to the ingestion of mind-expanding drugs—LSD and marijuana among others—partly on the basis of a rationalization that such drugs enhance creativity. Published examples of poetry and art produced under the influence of these drugs and controlled studies of creative performance do not, it is generally agreed, support this notion. Nevertheless, the belief continues because it is based in part on a widespread tendency to equate inspiration with the entire creative process. Since drug-induced experiences seem to be similar in some ways to inspiration, it is assumed that drug experiences will produce creations.

In correcting the emphasis on inspiration in relation to creativity, I would like to make clear that the term *inspiration* refers to an intrinsically dramatic experience. It indicates more than the simple achievement of a good idea. As many writers have pointed out, the term literally refers to the act of breathing, and the implication of vitality is bound into its meaning—that what is inspired, or taken in, sustains or imbues life. Suddenness, a sense of breakthrough, an impulse to action (usually writing something down but also running out of the bath shouting, "Eureka, I found it"), and an associated transient emotional relief (often associated with an actual physical sigh or voiced "Aha") are all, to some degree, invariant components of the experience. The term does not simply refer to the beginning of a thought process, although it is sometimes loosely used in this way. In other words, the popular image of the behavior accompanying an inspiratory experience is actually correct, but the popular as well as the scholarly conception of the *role* of inspiration in the creative process is incorrect. My subjects have reported that they seldom, if ever, have had an inspiratory experience when starting on a piece of writing, a painting, or a scientific project and that very few such experiences occur later during the course of the process of creation. Although the janusian process frequently occurs early and is usually accompanied by a sense of surprise and illumination, there are generally no dramatic effects. Similarly, when the homospatial process begins a creative sequence, it produces stimulation and a gratifying image or idea but little intense excitement or relief.

Also, with regard to the poetic creative process in particular, an extensive study of poetic manuscripts and biographical material covering many centuries carried out by Phyllis Bartlett has turned up much evidence indicating that inspiratory experiences have been an exception rather than a rule.[3] Careful study, from first manuscript drafts to final poem, indicates that the free driving quality of good poems is arduously achieved, not born in one piece. Statistically, it is probable that inspired ideas of all types are fairly common and widely found. Very likely, they have occurred rather frequently in the general population throughout the course of history. However, it has always been that true creators are those unique people who can work out ideas of any sort, inspired or uninspired.

The Role of Inspiration in the Creative Process

What is the actual role of inspiration in the creative process? I shall answer this by first reporting on what I have learned about inspiration in the writing of poetry and then bring in material about other creative activities. Inspiration is commonly linked to composing poetry, and what does or does not occur there has wide applicability to other creative fields. Generally, a poem first begins—before janusian or homospatial formulations—with a mood, visual image, word, or phrase. The poet usually refers to the formulation of a word or phrase as the earliest starting point of a poem because moods or images that are not immediately expressed in words become diffused or changed; they are forgotten or else do not remain associated with a specific poem. Occasionally, a poet reports that a poem began with a particular moral or intellectual statement. Some poets are embarrassed to admit this because of the popular belief that poems should not be constructed or contrived primarily to make a particular statement but should rather be spontaneous emotive outpourings.

The experience of beginning a poem differs from inspiration in that it is seldom accompanied by a sense of breakthrough, relief, or discovery. What degree of impulse to action there is appears in a variety of ways: interrupting a conversation or task to work on the poem until completed, jotting down some notes, or simply making a mental resolution to remember the word or words and work on the poem at some convenient later time. Rather than relief, however, the overriding feeling reported is that of tension. In part, this tension is about getting down to work and writing; it is relieved by the process of writing and primarily dissipated by the actual completion of the poem. It is also, however, a tension and an anxiety about *finding out what the poem is really about.*

What a Poem Is Saying

Over and over again, my subjects have told me that they seldom knew what a poem was really "saying" until they were well into the writing, until they had actually finished it or, in some cases, until months or years later. When they did find out what the poem was really saying, they then experienced a sense of illumination, discovery, and oftentimes, relief. The poets' allusions to *what the poem is really saying,* the meaning of this phrase to them, were quite variable. Although most of my subjects were understandably reluctant to spell out a prosaic or literal formulation of *what the poem is really saying,* they sometimes cited a particular line, phrase, or stanza in the poem itself as the embodiment of the idea. Often this line, phrase, or stanza was the final one in the poem, the punch line in a sense, but many other sections were also cited. Generally, *what the poem is saying* was an aesthetic statement such as, to give one out of myriad possible examples, Wallace Stevens's last line of *Le Monocle de Mon Oncle*: "But until now I never knew/That fluttering things have so distinct a shade." (Stevens has not been a subject of mine.) My *more* psychologically minded subjects referred to a particular line or set of lines and said such things as, "It's talking about cannibalism," and my *most* psychologically minded subjects said the same type of things but added, "These are my own concerns." My point here is that the discovery has always seemed to me to be a personal discovery or partial insight of some sort (not induced by my presence) even when given as an aesthetic statement. I base this conclusion both on what the most psychologically minded subjects have said and on my own knowledge of the less psychologically minded subjects' personalities and concerns.

Let me make it immediately clear that I do not mean that these later discoveries are true inspirations; quite the contrary. As I have said, true inspirations do occasionally occur both before and during the course of writing, but they are not equivalent to discoveries of the meaning or purpose of the poem. With these later discoveries, the poet is not generally impelled toward further action but, depending on the strength and certainty of what is found there is a sense of completion—a signal that the poem is finished or virtually so. These discoveries function to reduce and resolve a good deal of the tension and anxiety that were connected with starting and working on the poem (even when the discoveries occur several months later).

Although it is not immediately obvious, true inspirations are actually accompanied by a certain amount of anxiety. The heaving of sighs and sense of relief are so dramatic that anxiety is not apparent to the poet himself or to a casual observer. However, the other hallmarks of true inspiration—feverish activity and working on the poem—indicate that anxiety is present as well. This driving anxiety, I believe, is similar to that accompanying the usually nondramatic experience of starting the poem; *both anxieties are later reduced by the discovery of what the poem is really saying.* The discovery, in other words, provides emotional relief because it contains elements of real psychological insight (the nature of which will be clarified further in Chapters 10 and 12), whereas both inspiration and the range of thoughts associated with starting a poem do not.

Many people make comparisons between inspiration and the achievement of insight; on the surface, they appear to have many qualities in common. Both involve a sense of illumination as well as breakthrough accompanied by relief (for insight, it is saying or thinking, "Aha"). Nevertheless, the experiences are not psychologically equivalent. Insight involves bringing unconscious material into consciousness and understanding it, but inspiration only appears to do so or only does so in part.

Instead of bringing understanding of unconscious conflicts, both the thoughts that start a poem and the inspirations that occur along the way *embody* and *represent* the unconscious conflicts themselves. Poets are not aware that such thoughts relate to personal conflicts but see them primarily in artistic terms. They may have some general sense of a personal factor—psychologically sophisticated poets accept that as a matter of faith—but they are not aware of any specific unconscious issue involved at the time. Particular phrases, images, ideas, or poetic metaphors that constitute inspirations and beginnings of poems both represent and initially guard against recognition of personal conflicts. The personal importance of these phrases and other elements is felt, not conceived and, along with artistic considerations, leads the poet to use them in a poem.

Investigatory Evidence

I base my assertions on the following observations. (1) Initial words and phrases reported to me have often indicated a particular conflict. For example, a woman poet revealed that a metaphor (which I cannot quote because of difficulty in obscuring the authorship) connecting an invaginated structure and the color green was the first idea for a particular poem. This woman was, I had learned in previous discussions, quite concerned about her feminine status and had many anxieties about the vaginal bleeding of menstruation. Her phrase, *green————*, we later discovered, represented her conflict between a wish to have a verdant growing sexual organ rather than a red bleeding one and another wish to preserve her vagina and remain female, in fact, exotically female. (2) Both initial words and phrases, and inspirations, were consistently described as accompanied by the feeling of tension and anxiety I mentioned. The anxiety seemed clearly due to the underlying personal conflict and an initial feeling of pressure and risk about its coming to the surface. Subjects reported that a certain amount of relief accompanied initial ideas (more so in inspirations), but they also felt a tension that was later only resolved by finding out what the initial idea or the inspiration meant—finally succeeding in allowing the unconscious issue into consciousness. For example, another poet thought of an image relating roses to blood. The idea inspired a poem—she felt relief, a sense of breakthrough, and an impulse to write. However, she later described the poem itself as an attempt to find out what she felt about her own murderous impulses. (3) The reported discovery of *what a poem is saying* always appeared similar to real insight, or with some exploration it became the basis of a real personal insight. This insight was often directly related to the conflict underlying an original idea or inspiration. For example, a poet started a poem with an image about a man flying pigeons off his roof. He later discovered that the poem was about, *was saying,* something negative about God and by extension, older people. With minimal exploration, he related these negative feelings to feelings about his father, who never listened to him. Although we did not discuss the original lines about pigeons flying, my impression was that the image represented the poet himself, who let words fly off his roof (head). These words were not heard by his father and often, like pigeons, came back to plague him.

Although initial ideas for poems and inspirations represent and, to some extent, initially disguise personal conflicts, they contain the seeds that eventually spur the poet to insight. It is interesting that anxiety-laden initial ideas are courted by poets; they experience pleasure and excitement as well as tension when the idea occurs. Primarily, they are pleased that a poem (a highly valued achievement) is in the offing. Also, the fact that the idea is a way station leading to later understanding and some direct recognition of the reasons for anxiety produces the pleasurable anticipation of deep emotional gratification. Later discoveries are so pleasurable and useful to poets that they court the process of attaining them again and again.

Although inspirations and initial ideas both represent personal conflicts, inspirations are associated with a greater sense of relief. This is so because conflicts connected with inspirations come from deeper levels of consciousness. When inspirations occur late in the poetic creative process, for example, poets describe them as solving problems and bringing relief and pleasure. Notably, at that point, they have already worked and reworked their material and either brought unconscious material closer to awareness or succeeded in burying it deeper. Part of the sense of relief, therefore, is due to dealing with conflicts from deeper levels of consciousness than those at the beginning of the process.

The overall schema is as follows. Successfully creative poets start by drawing out or formulating tasks or problems that are simultaneously artistic and personal. If the tasks or problems are particularly difficult and fraught with anxiety, they may have an inspiration while working on the poem. This inspiratory experience is dramatic because it often comes from a deep level of consciousness and is truly a breakthrough, a binding up of the source of diffuse anxiety. However, there are many defensive and anxious aspects and a drive toward action—further writing and an attempt to gain resolution and insight. When resolution and insight are achieved—during or after the process—poets are no longer preoccupied with the poem.

In addition to the interview data I have already cited, some experiments I have done also bear on these conclusions. Using specially designed word-association tests derived from words in poets' poems in progress, I have obtained results indicating that they work in their poems with psychological material that is increasingly more anxiety-provoking to them as the writing process progresses.[4]

Inspiration in Other Creative Fields

The roles of inspiration and initial ideas in other types of literature, in visual art, music, and science are broadly similar to those in the poetic creative process. Novelists and playwrights start by visualizing a scene, a piece of dialogue, or an overall structure of a plot; visual artists start with shapes and colors, general composition, or an approach to visualization; musicians hear single chords, phrases, musical patterns, or overall compositions; scientists make and become absorbed in puzzles, mathematical equations, conceptual metaphors, and experimental methods. All of these beginnings, including—in a complicated way— scientists' preoccupations, have a personal and unconscious significance for creative persons themselves. Few artists would deny this nowadays, and in science, there are such strongly suggestive examples as Einstein's saying that—in developing the general theory of relativity— he found the differences between the Faraday and Maxwell-Lorentz theories to be "unbearable"[5]; Werner Heisenberg's saying he found the physical part of a theory "disgusting"; and Erwin Schrödinger saying he was frightened and repelled by a mathematical concept.[6]

In any occupation, scientific or otherwise, personal psychological factors always play a role in dictating particular interests or pursuits. Beyond this, the creative scientist has a tendency toward passionate involvement in the specific conceptual problems with which he works, and this indicates even more personal and unconscious involvement. In this, creative scientists are similar to musical composers who invest formal sound relationships with the deepest kind of personal emotion. Puzzling about the nature of unseen physical particles, how the cosmos was created, or the nature of synaptic transmission in the nervous system probably has the same type of emotional roots as fervent concerns with chromaticism and diatonicism in music.

As in the poetic creative process, artists of all types talk about the development of form and meaning as their work progresses. Although they do not necessarily refer to finding out what the particular type of artwork is saying, phrases such as *finding out what a painting is showing or displaying* and *what a piece of music is conveying* are used and are equivalent. Although the creative scientist does not generally employ such terms, he, too, is interested in what a discovery or theory may indicate about his own ways of thinking about himself and the world. In all these types of creative activities, inspirations in the sense I have discussed are rare. When they occur, they are imbued with personal conflicts that instigate further action and an attempt to dissipate anxiety. In the working out of this anxiety, creative effects are produced.

Inspiration and Mental Illness

At this point it may seem that I have demonstrated a linkage between creativity and mental illness. After all, have I not insisted that inspirations and initial ideas in the creative process are imbued with personal conflict? And conflict is intrinsically connected with psychiatric symptoms and illness, is it not? Also, in describing creative persons as engaging in the creative process partly in order to find out something about themselves, have I not indicated something like psychotherapy for illness?

No, a linkage between creativity and mental illness has not been demonstrated or certified here. Conflict is not at all a necessary matter of symptoms and illness, but it is embedded in our human condition. All persons, creative or not, experience personal conflicts at all periods of their lives without a real sign or indication of illness. Living life in the face of death and experiencing love, loyalty, success, and failure instill conflict between opposing wishes, thoughts, and feelings. No one escapes the pangs of indecision, anger at loved ones, or fear of freedom and responsibility. Conflict is universal, and one of the reasons art has deep and broad appeal is that it represents this universal human experience and state of being.

As for the creative process having therapeutic effects, this too pertains to the nature of our human condition rather than to illness. Although something similar to attaining insight occurs in successful creative work, that does not mean that people create primarily to make themselves well. Instead, they engage in creative activities partly in order to gain greater psychological freedom than they already possess. This often means that they ultimately become more free than the average person rather than signifying that they start from sickness and move to health. I shall have more to say about this matter of creativity and psychotherapy later (Chapters 12 and 13).

Also, there are many significant differences between the creative process and symptoms and illness. Artworks are communications in a sense that psychological symptoms never are or can become. Literary and artistic metaphors are unique, and they communicate universal truths and values. Although psychological symptoms have some uniqueness, they primarily reflect universal modes of dealing with anxiety. While communicating meaning to a skilled and sensitive therapist, they generally adhere to some obscuring conventional and time-honored pattern, for example, performing rituals, having physical impairments, or seeing visions. Such patterns primarily conceal meaning both from the ill persons themselves and from others. In contrast, literary and artistic metaphors and other aspects of an artwork stimulate both the author and his audience to seek meaning. A work of art may reduce anxiety to some extent for both creator and recipient, but it also stimulates the anxieties of both to a fair degree. Good art touches on emotionally laden issues and deep meanings and also is anxiety provoking for all of us to some degree. Furthermore, artworks communicate intellectual content, and scientific theories are widely useful factors totally lacking in symptoms. Scientific creations and discoveries change the environment in ways that symptoms and illness never do.

The creative process is decidedly not a form of therapy. Creators choose the conflicts they prefer to work on, and, more often than not, their ideas only touch an aspect of the personal issue. The poet, for instance, may achieve some insight and finish the poem, but he seldom allows the full impact of the insight to affect him. This is seen in the fact that poets often return, again and again, to the same theme or image. Robert Frost, in answer to the perennial question, "Why do you write poems?" has been quoted as saying, "To see if I can make them all different." By implication, Frost's whimsical reply is a criticism of the general literary tendency to be hung up on a recurrent theme and points to his own attempts to overcome this tendency. This hang-up, the need to return to the same unconscious conflict over and over again, is not an indication that poets or other creators are mad. It simply means that creators who are great expressers and interpreters of our inner and outer world and purveyors of joy and understanding are sometimes haunted.

4 ◆◇ The Mystique of the Unconscious and Creativity

Closely related to the emphasis on inspiration in creativity is the belief in the unconscious creative wellspring. Invoked more frequently in connection with creativity than with almost any other human action or experience, the unconscious is considered responsible for mysterious bolts from the blue, flashes of insight, waking from sleep with ideas already formed, and energy-releasing altered states of consciousness. Also, creative writings and works of art seem perfused with unconscious content such as Oedipus complexes, anima and animus, or sexual and aggressive symbolism. So ingrained is the idea that creativity arises from unconscious sources that investigators who present evidence for conscious factors do so at their peril; they run the risk of being rejected out of hand by both professionals and laity.

The belief in the unconscious roots of creativity is a mystique. Because creativity is unconscious, the adherents often also say, it cannot be explained or adequately understood. Moreover, this belief is closely allied to allegations about a connection between creativity and madness. Nietzsche's concept of the creative artist's Dionysian frenzy, for example, anticipates modern constructions of unconscious influences and emphasizes an extreme irrationality of the creative mind. These ideas, in fact, have a long and almost hallowed history. They go back to the philosopher Plato, who laid their groundwork in the following remarks to the poet Ion:

> For the poet is a light and winged and holy thing, and there is no invention in him until he has been inspired and is out of his senses and the mind is no longer in him; when he has not attained to this state, he

is powerless and is unable to utter his oracles. Many are the noble words in which poets speak concerning the actions of men; but like yourself [Ion] when speaking about Homer, they do not speak of them by any rules of art: they are simply inspired to utter that to which the Muse impels them, and that only; and when inspired, one of them will make dithyrambs, another hymns of praise, another choral strains, another epic or iambic verses—and he who is good at one is not good at any other kind of verse: for not by art does the poet sing, but by power divine. Had he learned by rules of art, he would have known how to speak not of one theme only, but of all; and therefore God takes away the minds of poets, and uses them as his ministers, as he also uses diviners and holy prophets, in order that we who hear them may know them to be speaking not of themselves who utter these priceless words in a state of unconsciousness, but that God himself is the speaker, and that through them is conversing with us.[1]

I do not mean to say that in this passage Plato formulated a concept of an unconscious or that he considered the roots of creativity to lie in some particular aspect of the human mind. On the contrary, he clearly considered creativity to be supernatural or divine in origin and, in another place, stated explicitly that the creative artist's performance was the result of "divine madness."[2] When performing creatively, the artist's own senses were not directly responsible for the product, and consequently the creative process was a matter of being out of one's mind and bereft of one's senses. Such emphasis on the seemingly possessed aspect of creative activity has been a basis for a long tradition citing both madness and suprahuman or external sources for creativity. It has, on the one hand, continued and fostered the classical idea of inspiration by the muse, and on the other, it has today culminated in a psychological emphasis on the unconscious aspect of the mind: rather than ideas being inspired by a source outside the creator himself, they have been located within the creator as another aspect of his mind. Although the idea of creativity arising from the unconscious is not the same as Plato's madness notion, it raises many problems.

The modern concept of the unconscious is associated with psychoanalysis and Sigmund Freud. Although Freud actually did not originate the concept—others such as Eduard von Hartmann[3] proposed it earlier—he was the first to develop a full and systematic theoretical account. Other theorists, notably Carl Jung, also attempted a systematic description of unconscious functioning, denying certain aspects of Freud's concept and adding cultural, historical, and other features. Although Jung's concept of the collective unconscious has had a prominent place in some modern theories of creativity, I shall not go into a recounting and assessment here of the differences between Freud's and Jung's theories of unconscious functioning. As the major thrust of the matter is similar for both, I shall focus on the Freudian unconscious and only touch on similarities and differences from the Jungian.

Freud and other psychoanalysts have believed that the unconscious plays a significant role in creativity. Turning to great works of art in order to corroborate findings about psychological processes derived from work with patients, psychoanalysts have long been interested in apparent manifestations of the unconscious in works of literature and visual art. In his initial presentation of his cornerstone concept of the Oedipus complex, Freud turned for illustration and support to Shakespeare's great play *Hamlet*. Citing Hamlet's inability to act against his uncle-stepfather, together with the intense relationship between Hamlet and his mother, Gertrude, Freud proposed that unconscious incestuous feelings toward Gertrude and murderous feelings toward his real father could explain Hamlet's doubt and torment. After this and other artistic analyses by Freud, numerous other psychoanalysts have attempted to describe myriad instances of unconscious phenomena in works of art. Because of the seeming universality of these instances, creative artists were alleged to be particularly sensitive to their own unconscious processes, and these processes were considered to play a critical role in artistic creation. Artists' own testimonies have also strengthened these considerations. Repeatedly, artists of all types report that they cannot trace the steps in their achievement of outstanding ideas and that such ideas seem to intrude into their awareness without warning or preparation. In many cases, important ideas are said to arise when the artist is not directly working on a creative task but rather while he is relaxing or occupied with something else. In effect, therefore, the Platonic idea of possession by an external factor has been changed to a factor that is external to awareness.

Here, however, I will insert a caution and a clarification regarding a distinction between the unconscious and the not-conscious. If something is simply described as outside of awareness or not conscious, it is only a negative factor. Saying "no," negating, or canceling out produces broad categories, and describing someone or something as *not tall* or *not hot* merely eliminates a characteristic rather than sharpening or clarifying the description. Although we often use negations as though they were opposites, *not tall* is not synonymous with *short*, and *not hot* is not equivalent to *cold*. The negatives of *tall* and *hot* include a very large range of height and temperature. Failure to recognize these differences has caused problems with respect to the idea and term *unconscious*. It is used both to mean an opposite of consciousness and (together with the old and misused term, *subconscious*) as a negative form roughly equivalent to not-conscious or *nonconscious*. With respect to creativity and madness, lack of clarity about the distinction has caused confusion and misconceptions.

The Unconscious in Creativity

The Freudian unconscious is not only the negative of consciousness, it is quite specific. Intrinsic to Freud's psychodynamic point of view is a definitely formulated and therefore positively defined unconscious, an unconscious that is *opposite* to the conscious. Freud's unconscious consists of elements derived from the individual's past which are kept out of awareness for a reason. These elements, designated as drives, wishes, memories, and affects, remain unconscious to the individual himself because they are unacceptable, either personally or socially, and therefore cannot be *tolerated* in consciousness. They are kept unconscious by so-called *repression*, an active psychological process or barrier.

Also, elements in the unconscious have *a diffuse and controlling* effect by virtue of being kept out of awareness. These elements exert a consistent and potentially broad effect on conscious thought and behavior precisely because they remain unconscious. Once an element becomes conscious—once its form and substance are known—then it can be changed and modified by intentional control. When unacceptable personal memories, wishes, and affects are kept out of awareness or repressed, they still have force and influence, but they exert an involuntary effect. And the more strongly they are prevented from coming to awareness, the more broad and diffuse is their effect. Strongly repressed unconscious drives, for instance, tend to influence all conscious thought and behavior. Although the matter is somewhat different with respect to the Jungian collective unconscious, the contents and themes of this type of unconscious are derived from the past, too, and they also exert a controlling effect on individual consciousness.

Now, if this type of unconscious were fully responsible for creativity, as many theorists contend, what would that really mean? What would that signify about the nature of creative processes? For one thing, with this type of unconscious and the controlling force of past events as entirely responsible for creative activity, we would have to restrict the definition of creativity severely. True newness, consisting of a complete break with the past, would not be a characteristic, or even a feature, of the creative process or of creations. Creations could not be truly new because they would be the direct product of past and *preexisting* unconscious factors. A meaningful definition of creativity should include the possibility of human beings producing truly new ideas, theories, artistic styles and forms, or inventions. Consequently, the contention does not work.

A second more telling result of this theory would be that the unacceptable and, in fact, the ordinary and banal contents of the unconscious would be the basis for great works of art and other important human achievements. Although this proposition is not as offensive right off the bat to me as it is to some, on serious consideration it produces thorny problems. Works of art are decidedly not offensive or unacceptable or banal, and therefore some type of transformation or change would have to occur on the way from the unconscious to the final product. Rather than the unconscious, the particular transforming factor—whatever it is—would become the real cause of creativity.

The biggest problem with accepting this idea of unconscious causes of creativity is the tied-in feature of a broad controlling effect on conscious thought and behavior. For although this control could plausibly account for representation of unconscious factors in the content of an artwork, it could not account for *artistic form*. A primary function of the Freudian controlling mechanisms is to conceal unconscious content: they alter and distort unconscious material so that it cannot be recognized in consciousness. But artistic form—the shapes, patterns, styles, and compositional features of artworks—has an opposite function: it uncovers and reveals deep meanings and psychological processes. It shows the organization of the feelings and actions of human beings as well as of the sounds and sights of nature. Independence from unconscious control of the processes responsible for form is necessary in order to produce revelation rather than concealment and the lucidity of art rather than obscurity. Also, a broadly controlling unconscious force could not produce intrinsically important unities in art, but, because the unconscious is essentially disunified, it would result in disunity or monotony.

Although Jung's collective unconscious is not necessarily a repository of unacceptable affects, drives, and memories, there are similar problems with that formulation. Characteristic themes of the collective unconscious such as *the wise old man, the great uroboric or unisexual mother*, and *the birth of the hero*, must also be transformed or changed to have a creative effect. According to Jung, these themes have been transmitted throughout history and are embedded in the past of particular racial and cultural groups or of the human race as a whole. He says the artist uses unconscious "autonomous complexes" to transform these themes into art.[4] This formulation, unfortunately, is redundant and circular and will not do. According to this, *autonomous* unconscious factors produce both *autonomous* form and content in art.

Despite all these difficulties, there is something to be said for the theories. Aspects of these positively defined types of unconscious functioning, Freudian and Jungian, must play some role in artistic creative production. Ordinary conscious thinking is too stepwise, too free of affect and emotion, and too focused on the natural world and on things as they are to provide the kind of remote and unusual connections and penetrating affective experiences characteristic of art. Emotion-laden operations of the Freudian unconscious which link childhood and adult thoughts and experiences together, infuse feeling, and produce constant shifts in thinking without regard to specific goals play important roles in various phases of the creative process. Also, as I said at the end of the last chapter, there is little doubt that artists' unconscious conflicts (and perhaps also the contents of the collective unconscious) determine their characteristic preoccupations with recurrent themes. All types of artists return over and over again to themes having the basic structure of some unconscious element, be it the Oedipus complex, bisexuality, castration, reunification with a mothering or fathering figure, or the themes of the collective unconscious. The Oedipus complex, for instance, was not only the concern of Sophocles and Shakespeare, but more recent writers such as Nathaniel Hawthorne, Herman Melville, Eugene O'Neill, Edgar Allan Poe, Samuel Butler, Fyodor Dostoyevski, Arthur Miller, Tennessee Williams, Harold Pinter, Edward Albee, and Samuel Beckett show definite preoccupation with various aspects of this theme, as do other types of artists as well.

The Nonconscious and Conscious in Creativity

The other type of unconscious functioning is the one that is designated simply as *nonconscious*. Distinguished scientists such as Walter B. Cannon and Charles S. Sherrington have both argued extensively that creative ideas arise from the nonconscious portion of the mind.[5] Unfortunately, the concept of the nonconscious is, as I said, a negative one and is therefore very broad. Proposing a nonconscious mind without any specific attributes like those described by Freud and Jung has only increased the mystery. Discovery of the specific homospatial and janusian processes in creativity, however, does help to solve this problem directly. Neither of these processes appears directly in awareness, and neither of them arises directly from either the Freudian or the Jungian unconscious. Neither follows the patterns of ordinary stepwise or productive thinking.

With either or both of these processes, creators are only consciously aware of the *products* of their thinking. Only the resulting metaphor, characterization, plot idea, visual image, musical phrase, or theoretical formulation appears in consciousness, not the structural features of these processes such as searching for opposites or superimposing mental images. Because the creators are not aware (and do not need to be aware) of the structure of their thinking and seldom if ever retrace particular thought sequences leading to creative ideas, the ideas seem to them to result from factors out of their control. Because creative persons have intentionally not distracted themselves in order to focus on, or become aware of, the detailed nature of their thinking, they have never described these processes in their own writings and testimonies about creativity. Only through extensive and painstaking cooperative interviewing and sequence reconstruction together with observation and experimentation have the processes been revealed to me.

The structural features of the janusian and homospatial processes account in part for the numerous reports—adding to and abetting the mystique of unconscious creativity—of something coming from out of awareness. In the case of the janusian process, there is a leap of thought in which the multiple opposites or antitheses are brought together at once. Ideas, images, or propositions traditionally considered valid or real are juxtaposed with their polar opposite or opposites; the coming together of such widely disparate elements produces a feeling and experience of something coming out of nowhere. Because the polar opposite has not been seriously entertained previously to be true or meaningful—sometimes not even to exist at all— it is held at the periphery of consciousness. Bringing it together with an idea that is in the focus of attention produces a sense of sudden insight or a leap of thought.

In Albert Einstein's development of the general theory of relativity, for example, he had considered all the characteristics of gravitation and motion prior to formulating the key step. He had pondered moving objects, speed, acceleration, and especially the motion of magnets in an electrical field. Rest, the opposite of motion, was the limiting condition at the fringes of the matter until he brought rest and motion together in the image of a person falling from the roof of a house—at rest within his fall. And he described this idea as a thought that came to him while he was working on an essay—he was focused only on the new understanding he had achieved, not on how he had achieved it. Certainly aware that the idea seemed contradictory—in the report I cited earlier he carefully took up each discordant detail—he was nevertheless moved by his thought. The experience of extreme disparity, the turning around of what was previously believed to be totally untrue or contradictory, is what accounts for the strong feelings of suddenness and strangeness and, in many cases, the sense of outside influence.

The scientist Edwin McMillan also spoke in our interview of a sudden realization in his discovery of the principle of phase stability. He thought of a particle being out of phase and conceived that it shifted to the "opposite sense." This idea was the breakthrough that led to his recognition of constantly oscillating particles that were in a stable state. Going over the sequence in his thinking several times in order to be sure I had made no mistake in interpretation, I asked him whether he knew that he had conceived of an opposite direction and of simultaneously opposite energy levels. Acknowledging retrospectively that these were his conceptions at the time, he then went on to elaborate on the product of his thinking—the actual phase stability principle he had discovered. In response to further questions, he also made absolutely clear that he was fully conscious and rational at the moment he developed the idea but thought about the content rather than the way in which he had achieved it.

Similarly, the poet whose initial idea for a poem was that horses are animals who "renounce their own kind in order to live our lives" did not initially comment to me on the oppositional characteristics of this thought. He had been reading a poem about men and horses written by another poet when he developed the formulation. When I then pointed out the simultaneous opposition in the structure, he completely agreed that it was there and, like McMillan, went on to elaborate on extensions of his conception. Animals, he said, were often more gentle than human beings, and humans often behaved in what were considered "bestial" ways. In this case, the lack of focus on the structure of his thinking was more striking to me than with other creative subjects with whom I had worked because this poet had openly revealed to me previously his tendency to use opposites in his poetry. When using opposites, he said, "you can have it both ways." Despite that, at the moment of developing his janusian idea about horses for a particular poem, he had not stopped to think about the oppositional structure of his thinking. Appropriately, he was only intrigued by the poetic notion itself.

Creative thinking is nonconscious in this respect primarily. In each case, creators are not generally aware of the specific structural features of the unusual modes of thought which they use in producing a creation. These types of thinking occur, however, when they are fully conscious and in possession of their senses. Neither dreaming nor in a special altered state of consciousness in which unconscious material becomes available, they are not engaged in "regression in the service of the ego."[6] According to that theoretical formulation, unconscious processes erupt into consciousness and, in an unexplained and mysterious way, are controlled by the ego for creative purposes. Instead, the creator characteristically tends to formulate simultaneous oppositions and superimpositions in the creative process without paying attention to how he does so.

The overemphasis on the unconscious, the mystique, and its related idea of possession, is therefore a mistake. But that is not the complete story. All conscious thought is in some way influenced by unconscious processes, and janusian and homospatial types are not exceptions. For instance, there are often unconscious factors influencing a creative person's focus on a particular task, his choice of a particular set of opposites, or the elements superimposed in the homospatial conception. At times, these particulars may be derived from unconscious conflicts. Although the relationship of both janusian and homospatial processes to unconscious material is primarily an independent one, unconscious factors do play a role. Also, many aspects of a work of art, and of a scientific theory as well, are derived from unconscious material.

To come full circle, Plato's description of the matter was not really so far off the mark. Only his conclusions regarding madness and the tradition he fostered, which emphasize a source of creativity completely external to consciousness, are found wanting. The reason the creator is unaware of the specific factors accounting for his skill or art is that he does not think of the particular structural qualities of the thought processes he uses in producing his creations. They are part of that diffusely negative nonconscious aspect of his mental functioning, and to some degree, they are derived from the specific and positive unconscious defined first by Freud. The creator is, however, neither out of his mind nor bereft of his senses. He is a more sensitive and flexible thinker than the rest of us and is capable of using thought processes and blending modes of thought in unusual and exciting ways.

5 ◆◇ *Psychosis and the Creation of Poetry*

*S*chizophrenic Patient—
Verbatim Transcript

I've never been confused as much as I have been recently. Confusion
was nothing to me. It was fun. I loved art, I loved to have my hands in
every single thing I could get them in. And when I'm here I don't have
the facilities to dig in the garden and put my feet in the mud and I just
can't stand that . . . feeling. I, I need to be free like most of us do,
because I feel like a bird when I'm up in the air for any length. I feel
like a bird when I'm skiing, I feel like I could fly if I really tried but I
wouldn't try because—hee, hee—it's beyond my power. Maybe someday they'll perfect it so that a person can fly without . . . walking. But
they better hurry up! Because there's too many guys on the road right
now."

There is no doubt about it: people suffering from schizophrenia
say the darndest things. As a matter of fact, people suffering from
schizophrenia often say or write things that are intriguing, ambiguous, even metaphorical; seemingly poetic, profound, and meaningful
words and ideas virtually pour out at times. Also, as I have said, very
good poets, even great ones, are sometimes quite disturbed. Several
poets in recent decades have committed suicide, spent large portions
of their lives in psychiatric hospitals, or dissolved themselves in drink
to such an extent that suspicion arises that these people particularly
are trying to relieve the enormous tensions and the attendant delusions and hallucinations associated with schizophrenia.[1] Does this
mean we have to take sides? Despite what I have said about specific

nonpsychotic janusian and homospatial processes in creativity, do we have to grant that there may be some particular affinity between the poetic imagination and schizophrenia? Or, should we take up lance and charge St. George-like against monstrous intimations about the poets and the poetry we love? Worse still, do we assert that schizophrenia and related conditions are valid states of being in a crazy world and that the suffering of the severely disturbed person is yet a noble and necessary concomitant of greatness, poetic vision, and true morality?

None of these positions is valid with respect to poetry or to any other field of creativity. For some poets, it appears that illness does feed and nurture their gift; visions, conflicts, and "dark forebodings" dictate the subject matter of their work, and the loose, unusual thought sequences generated by tension and anxiety lead to new and telling combinations and structures. Other poets, free of mental illness, follow other paths. Furthermore, asserting that a poet is schizophrenic or that a poem grew in part from schizophrenic thought processes should not be a value judgment about the poet or the poem; poetry and people are judged by their effects, not by illness or any other forces that made them the way they are. Rather, ill people are judged by what they do about their illnesses.

The payoff in considering the relationship between schizophrenia and poetry comes from a quarter other than the time-worn arena in which heroic accusations and counteraccusations are fought out. It is often alleged these days by poets, teachers, and mental health professionals that poetry is—or should be—a direct outpouring of unconscious processes, a precept derived from the mystique of the unconscious sources of creativity. As a result, some classroom teaching of poetry writing emphasizes helping students to "free up," become unstifled, or to get in touch with their basic feelings and conflicts. Refraining from direct criticism of students' poetry, teachers—as often as not, teachers who are themselves poets—focus on students themselves and, in a supposedly therapeutic way, talk with them about their lives, their experiences, and their problems. Now, the schizophrenic psychotic condition happens to be the natural testing ground for the kind of position these therapist teachers take. In a technical sense, direct outpouring of unconscious processes is the *sine qua non* of schizophrenia because persons suffering from this condition are unable to marshall the defenses and other adaptive forms of mastery which keep these processes under wraps for most of us. If poetry were really the result of a direct outpouring of unconscious processes, schizophrenia and poetic creativity would be equivalent.[2] But there is no need to invoke such an easily rejected straw man to justify a consideration of poetry and schizophrenia or, more specifically, poetry composed by persons with schizophrenia; teaching poetry writing is complicated enough, and despite the weakness of their theory, some teachers may help students with a quasi-therapeutic approach. As a matter of fact, teaching poetry writing to schizophrenic students is dazzlingly difficult, but it highlights problems of the everyday poetry classroom on the one hand and of coping with the shifts in psychotic people on the other, exactly because so much of these students' writing seems so good.

Poetry Writing by Schizophrenic Patients

Let us look at the matter further. The setting is a school in a psychiatric hospital. Students attend this school while living in the hospital, sometimes for rather long periods of time, and an attempt is made to keep them coming to school regularly regardless of the degree of their disturbance and the vicissitudes of their illnesses. They are high school age or a bit older and suffer from many types of psychiatric illness. Here is a response to an assignment in English class—"explain a popular saying"—by a schizophrenic student:

> Two heads are better than one—one for public use, one for personal use: then you [*sic*] called schizophrenic.
> Moral: Keep it all under one roof.[3]

From a psychiatric point of view, the response is particularly interesting (as is the assignment itself) because proverbs and popular sayings have often been used in mental status examinations for the purpose of diagnostic assessment, especially to assess schizophrenic thinking. Impaired ability to think abstractly has traditionally been considered a hallmark of schizophrenic thinking, and a literal and idiosyncratic explanation of a proverb, therefore, has been seen as a diagnostic response. There is no need to haggle about such diagnostic procedures or bald interpretations; they have been modified by modern psychiatry, and this student's rejoinder shows one of the reasons for the modification. Clearly, the response is abstract: the student attempts a justification of his illness and couches it in philosophical and poetic terms. Introducing and metaphorically using an aphorism in reply to an aphorism is vital and ironic, and the substance of the whole response is expressive and—at the very least—poignant. Here is another example of this student's use of metaphor, again in response to an assignment:

> How I envision myself. I see myself as a cup of tea. The cup is made of glass and is colored in off white. The cup also has a thin handle. The

tea inside is plain orange pekoe. The cup is slightly hot but warm. There is a silver spoon in the cup. Tea has formed and stuck to the outside of the bottom of the cup. The light from above shades the cup and also reflects light inside forming a three-fourth diameter in contour. You can see through the white cup because it's transparent.

The glass is artificial, but made of natural resources. I have an attitude phony at times by not showing my real feelings. The tea is slowly matured in the sun and has a nutty, deep taste. My inner self.

The spoon has a metallic warm which sometimes I do, although sometimes I don't.

The warmth of the tea my mental scars of being show up in the hot anger which is covered by the mellowness of the warmth. The spilt tea is anger shown consciously and unconsciously. The shade of the light on the cup: my feelings of everything being black and white at times. At other times, gray lives or different feelings colors give off.

The transparency of the tea through the cup is me seeing through my own walls I have built up past the time when I needed them for protection.

Taken as a whole, the piece is not poetry. There is too much prosaic spelling out of the metaphor and, in fact, too much literal thinking. By literal thinking here, I mean the tendency to elaborate details of the metaphor such as the "metallic warm" of the spoon in relation to himself. The feeling is that the writer does not distinguish himself from the cup of tea, or he is afraid the reader won't make the distinction and he is at pains to clarify what applies to himself and what doesn't. This, in fact, is one of the major issues in defining a borderline between schizophrenic thinking and poetry.

Taken out of context, many phrases in schizophrenic utterances are interesting and evocative metaphors, for example, the student's "spilt tea is anger." But it is not clear from the writing or the complete utterance whether such a phrase is really posed in a figurative sense, and of course the figurative nature of metaphor is its poetic essence. Furthermore, the entire piece has a quality that is surely not poetic. The writer seems to be trying to communicate particular things about himself to someone who could help him—not unexpectedly, you might say, since he is in a psychiatric hospital—and there is no progression, no unified meaning, merely disjointed and sometimes over-dramatized statement. Yes, it says something about his being ill and trying to communicate to a helping person, but such statements are not distinctive or literary; they are also present in the writings of non-hospitalized or nontreated schizophrenic persons as well as in bad poetry. So far, however, I have only presented this student's attempts at "expository" writing, not his self-conscious attempts at poetry. He did the following in class also:

> time for some concern for her wishes, hopes;
> time for cry for the pain he caused.
> time to be at peace with my disappointments.
> time for the good-bye embracement I never had.
> time for my wander soul to be reborn into something better than
>   the past
> time to catch the sunrise a few times
> time to catch the sunset at its peak
> he waited for you, he sat there crying while
> he was expecting you to come out and see
> him throwing dirt balls at the wall like
> a child, and you his first and only friend
> sat here with him throwing dirt balls and
> asking him sympathetic questions.

> fragrant lesbians walk by
> chrome and spark plugs ignite explosive thoughts
> sometimes I wonder where my
> father is but know his sanity
> is on vacation with him.
> my anorexic girlfriend
> vomits in her hatred of me.
> my mother tells me to paint
> on her canvas but has blown off
> my hands with the shotgun that
> she holds cocked in her hands
> aimed at my legs which are quivering
> with fear of my long awaited journey
> to jerusalem.

This piece has some of the same problems as the student's other writing: is the arresting image of the mother with the gun in her hand too strong or overdramatic for the rest of the poem, or is it the best part of the poem and requires more prior development and coherence with the other images used? Here, the psychiatric question comes to the fore: is the student so motivated to communicate his difficulties to a prospective therapist that the thought about his mother intrudes to disrupt the instances of tight and exciting poetic language and structures of the stanza, "fragrant lesbians walk by"; "spark plugs ignite explosive thoughts"; "his sanity is on vacation with him"? With respect to this question, it is important to note that the anorexic girlfriend was also a patient in the hospital, and the reference to her probable secret has elements of a request for help for her as well as for the writer himself.

Make no mistake about it, the psychiatric question about this section of the poem is a teacher's question as well. Should the teacher try to help this student with the poem by entering into a discussion of the thoughts and feelings alluded to in these lines in the hope that further revelation and/or resolution of those feelings will make for better poetry (and possibly be therapeutic for him as well)? No, that seems to be the wrong tack. Year after year in numerous hospital settings, such an approach has been tried, and the result has been that neither the patient nor the poetry gets any better. There are complex reasons that this should be so, but the essential matter is the nature of the student-patient's enterprise: he is consciously attempting to write poetry, not engaging in therapy. A teacher's focusing on the communication of problems reinforces rather than alleviates a disruptive tendency in his poetry writing and, in the end, frustrates him.

There are many ways around this difficulty. One of the ways my colleagues and I have found to be meaningful is to emphasize the goal of poetic unity. To illustrate this approach:

The last stanza is, we think, quite exciting. There are many vivid images, and the emotional impact is strong. But let's look at some of the images to see what's going on:

> *fragrant lesbians walk by*
> *ignite explosive thoughts*
> *his sanity is on vacation with him*
> *vomits in her hatred of me*
> *paint on her canvas*
> *blown off my hands*
> *my long awaited journey to jerusalem*[4]

Do you see any difficulty here? No? Well, sure, taking something in poetry out of context always distorts it, but let's forget about that for the moment and see if we can understand something about what seems not to work in the poem. You can't? Well, here's the question: do all these images fit together? The phrases "fragrant lesbians walk by," "chrome and spark plugs ignite explosive thoughts," "his sanity is on vacation with him," and "my long awaited journey to jerusalem" all seem related to each other and to the context of the poem. You, the poetic subject, are sitting and waiting; these images all relate to something about that, for example, people walking by, cars passing, going on vacation, taking a journey. Oh yes, there's another theme: you move from lesbians to your girlfriend to your mother. And, of course, the shotgun aimed at your legs has a good deal to do with your waiting, your journey, and perhaps even your father's sanity being on vacation with him. So what? Well, how does the anorexic vomiting fit in, or, interesting and evocative as it is, how does your mother telling you to "paint on her canvas" sound in relation to these other ideas and images?

What should you do? Work on the poem more, we think. The images we talked about, some of them, are very telling and poetic: the sanity on vacation, the shotgun aimed at your legs, and perhaps even the fragrant lesbians. See what more you can do with it all.

At this juncture, we make no effort with the student-patient to do anything about the cliché, "journey to jerusalem," nor even about the monotonous cliché rhythms and repetitions of the first stanza because, after we have pointed out the disunities and excited some interest in improving the poem, a major hurdle consistently appears. It is a hurdle that arises so universally and consistently in work with schizophrenic patients that I feel justified in calling it a characteristic of the illness; not that it doesn't occur with other people, sick or well, but, as an initial response, it is virtually invariant here. The hurdle is: *schizophrenic patients won't revise.* Not on your life, not in a million years.

The probable reasons for this are interesting in that they shed some light on the difficulties about writing poetry in the first place. The poem as written is apparently experienced as a direct extension of the person himself (recall my earlier interpretation regarding the spelling out of the cup of tea metaphor). Just as the person feels he must be understood, even loved, unconditionally, that is, he must be understood without making an effort toward achieving understanding (indeed, just the opposite occurs: schizophrenic communication is often highly distorted), so too neither the poem nor the person can, or should be, changed. And the reader is not only charged to do a lot of the work of integrating and clarifying, he must do almost all of it.

Fear, defensiveness, and compulsiveness all play a role. And, fortunately, although the refusal to revise is characteristic, it is not insurmountable. Some reworking of the poem eventually will be done if we care enough about the patient, do not work on too much at once, and keep our focus on connections and unifications. Included in connections and unifications, of course, are unities of sound and rhythm. The repetitive rhythms of the first stanza of this student's poem should eventually be sounded back to him in connection with the other rhythms of the poem, and unity or diversity of sound patterns should be discussed. Sometimes there is no revision, but a new poem is begun.

Mixing Madness and Poetry

The teaching exercise here illustrates some of the issues in the crossover between schizophrenia and poetic creativity. The unleashed unconscious processes coming to the surface in schizophrenia undoubtedly account in part for some of the startling and vivid combinations of words and images in speech and in writing. For example, I suspect that the student's reference to his mother telling him to paint on her canvas concerns a childhood memory of an actual event, whereas the shotgun blowing off his hands concerns his previously unconscious, now conscious, fear of mutilation by his mother. In context, these lines are poetically effective partly because they lead back in the next lines to ideas about locomotion begun earlier. But the writer's associational route to these lines seems to have been from father (or lesbians perhaps) to girlfriend to mother rather than through the poetic constructions of the earlier lines themselves. In other words, the patient's problems *have* disrupted his poetry; his thought travels along lines dictated by his anxiety and his dependence on some ideal reader to understand him rather than along the lines of the categories dictated by the poetry itself. Cardinal among the difficulties in schizophrenic thinking—in all unconscious thinking, if you will—is such difficulty in developing and using categories pertaining to the external world. Unlike the janusian and homospatial processes—which consistently recognize and employ logical, useful, and aesthetic distinctions and categories—words, thoughts, and objects are brought together on the basis of superficial (or personally meaningful) resemblances. Consequently, schizophrenic thinking often produces disjunctive and idiosyncratic combinations, some of which seem vivid, poetic, or dazzlingly abstract; but the indiscriminate violation of external categories produces disunity in ordinary discourse, sometimes actual incoherence, and disunity in poetry as well.

Another student, very caught up with alliteration—the use of similar sounding consonants—produced a poem with some typical forms of idiosyncratic combination, word coinages, or neologisms:

> yellow kanabaris
> squared rambrewfully
> words written in tears
> elaborating on boxes

tomorrow and today
light up your cigarettes
frantic fuckers filling space
time warons ticking
remembering he who's lost
insulting impenetrable virgins
bangers on the brain
tall walls crumble cumbersomely
as metallic metaphors are slaves to all.

And, in another poem he pushed alliteration further.

majestic marmelade man
what's that sparkle in your eye
sadly lost souls sink
while collaborating caucases condemn
peal off paper past
repent remorse regret
mainlining memories maim
as crystallizing cages conceal all convictions
hopeless healing hickeys
mordacious morbid mothering myth
demoralized dimensions diluted by tears
sorry yesterday
try and forget your loneliness.

In the first poem, the words *rambrewfully* and *warons* are clear examples of word condensation or combinations based on some private emotionally meaningful resemblance. In context, they are not equally problematic: *rambrewfully* seems to convey some concrete aspects of the drug experience of the poem, but *warons* is totally incomprehensible. Working with this student, we would not necessarily pay much attention to these words except for letting him know that we did not understand *warons* at all (is it from "wears on"?). But we would be concerned with the alliteration in both poems because it is here that the poet seems to lose hold of a category that is potentially quite powerful. Linking words and thoughts on the basis of alliteration comes very easily in schizophrenia; it is a cardinal characteristic of so-called clang associations and a general tendency to pay attention to superficial sound resemblances. But alliteration in poetry is distinctly more than that. Therefore, we would approach the alliterative sequences in the following way. First, we would repeat back to the student the monotonous rhythms, particularly the penultimate lines in the second poem depending on the *m* and *d* alliteration, and ask if they related well to the rhythms before and after them. Then, we would break down the alliterative sequence and ask about such combinations as *demoralized dimensions* and *dimensions diluted* to see if the poet really felt they fit together. The fruits of such labors are rewarding because the student learns that sound and alliteration are not arbitrary matters and that such connections as the word *tall* and the component portions *tall* of *metallic* do not justify the use of the forced and intrusive last line of the first poem. In the face of the unreality of the psychotic world, we would explain that poetic categories of sound, rhythm, and imagery are just as real as any other categories in the external world.

It turns out, then, that the attempt to help the schizophrenic poet organize his original images, words, sounds, and metaphors into a poetically meaningful unity is directed at a basic thinking problem and is therefore therapeutically as well as artistically sound. But let's not be antiseptically formalistic about it; the things the poet is saying bear scrutiny as well. And here we run into very tricky complications that in the end may only be resolved by taste, intuition, and other imponderables; for despite what I say about the problematic intrusion of the student-patient's problems into his writing, poetry should be personal, introspective, and arresting. The line between the pathological and the powerful or the poignant is often microscopically fine, and when confronted with a decision in a particular case, there is a great temptation to withdraw and be *laissez-faire*—if not helping, at least doing no harm.

Sorting Out the Differences

I think the key to resolving the issue lies in an assessment of the emotional burden the poet is placing on the reader. Clearly, I am not now referring to the degree of difficulty in understanding a poem or resonating to it, but rather to the feeling that the poet is primarily hanging out his dirty linen, asking the reader to *do* something for him, respond to him as a person rather than to the poem or the world of the poem. It is an important distinction, and I shall take it up further in the next chapter. Along with students like those whose works I have discussed, we have also had some who have suffered as a result of a teacher's misplaced indulgence or fear of harm. In one case, a student's writings prior to hospitalization were filled with gory spectacles of disemboweling, murder, and unmistakable references to her own suicidal intent. Her high school teacher, clearly confused, and out of a misplaced desire to encourage the student's "talent," returned the writings to her with the comment, "I do believe that you can out Poe Edgar

Allan." But the student could only experience this comment as a rebuff: the teacher, in a manner similar to this student's overambitious parents, was ignoring the insistent overall message and inappropriately paying far more attention to her artistic products than to the student as a person. The girl's illness progressed, and not long after, she did attempt suicide. This is not to say that the teacher should have known exactly how she reinforced the parents' position to the teenage girl; by paying attention to the message, however, the teacher could have helped the student earlier. Learning to distinguish psychotic from aesthetic power is important for the teacher, the poet herself, and for the rest of us, as well.

6 ◆◇ Self-destruction and Self-creation

C*reation and* destruction, although opposites, are closely related to each other. Patients of any type who are engaged in psychotherapy often come to a point when they are preoccupied with thoughts of suicide. Yearnings for death, oblivion, escape, or declaimers of total surrender fill the therapy hours. It is a frightening time for the patient and sometimes for the therapist as well. But such thoughts often signal a turning point: the patient is confronting basic conflicts and the full brunt of his fear of change. With sudden impact, the patient has come to see that the locus of difficulty is within himself. Although the source of his problems may originally have been external—harried by an overbearing spouse, cursed by bad breaks or faulty upbringing by unfeeling parents—the patient realizes that only he can set things right. He feels that he must change himself, and he is terrified of change; death seems a far preferable alternative. For the patient in the throes of such an experience, the options are overwhelming. He feels a total dissolution of the person he has been and a simultaneous sense that he could make himself anew; he could mold himself totally into a person he wants to be. In the face of such unlimited potential and freedom, the patient yearns to retreat into oblivion. He is hovering between self-creation and self-destruction.

Creation and destruction are intimately related to each other in the experience of life, and in artistic production too. Artists knowingly set out to destroy a previous style by the creation of a new one, and in an essential sense, the production of anything radically new always involves destruction of the old. Art involves nullifying the modes and forms of the past and our ordinary ways of looking at the world. Poetry shocks our sense of grammar and syntax, music our sense of functional sounds, and even representational art changes our view of a face or scene. Scientific creation even more clearly results in radical change or obliteration of existing beliefs and practices. Although destruction, in this sense, may seem somewhat abstract and impersonal, there is a personal and concrete relationship between it and creation in art as well. While they are engaged in creating, artists must frequently cope with destructive feelings, both consciously and unconsciously. The artists' wishes to hurt, maim, humiliate, even to annihilate other persons often provide fuel for the creative process. As I shall clarify further in Chapter 12, creating always involves a movement toward basic self-knowledge, a process of simultaneously unearthing unconscious material through dynamisms such as the homospatial and janusian processes while attaining artistic and pragmatic goals. A key motive for engaging in creative activity is often an attempt at unearthing and working through the sources of destructive feelings particularly. In other words, artists and other types of creators frequently create in order that they not destroy; or they explore a scientific problem, literary theme, visual image, musical idea, or poetic metaphor as an unconsciously motivated means of uncovering the sources of disturbing, frequently destructive feelings. For example, a poet subject of mine, mentioned earlier, was moved by the experience of seeing a horse appear suddenly at a barren desert site. He decided to write a poem about the incident, and in the course of writing it, he became dimly aware of hostile feelings toward women; he sensed that, in some way, the horse unconsciously represented some specific women in his life. In another case, a novelist, writing about college students, gradually became aware of a resemblance between one of the characters he created and his own brother. Unwittingly, he had given his highly negative character—the villain of the piece in fact—some of his brother's attributes. Realizing this, he became aware of some long-standing feelings of sibling rivalry and hostility. As a third example, a scientist—here my data are inferential rather than direct—shifted to a dramatic and creative solution to a problem in the presence of someone toward whom he had destructive feelings. While working in his laboratory, he looked up at one point because he heard someone come in. Rather than being his expected collaborator, the visitor was a representative of his scientific rival, a man who had criticized him sharply. Then, while the visitor worked in another part of the laboratory, the scientist arrived at a ground-breaking solution of a problem he had worked on for years.

Scientists, of course, seldom become aware of the unconscious roots of their ideas because of the nature of the scientific enterprise.

The problems they deal with seem completely external to themselves, and there is rarely a reason to explore a specific idea or image in a way analogous to the extrapolations and explorations of art. Yet creation in any field is a healthy means of dealing with destructive feelings. Because creation has the *potential* for increasing self-knowledge, there is the possibility of creative persons freeing themselves from their psychological past and making themselves, or aspects of themselves, anew. In other words, creation in the arts and sciences can facilitate self-creation. As Yeats wrote,

> Those friends that have it I do wrong
> Whenever I remake a song
> Should know what issue is at stake
> It is myself that I remake.[1]

The Case of Sylvia Plath

The poet Sylvia Plath was unable to turn creation into self-creation. Although much of her poetry is full of vibrant and beautiful images, there is another strain in her work which, I think, foretells her tragic suicide at the age of thirty-one. Strong drives to destruction as well as creation appear in her poems. There are new images of the ominous, deadly side of homely kitchen things and of living bodies and flowers. These images transform both the living and the deadly: they make death seem beautiful and life seem threatening. The quiet, resigned rhythms of her lines contrast with the bitterness, resentment, hatred, and annihilation in and behind the words, producing a strange excitement and vitality. But, while her destructive feelings are often fused into poetic creations, there is little working out of them and little indication of any insight and unearthing of the unconscious sources of her concerns. For example, in one of the poems she wrote shortly before she took her life, *Edge*, there are striking excesses.

> The woman is perfected.
> Her dead
>
> Body wears the smile of accomplishment,
> The illusion of a Greek necessity
>
> Flows in the scrolls of her toga,
> Her bare
>
> Feet seem to be saying:
> We have come so far, it is over.
>
> Each dead child coiled, a white serpent,
> One at each little

Pitcher of milk, now empty.
She had folded

Them back into her body as petals
Of a rose close when the garden

Stiffens and odours bleed
From the sweet, deep throats of the night flower.

The moon has nothing to be sad about,
Staring from her hood of bone.

She is used to this sort of thing.
Her blacks crackle and drag.[2]

The lines beginning the poem are beautiful but chilling: "The woman is perfected/Her dead/Body wears the smile of accomplishment." Looking at these lines retrospectively, with knowledge of her suicide shortly thereafter, we can, of course, see a clear statement of her intent. But this is not the excess I am talking about, because there is poetic creation in these lines despite their macabre tone. The lines are paradoxical, exciting, and stimulate a progression of thought. Soon after these lines, however, there are the strange and disjunctive ones: "Each dead child coiled, a white serpent,/One at each little/Pitcher of milk, now empty./She has folded/Them back into her body as petals/Of a rose close when the garden/Stiffens and odours bleed."

I believe these latter lines to be uncreative because, in them, destructiveness has become excessive. The children are returned to the mother's body simply because she can give no more. She and her breasts—the pitchers of milk—are empty and dried up. The children are enfolded back into her womb, back into the past, because that is where they came from. They are destroyed simply because she is destroyed. Furthermore, they are called *serpents*, a name whose negativity is only slightly modulated in this context by the adjective *white*. In parallel with the destructive exorbitance in these lines, the poetic images introduced are inconsistent and jarring. Serpents do not go with pitchers of milk, and the petals of the rose do not close as other flower petals sometimes do. It seems that the rose is used primarily because of its rhyme with the word *close*; such rhyme disjoined from meaning is, I think, distinctly unpoetic and uncreative. The images and metaphors are fragmented, and the ideas expressed, negative and hostile.

I call attention to these lines to show how precarious is the balance between destruction and creation in art, just as the balance between self-creation and self-destruction is precarious in life. Sylvia

Plath begins her poem with an assertion of triumph over death, the *smile of accomplishment,* but she cannot carry her triumph further. A sense of victory over death is, and should be, associated with a subjective sense of freedom—for most of us, that is. In this poem, however, there is no freedom; there is only the bringing of the children back to their origins, back to entombment in the past.

There is reason to believe that the aesthetic problem with destructive feelings in this poem closely reflected Sylvia Plath's problems with destructive feelings in her life. She committed suicide approximately seven months after her husband, the poet Ted Hughes, separated from her. Left with the total responsibility of caring for her two very young children, she seems to have been constantly embroiled in a struggle with hostile feelings toward them. Many of her unfinished poems during this period suggest such a struggle, and the circumstances of her suicide indicate it as well. Here is an excerpt.

> She hates
>
> The thought of a baby—
> Stealer of cells, stealer of beauty—
>
> She would rather be dead than fat,
> Dead and perfect, like Nefertit[3]

Turning on the gas in the kitchen stove early in the morning while her children were sleeping nearby, she made no provision for protecting them from the fumes that took her own life. They only survived by chance when an *au pair* woman came to the house. It is impossible to know now whether or not Plath had consciously intended to murder her own children, but there is little doubt about the expression of that type of destructive feelings toward children in the poem *Edge.* The *serpents* are white and are unbrutally enfolded into the mother, but they are murdered, nevertheless.

I believe that Sylvia Plath could not turn her hostile feelings into poetic creation in these lines because she was using poetry primarily to *control* rather than create. In other words, she attempted to express destructiveness in poetic form in order to expel it. Such an attempt at expiation and indirect expression functions only to exert control over feelings, not to change them; it strives for balance—a static rather than a progressive state. Good poetry does not do this; it both expresses and gets beneath the feelings—provides understanding, and develops and uses them in a dynamic way. The writing of good poetry involves the poet's freeing herself or himself up from the past through attaining a degree of understanding—partly through the use of the homospatial and janusian processes—and involves a movement into the future. One of the sources of our own enjoyment of poetry is our vicarious identification with the poet's personal struggle for understanding enlightenment and freedom. In the case of this particular poem, Sylvia Plath could not fully turn destructiveness into creation and could not liberate herself enough from the past to move toward the future. As we now know, this state portended her self-destruction.

Just as a need to control interferes with turning destructiveness into creation in art, so it interferes with turning self-destructive feelings into a process of self-creation in life. The following case of a patient yet unable to create any type of art illustrates this.

A Suicidal Patient

A seventeen-year-old college girl sat on the ledge of her window on the second floor of the dormitory. It was pitch dark, and no one saw her sitting there, including those in a nearby dormitory room. For a long time, she sat there thinking about jumping and flying and vaguely about killing herself. Several times, she wondered whether anyone would come by and notice her there. For what seemed like hours, nobody did; she jumped.

Although she did not kill herself, she seriously injured her back and pelvis. Immobilized in a body cast for seven months, she also began intensive psychiatric treatment. For some years prior to the jump, the girl had suffered from symptoms of incipient schizophrenia. She had experienced severe disturbances of thinking, including delusions about religion and about food. Following her jump, she began the heavy use of psychotropic drugs such as marijuana, LSD, and amphetamines. Finally, drug use and schizophrenic disturbance led to the need for her psychiatric hospitalization.

She was a highly intelligent girl, able to maintain excellent grades at a very competitive Ivy League college in spite of her symptoms and drug taking. Her ambition was to become a great writer, but unlike Sylvia Plath, she had done very little actual writing. The few poems she had completed showed some measure of talent, but she had never made any sustained effort at the novel she hoped to write.

In the course of psychotherapy, she revealed an exceptionally entangled relationship with her mother. Both were highly interdependent on each other in the manner often referred to as *symbiotic*. In spite of many attempts at becoming independent, she found that she was constantly at the mercy of other people, especially her mother. She tried constantly to fulfill (what she thought were) her mother's expectations. Also, she hated her body but engaged in sexual activity because "others" wanted her to. At the time she jumped from the window ledge, she fully believed that she might fly, and she did feel a distinct sense of control over both her body and the environment while falling.

As this patient improved, she gradually became aware that one of the underlying reasons for her jump was an overwhelming fear of death. Paradoxical as this may sound, she felt so much at the mercy of death, so much at the mercy of forces outside of her control, that committing suicide was for her a means of establishing control. Rather than waiting for death to take her, she would take command and kill herself. Either flying through the air or choosing her own death would amount to the same thing: she herself would be in control.

Persons who engage in rational discussions of suicide often insist that killing oneself is an act of freedom. Arguing that self-destruction is a basic human right, they push further to assert that it is also an act of free choice. Although I do not intend to enter into a discussion of the morality of suicide here, I will assert that it seldom results from a state of subjective freedom. Almost invariably, it is an attempt to regulate psychological forces over which one feels one has no control. It is a state of subjective fatalism or determinism wherein no alternatives are possible except those already given. One merely thinks of directing the given rather than transforming it. Destructive feelings toward others, for example, are turned against the self rather than being understood and thereby overcome. Sylvia Plath's hostility toward her children could have resulted from her conscience-motivated enslavement to her motherhood (rather than from the heightened feminine con- sciousness wrongly attributed to her by women's liberationists). Knowing this and forgiving herself for it, she might have been able to become a different kind of mother.

Self-creation

As the student-patient I have described continued to improve, she again became preoccupied with thoughts of suicide; but now she was hovering between self-destruction and self-creation rather than only trying to control feelings and impulses derived from the past and her need to feel and do only what others wanted. I say this because she experienced an important turning point into self-creation when she became aware, in a therapy session, that one of her reasons for want- ing to give up and not change was her fear of death—the same fear previously underlying her suicide attempt. If she did not change—if, in other words, she never grew up—she would never have to face death. Irrational as such a position is, it is one of the unconscious bases, universal in people, of a fear of growing up and changing.

Death is the ultimate and absolutely fated event in life. When we feel totally at the mercy of forces from the past in our life, we also fear death most intensely. In such a subjective state rather than one in which we feel the strength of a sense of freedom, we resort to attempts at control. These attempts, whether they are aimed at overpowering death by choosing our own time to die or at harnessing destructive feelings—overwhelming destructive feelings are almost invariably derived from past attitudes and orientations—by denying them or turning them against the self, are only efforts to gain power and a false sense of freedom. Control, as I have said, is static; it keeps past forces in check but does not change them.

Nothing can, or will, alter the fact of death, of course; and that is just the point of engaging in self-creation, of choosing to make oneself into the person one wants to be. Self-creation does not deny the fact of death; it rather removes death's determining effect on life. In opting for self-creation, we accept the inevitability of death but move on through our exercise of freedom to experience life in its fullest. Recognizing and accepting fear of death as underlying her fear of change, the patient began, slowly and arduously, to explore new situations, to try new ways of reacting to people, and to make choices that helped her define herself.

Self-creation comes out of diverse types of activities. Hardly is it necessary for everyone to engage in psychotherapy in order to become self-creating. Seldom, in fact, except in psychotherapy, is self-creating dramatically opposed to self-destruction in the manner I have described. Engaging in artistic creation often facilitates self-creation because good artists use their art to help them define themselves and achieve better understanding of their own feelings and thoughts. Artistic creation is frequently an exercise in experiencing a subjective sense of freedom, and this is one reason why persons facing death do well to engage in creating art, even if they have never done so before.

But artistic creation can offer traps for self-creation as well. If art is used primarily for control of unacceptable feelings, as in the lines I presented from Sylvia Plath's *Edge*, it serves a constrained and constricted subjective state rather than a free one. Furthermore, if artistic creation is undertaken primarily for its effect on others, primarily to get something from others that one cannot find in oneself—I am not now talking simply about getting accolades or recognition of artistic achievements—it defeats self-creation. Such a purpose is evident in the poem *Edge* and, up until the present time, in the young patient's ambition to be a great writer.

The final portion of the poem *Edge*, "The moon has nothing to be sad about/Staring from her hood of bone./She is used to this sort of thing," reads, to me, like a simultaneous anguished lament and a call for help. The poet was crying out against an indifferent universe, one that does nothing about death or troubling destructive feelings and acts. In this poem, as in many of the others written shortly before her death, Plath was writing a kind of suicide note. By *suicide note* I do not mean a piece of writing that explains a person's self-destructive act after the fact, but rather one that is meant to be discovered. Such a suicide note is a cry for help that says, "please stop me." Another such poem, *The Detective*, which presents clues to a suicidal purpose, was published posthumously.

> What was she doing when it blew in
> Over the seven hills, the red furrow, the blue mountain?
> Was she arranging cups? It is important.
> Was she at the window, listening?
> In that valley the train shrieks echo like souls on hooks.
>
> That is the valley of death, though the cows thrive.
> In her garden the lies were shaking out their moist silks
> And the eyes of the killer moving sluglike and sidelong,
> Unable to face the fingers, those egotists.
> The fingers were tamping a woman into a wall,
>
> A body into a pipe, and the smoke rising.
> This is the smell of years burning, here in the kitchen,
> These are the deceits, tacked up like family photographs,
> And this is the man, look at his smile.
> The death weapon? No one is dead.
>
> There is no body in the house at all.
> There is the smell of polish, there are plush carpets.
> There is the sunlight, playing its blades,
> Bored hoodlum in a red room
> Where the wireless talks to itself like an elderly relative.
>
> Did it come like an arrow, did it come like a knife?
> Which of the poisons is it?
> Which of the nerve-curlers, the convulsors? Did it electrify?
> This is a case without a body.
> The body does not come into it at all.

It is a case of vaporization.
The mouth first, its absence reported
In the second year. It had been insatiable
And in punishment was hung out like brown fruit
To wrinkle and dry.

The breasts next.
These were harder, two white stones.
The milk came yellow, then blue and sweet as water.
There was no absence of lips, there were two children,
But their bones showed, and the moon smiled.

Then the dry wood, the gates,
The brown motherly furrows, the whole estate.
We walk on air, Watson.
There is only the moon, embalmed in phosphorous.
There is only a crow in the tree. Make notes.[4]

Knowing that she did show some of this type of poetry to others before she died, it is reasonable to assume a cry for help along with the artistic purpose.[5] I do not, however, mean to pass a moral judgment for having such a purpose in these poems; I want to point out how the writing of the poem subverted self-creation rather than facilitated it. Writing a suicide note in the form of a poem is a self-destructive act: while bewailing people's misunderstanding and indifference, it creates further misunderstanding. If a person hearing the poem calls it a suicide note, the poet as artist is misconstrued; if it is heard exclusively as a poem, the person crying for help is ignored.

This is an extreme example, but as I pointed out about schizophrenic writing, artistic works often fail because they make an undue demand on their audience. Works that in large measure display the conflicts and disturbances of their authors, works that invite the audience to justify or accept them rather than be stimulated or learn from them, are failures as artistic creations and subversions of self-creation.

So, too, the young patient's ambition to be a great writer has not yet served her turn toward self-creation because it is based on a need to affect others and control her feelings. She has felt she must become a great writer in order to prove her worth to the world. Her feelings of lack of worth have been so consuming that nothing short of overwhelming greatness could make her feel acceptable at all. As with her fear of death, she has sought to control and compensate for feelings of worthlessness through fantasies of greatness.

Someday, she may be able to use artistic creation in the service of self-creation; but there are many other routes available to her and to all of us as well. Primarily, we create ourselves in the everyday choices that move us on in life. We create ourselves when we risk an alternative that closes off the manifold potentialities of childhood and when we strive for understanding rather than control. In the face of powerful urges to adopt a stagnant, backward-looking subjective state ultimately connected to self-destruction, we create ourselves in our acceptance of our freedom and our death.

7 ◆◇ *The Perils of Psychoanalyzing (or Scandalizing) Emily Dickinson*

*A*nother *female* writer, Emily Dickinson, has long posed a baffling and exciting literary puzzle and provided an intriguing psychiatric and psychological challenge as well. Totally unknown as a poet during her lifetime, she was the daughter of Congressman Edward Dickinson, Amherst, Massachusetts's leading citizen. The latter portion of her life she spent entirely as a recluse in her parents' house and characteristically dressed only in white. Outside of her sister, Lavinia, who lived with her, and some special family and friends who visited her, she saw no one. Even Mabel Todd, the person who was later to become the major organizer and editor for her poetry and to whom she wrote several poems, never talked with her in person, although Mrs. Todd visited the house many times. The poet once flitted by the living room dressed in a white gown, allowing Mrs. Todd a quick glimpse, and on another occasion, she called down from upstairs to thank Mrs. Todd for playing a piece on the Dickinson piano. Never seen on the streets of Amherst during the latter part of her life, Emily Dickinson was referred to by the townspeople as "the Myth."

When her poetry was published after her death, it was largely rejected by critics of the time but soon received enormous popular acclaim. She is now accepted as one of the greatest of American poets. If ever a creative person invited psychiatric interest, Emily Dickinson is the one. Her extreme isolation and the lack of public exposure of her poetry during her lifetime provide the circumstances for a rare type of naturally occurring psychosocial experiment: she seems to have written poetry primarily for herself, yet she achieved great aesthetic power and popular appeal. Also, her life was so unusual that even literary historians and critics have felt constrained to speculate about her psychological makeup. Many have indeed considered her to be quite mad.

Was Emily Dickinson mad, or more precisely, psychotic? Unfortunately, psychiatric and psychoanalytic studies have so far not met the challenge of providing meaningful understanding of this question or of other matters regarding this fascinating woman for reasons that must be laid at their own scientific doorstep. The approach used to investigate her psychological makeup and her poetry has generally been seriously flawed. Indeed, since the time of Freud, many psychoanalytic studies of literary figures have suffered from similar types of scientific defects.

Psychobiographical Approach

Sigmund Freud was a highly cultured man and a lover of art and literature. In the early days of psychoanalysis, when he was attempting to formulate and corroborate his far-reaching concepts about the nature of man, he turned respectfully to the analysis both of great works of art and literature and the lives of great creative persons. He believed that great works of art and literature contained universal psychological truths and that the study of artists' and writers' lives would reveal basic psychological truths in persons of heightened sensibility and talent. Imagine his excitement and delight, then, when he thought he saw evidence for such processes as the Oedipus complex in the works and lives of Leonardo da Vinci, Fyodor Dostoyevski, and William Shakespeare or thought he could explain some of the dynamic tensions of the Michelangelo sculpture *Moses* by means of the psychoanalytic concepts he had formulated!

Freud was a fine writer himself, and this delight and excitement come through in all of his works on art and literature. But Freud was notably cautious in his approach to psychological evidence, and he stipulated carefully the limits of psychoanalytic investigation with respect to art and literature in his famous disclaimer, "Before the problem of the creative artist, psychoanalysis must, alas, lay down its arms."[1] He was primarily interested in corroborating his psychoanalytic findings about patients in the vivid and wide-ranging documentation of biography and great works of art, rather than especially contributing to aesthetics or literary criticism.

No such caution is found in many psychoanalytic studies of art and literature by his followers. In the last sixty or seventy years after Freud's monumental works, psychoanalysts have analyzed and reanalyzed the biographies, paintings, sculptures, poems, novels, plays, and musical compositions of almost every great creative artist in the last two centuries. Although the widespread existence of an Oedipus complex has certainly been demonstrated through these studies, and many other valuable insights about psychological functioning have resulted, it is questionable how much such studies contribute to the appreciation and understanding of art and literature. For one thing, it is doubtful that they tell us anything about the psychology of the process of artistic creation.

The great strength of psychoanalysis as a science is that it derives evidence about psychological processes through a *collaboration* between the psychoanalyst and his patient, which allows the patient to correct and refine the analyst's understanding of unique personal processes. The clinical psychoanalyst obtains a wealth of corroborated information that is not obtainable in ordinary interpersonal discourse or even in works of great literature or letters of eminent artists. Furthermore, psychoanalysts gathering evidence from patients pay exquisitely sharp attention to the context of the patients' remarks; they base their understanding of these remarks on a full consideration of the meaning of that context. For example, if a patient quotes a comment he made to his mother, the analyst does not necessarily take the comment as a statement of fact but tries to grasp the patient's intent in repeating it at that moment, and he also considers other possible distorting factors. So, too, when an artist paints a picture or a poet writes a poem, or when either writes a letter to his mother, the analyst must pay attention to the context of these acts.

So far, however, few psychoanalysts have shown this type of sensibility to art or literature, and often they have not given adequate consideration to the circumstances in which artists', composers' and writers' letters have been written. Another problem adding to the weakness of their scientific approach, therefore, is that they have contributed little to the understanding and appreciation of the creative arts, and unlike Freud, they lack the excitement of original discovery.

Dickinson as Subject

To discuss the question of Dickinson's mental illness as well as the types of flaws that have appeared in psychoanalytic psychobiographical approaches, I shall focus on one famous commemorative year study of Dickinson, *After Great Pain*, by Dr. John Cody.[2] This discussion will also reveal the kind of thinking by both professionals and laymen that has traditionally connected creativity and madness.

Cody unequivocally labels Dickinson as psychotic (along with some other diagnoses), and he attempts to indicate some of the processes that led her to have, in his opinion, one or more particular psychotic episodes in her life. Searching for possible noxious influences in the poet's childhood, Cody begins by paying considerable attention to Dickinson's relationship with her father, who was known to be somewhat stern and remote from his family. Pointing out that the father's sternness and remoteness would not necessarily have produced severe psychological wounds in the young poet, Cody then shifts to the less well-known and less clearly defined mother. He emphasizes that a good deal is known about the personality of the father through previous biographies and family letters and suggests that the virtual absence of information about the mother could, in itself, indicate that she was weak and ineffectual in the family scene. Her weakness and withdrawal may have been experienced by Dickinson as severe rejection.

So far, so good. We know that a parent who is stern and strongly disciplinary to children is often remembered vividly and somewhat harshly but that such a parent may convey more concern and interest in the children than one who is withdrawn and passive. When little reference is made to any member of a family, particularly a mother (even in the female-denigrating nineteenth century), we begin to suspect that the unmentioned member may have had a more important and insidious effect than one complained about vehemently. Early in his book, Cody attempts to support this clinical hunch with copious quotes from the poet's letters and poems as well as from letters by other members of her family. But here a fairly typical and serious flaw in the approach to evidence appears: quote after quote is taken out of the context of the letter or poem and elaborated with inference after inference. Finally, Cody tries to describe the young poet's upbringing by extensive quotations from a book on childrearing in the Dickinson library which, without other evidence, he strongly implies Mr. and Mrs. Dickinson followed to the letter!

In the end, the only reasonably direct pieces of evidence for maternal rejection produced by this investigator are two written remarks the poet made as an adult to her erstwhile literary adviser, Thomas Wentworth Higginson. Cody refers to both of them frequently. "I always ran home to Awe as a child, if anything befell me. He was an awful mother, but I liked him better than none," and "I never had a mother." Strong as these two remarks are, even if viewed along with some of the poet's highly strange behavior, they are far from proof of maternal rejection. Accepting them as literal statements of the poet's true feelings about her mother ignores the context in which they were made. They are the remarks of the adult poet to the man she was trying very hard to impress (note, by the way, that she uses a poetic play on

the words *Awe* and *awful* in the first remark) and not the confidences of
a patient to her analyst. Such an oversight is unaccountable since
Cody, along with other Dickinson biographers, readily acknowledges
that the poet made remarks to Higginson in order to produce a dramatic effect—most notably her strange assertion that her father never
let her read any books but the Bible when she was a child!

Was She Psychotic?

With regard to the question of psychosis, the overall configuration of
her life—the long period of intense seclusion and the strange habit of
dressing solely in white—would lead most psychiatrists to assume
that she had been psychotic at some point or, at least, that she bor-
dered on psychosis. In fact, many of the lay people of Amherst assumed that very thing during her lifetime, and certainly many lay
people knowing her story would think the same today. As Cody sali-
ently points out, it is primarily the poet's family and editors as well as
the idolizing literary critics who argue against a serious psychiatric
illness. Here, this psychoanalyst-investigator is to be applauded for an
unsentimental scientific concern for the truth that potentially ren-
ders the poet into a real human being rather than a mysterious saint.
But, again, he must be jeered for the way he attempts to prove his
point.

Arguing that she had one or more psychotic episodes during the
period of 1857 to 1864 when a large number of her poems were written, he turns for proof to a literal interpretation of the poems themselves! Quoting such phrases as, "And then a Plank in Reason broke," "I
felt a Cleaving in my Mind/As if my Brain had split," and "I thought/My
Mind was going numb," he asserts that Dickinson was literally describing her own experience of going out of her mind. Recognizing that the
poems containing these lines are eminently coherent, of course, he
goes to great lengths to point out and develop the well-established
clinical observation that psychotic people are not disorganized and
irrational at all times during the course of their psychosis. Specifically,
he justifies his interpretation of these lines as follows:

> We must ask ourselves whether anyone, even a poet, can portray a
> feeling state that he has not himself undergone. And if one grants that
> this is possible, what could possibly motivate a person to attempt to
> express what he never felt? It may be replied that Emily Dickinson
> knew what ordinary depressions were and may even have had some
> acquaintance with certain severe neurotic ones and that, drawing on
> such experiences, she could imaginatively have extrapolated and pro-

jected the psychotic intensification of depression that is expressed in the phrase "I thought/My Mind was going numb," and the sense of estrangement conveyed by the image of the universe resonating with the poet's projected despair like a mighty tolling bell convey an intensity of disintegration and a confounding of inner experiences with outer reality which reflect the profound insight into the specific pain of the psychotic state. Where could this insight have come from if not from Emily Dickinson's own inner life? The simplest and most natural explanation is that in this poem Emily Dickinson is talking about herself, that she is describing a real experience which happened to her, and that, in the line "And then a Plank in Reason broke," she is revealing that she had been a victim of a psychological crisis that was not an ego-sparing and relatively benign neurosis, but a reason-disrupting, prostrating psychosis.

Poem Number 937 . . . [beginning with the line "I felt a Cleaving in my Mind"] gives further support to this conclusion in the perfection of its description of a psychotic thought disorder.[3]

Although it is certainly correct that many people who are psychotic write poetry and are coherent, I do not believe that this investigator realized that his phrase *simplest and most natural explanation* naïvely explains away the whole secret of literary creativity. If poetry and other types of literature were simply descriptions of actual experiences that authors had undergone, we would have no such thing as imagination, nor would we marvel at writers' capacities to rise above their own experience and use it to convey insights, feelings, interactions, events, and values that are new for them as well as for us. And although the motivation to describe a state or experience one has never had is surely complex, it lies at the heart of the creative impulse. The poetic phrases Cody quotes must have a complicated relationship to Emily Dickinson's inner life, but he is unjustified in assuming that they describe an actual psychotic experience.

Although this investigator does not prove his point about psychosis, he does help elucidate the strange and important period of 1857 to 1864 in Emily Dickinson's life and the onset of her bizarre seclusion. Here, he is effective because he relies largely on her letters and his clinical judgment. Rather than following the popular story that the poet was disappointed in a great love affair at this time, he turns to her relationship with her brother and his wife. Marshaling a good deal of convincing evidence from copious letters written by all three of them and following his own hunch about the poet's need for a mother substitute, he suggests that the poet had been devastated by the marriage of her brother to her friend Susan. This analysis of Susan's importance as a maternal figure for Dickinson and of the impact of this relationship on her psychological state for the remainder of her life is so convincing that it tends to support his thesis about maternal rejection.

Assessment of the Psychobiographical Approach

The problem with many psychoanalytic biographies of writers, composers, and artists is that they are misconceived and misguided. They are not, as some would have it, prying and disparaging expeditions into the private lives of hallowed figures of history. The problem is not even that the writers of such biographies are poor clinicians in terms of their approach to psychiatric illness (I only seriously considered this possibility once in Cody's case when I found that he had used fully *six* different, and in some instances incompatible, diagnostic terms to apply to related aspects of her behavior: depression, manic behavior, agoraphobia, pseudologica phantastica, catatonic schizophrenia, and psychogenic eye disorder) but that they lack literary and aesthetic understanding. Since the clinicians are working in a literary and aesthetic context, of course, this charge is not directed at their competence as psychoanalysts, but from a more general point of view, their studies are often tasteless bull-in-the-aesthetic-china-shop excursions.

Frequently, these psychobiographers approach poetry as though meaning were the sole aesthetic consideration for the writer or the reader of the poem. Showing little awareness of meter, assonance, alliteration, or other structural issues in poetry, they ignore the unity and organicity of a poem and the important interrelationship of lines and images. In the search for psychological meaning, they too often feel justified in taking phrases out of the context of the poem, paraphrasing them in prose, and considering them to be direct statements of the poet's experience or internal state.

One example of this—not related to the issue of psychosis—comes from Cody's analysis of the Dickinson poem that begins, "I had been hungry, all the years." Regarding the following lines in stanza 4, "As Berry—of a Mountain Bush/Transplanted to the Road," he says, "It is difficult to see why the idea of being in an unsuitable and alien situation (conveyed by the word 'transplanted') should involve the symbol 'Berry' when so many other objects in the natural world are susceptible of being transplanted to unaccustomed and uncongenial environments. And why precisely a berry from a 'Mountain Bush'?"[4] This is an interesting question, but rather than observe the telling alliteration between the words *Berry* and *Bush,* an alliteration that paradoxically links the transplanted berry and the bush, he decides only that the berry symbolizes hymeneal blood.

The "Cleaving" in Her Mind

I shall try to demonstrate an alternative approach to the literal interpretation of Dickinson's poetic phrases by looking in some detail at one of the poems containing a line Cody cites as evidence for psychosis. This is the poem that begins with the lines, "I felt a Cleaving in my Mind/As if my Brain had split." Here is the entire poem.

> I felt a Cleaving in my Mind—
> As if my Brain had split.
> I tried to match it—Seam by Seam—
> But could not make them fit.
>
> The thought behind, I strove to join
> Unto the thought before—
> But Sequence ravelled out of Sound
> Like Balls upon a Floor.[5]

Beyond the particular references to mind and brain, a reading of the entire poem indicates another pervasive theme—the theme of sewing. The third and fourth lines of the first stanza refer to matching and fitting seams, the first two lines of the second stanza refer to joining, and the last two refer to balls of thread or yarn ravelling upon a floor.

Are we now to assert that this poem is literally focused on the art of sewing? No, not quite—certainly no more so at this point than asserting that it is literally focused on psychosis. But, bringing all the parts together, we can say that the poem is representing something about a state of mind or a figurative state of existence. A metaphor pertaining to sewing is used to convey both meanings and feelings regarding that state of mind or existence.

What are the meanings and feelings conveyed? One possibility is that the poem describes a person's dissociated and fragmented mental processes, which she or he is desperately trying to sew up or bring together. I believe, however, that in this poem there is a mysterious sense of an undertaking more important than sewing up separated fragments, and that interpretation, therefore, seems weak. For one thing, the sewing interpretation does not account for the reference in the second stanza to trying to bring a proper *sequence* to the thoughts. Sewing fragments or thoughts together does not necessarily put them into temporal succession. Also, this interpretation does not get at some of the evocative sound qualities and enigmatic meaning of some particular words in the poem.

The words I have in mind are *cleaving* and *ravelled*. These words are important in the context of the poem because of the precise manner in which they are used. With regard to sound qualities, a centrally located *v* sound is strong in both, and, as each is located close to the beginning and the end of the poem, they form a sound linkage or unity between start and finish. Notably also, both words have double meanings; and beyond that, these double meanings do not only differ from each other, but in each case, the pairs of meanings are diametrically opposed! The word *cleaving* means both parting or separating forcibly and its opposite, a uniting or coming together strongly. Persons or things may be cleaved apart, or they may cleave unto each other.[6] And the word *ravelled* has opposite meanings as well, referring both to bringing threads together and to separating them.[7] Ravelled threads may be either tangled or untangled.

Thus, there is a subtle dual connotation that the person of the poem is simultaneously trying to mend a rift and adjust a disordered temporal sequence. At the start, the fragments of the mind are cleaving. According to the double and opposite meanings of cleave, this suggests that the mind is both splitting apart and being brought together after a previous separation. Focusing on this second meaning, that is, "I felt a Cleaving [bringing together] in my Mind/As if my Brain had split," the succeeding lines of the poem then tell of an attempt to match all the brought-together parts of the mind and, following that, to put thoughts into a proper temporal order. Finally, however, the sequence becomes hopelessly tangled and lost, out of sound (or reach) "Like Balls [of thread or yarn] upon a Floor."

At the same time in this richly suggestive poem, the opposite of a tangled sequence is also indicated. According to the other meaning of *ravelled*—loose or separated threads or yarn—the thoughts silently spread out somewhere upon the floor. Varied interpretations emphasizing the tangled and untangled meanings of this word are also suggested.

Are these interpretations of multiple and deeper meanings purely speculations with the same degree of validity as Cody's (and others') literal reading of a description of a psychotic experience? That this poem represented more than that literal description of psychosis was brought home to me even more forcibly when I discovered that Dickinson had written a remarkably similar poem almost a year later. This entire poem (number 992) is identical to the second stanza with only two words substituted, *Dust* and *Disk*, as follows:

The Dust behind I strove to join
Unto the Disk before
But Sequence ravelled out of Sound
Like Balls upon a Floor—.[8]

This poem and its modifications surely evoke a different experience than the split brain and disordered thinking which, to Cody, suggested the literal description of psychosis. The poem adds another dimension to the theme of the previous poem, but it does not put the meaning question to rest immediately because another puzzle emerges. What is the meaning of the reference to joining *Dust* and *Disk?* The sewing or knitting metaphor is continued in this poem with the reference to the "Balls upon a Floor," but the words *Dust* and *Disk* do not connect with sewing or even, in terms of any modern usage, with each other. Is this later poem an incoherent psychotic production, and is Cody therefore proved correct on a basis other than what he claimed?

I realized that the only way to solve this puzzle was to find out, if I could, what meanings these words might have had in Emily Dickinson's time and, equally important, in the context of word usage throughout her poems. This led me to search for the answer in the extensive holdings of the Emily Dickinson Collection at the Jones Library in Amherst, Massachusetts. There, I discovered the following interesting facts. (1) In the edition of Webster's dictionary used during Emily Dickinson's lifetime, the *first* definition provided for the word *Disk* was the "the sun."[9] Also, in numerous other poems, Dickinson herself had used that same word to refer clearly to the sun. (2) The Dickinson concordance of her word use in her poems showed that she had almost invariably used the word *Dust* to refer to death.[10]

These word meanings help clarify the later poem. The coherent central poetic image therefore consists of trying to join together death and the sun in some type of temporal sequence. Given the context, I believe that the sun or *Disk* represents life or life forces, and hence the attempt is to bring together or understand the sequence of life and death. Further weight to this particular idea comes from the knowledge that this poem seems to have been a death dirge. It was probably sent by the poet to Susan on the occasion of the death of Susan's very young daughter.[11] Deeply philosophical, the poem raises the question of the joinings, both temporally and substantively, between death and life. As a poem of mourning, it asks how bright and shining life as represented by the sun (in this case, probably the young life of her niece) could be joined to, and followed by, dust and death.

Although this later poem stands alone as a creation in its own right, I believe that the identity of structure with the earlier poem indicates shared overtones and meanings. In the earlier poem, the statement that the person's experience and mind are cleaving, in both the separating and bringing together senses, is followed by the idea of trying to join up and understand thought sequences. Therefore, that poem, too, is a mediation and questioning of the reasons for sequences in life: how does one experience lead to another? The sewing metaphor: how can thought and life be mended up after death or separation from loved ones cleaves them apart? Also, when disparate experiences begin to cleave together in the mind, can we then sew them carefully together into an integrated whole? As we try to put the parts into an ordered temporal sequence, we find them having become both tangled and untangled and eventually not available. They are out of reach, "Like Balls [of thread] upon a Floor," and not amenable to use or understanding.

Creativity as a Healthy Process

Many psychoanalytic and psychiatric investigators, by literal readings similar to Cody's of poetry or other forms of literature, have developed allegations that an author was ill or psychotic. Even stating that the surface meaning of the poem is a description of a psychotic state of mind—literal or surface meaning is, of course, also part of a poem's impact—would not argue for psychotic illness in the author and would not take into account the multiple levels of meaning and coherent aesthetic impact of that poem. The use of the words *ravelled* and *cleaving*, with their diametrically opposed double meanings, suggests that Dickinson employed the janusian process during the creation of this poem. She conceived of cleaving the mind—both splitting it apart and bringing it together—simultaneously, and this idea either evoked or fit in with other notions pertaining to the sequences of life and thought. She formulated a ravelled sequence, simultaneously tangling and untangling time, and this either generated or developed further issues pertaining to life and death.

It was the use of the healthy and adaptive janusian process and other creative processes rather than psychotic thinking which produced the aesthetic effects of this poem. The poem was not a confession or simple description of a psychotic state. Even if Emily Dickinson had been psychotic at some point—and that is not at all proven—much about the transition from psychosis to the creative achievement in this poem would have to be explained.

Unfortunately, because of the method Cody and other investigators adopt in which aesthetic considerations are glossed over or not fully considered, creative processes such as the janusian type of cognition are not identified. Reductionistic clinical assumptions are used and often contribute to the mythology connecting mental illness and creative work. Cody attributes Dickinson's creativity to maternal rejection. How? He argues that her basic sense of rejection led her into seclusion and isolation and that she therefore had time to devote to writing. Furthermore, he believes that her psychotic withdrawal from human relationships led her to value and rely on written communication, while her personal unhappiness induced her to focus on her inner psychological processes. Fortunately, such gross oversimplifications are not characteristic of all psychobiographical explorations.

If Not Mad, Scandalous

Actually, psychoanalytic biography is quite productive when it adopts the principles of good detective work, elucidating missing links and providing answers to artistic and psychological puzzles. Unfortunately, however, these principles are also not always easy to come by. Even detective writers do not always follow them when they explore literary biography.

In the commemorative-year biography, *The Hidden Life of Emily Dickinson*,[12] John Walsh, winner of the Edgar Allan Poe award for detective fiction, attempted neither a psychoanalytic nor even a psychologically sophisticated study but a manifest piece of literary detective work. However he seems to have been intent on creating a literary scandal. Unlike Cody, who explicitly refrains from speculating about the identity of Emily Dickinson's mysterious lover—the addressee of her famous "Dear Master" letters—Walsh points directly to Judge Otis Lord, a married man and friend of the poet's father. By a clever set of inferences about the wording of her letters and by logically excluding other persons who have been implicated previously, Walsh insists that her lover had been the man to whom she almost became betrothed later in her life. After his wife died, Judge Lord and the poet carried on an open courtship. Interestingly, Dickinson wrote the "Master" letters, presumably to this man, during the period of her greatest poetic output, a period during which Cody has suggested she may have been psychotic. Such a focused interaction with a real lover, however, is seldom characteristic of periods of psychosis.

This detective writer has also avowedly discovered that Dickinson borrowed extensively from Elizabeth Barrett Browning's epic poem *Aurora Leigh*. He refers to many similar passages in the Browning poem and various early Dickinson poems to establish this case. Although shying away from accusing Emily Dickinson of plagiarism directly—"plagiarism, but whisper it soft,"[13] he says—his goal is to demonstrate that she was not as original as she has generally been taken to be.

The accusations regarding Dickinson's borrowings are less convincing than the Judge Lord-as-lover argument. The similar passages in Browning and Dickinson which Walsh cites indicate that there was some clear poetic influence but not enough to warrant a charge of direct borrowing or plagiarism—even a "whispered charge." Also, little evidence is shown of any Browning influence on the scores of later poems that helped establish the Dickinson reputation for originality.

The detective writer's picture of Emily Dickinson's personality provides an interesting contrast to the psychoanalytic profile by Cody. The former sees her as an overly dramatic, rather naïve girl who desperately sought for fame. She then felt so rebuffed by Higginson's lack of encouragement that she gave up trying to have her poetry published. Although Cody's tortured, sensitive psychotic might also have felt rebuffed by lack of encouragement, she was neither presented as being dramatic nor were her remarks taken with a grain of salt.

In Commemoration

The same year that these two books were published, the Emily Dickinson commemorative stamp came out as part of an American poet series. Unfortunately, neither book was an especially fitting accompaniment for such an event. Cody's sober scientific analysis was a somewhat welcome relief from the romanticism that has clothed Dickinson's life throughout this century, and Walsh provided a skillfully written book about unknown aspects of her life and work. But overall, there was a debunking quality in both: the psychoanalyst tried to account for all of Dickinson's behavior, including her creative achievements, through descriptions of psychological processes present in everyone, especially patients in the clinic; the detective writer tried to insist that she was a borrower. The best that can be said of reductionistic psychoanalytic works and scandalizing literary ones is that they try to put some flesh and blood onto the mysterious ethereal figure of a writer such as Emily Dickinson; she is treated as a human being rather than a goddess. Such a view neither hurts her nor detracts from appreciation of her poetry; it helps us all feel a little closer to the deities.

8 ◆ The Psychosis and Triumph of August Strindberg

The Swedish playwright August Strindberg has been generally considered the "Father of Modern Drama." Initiator of the modern theatrical style called expressionism, he also developed the naturalistic style of drama into the intense form used by many modern playwrights. However, unlike Emily Dickinson, for whom the evidence of mental illness is equivocal, August Strindberg clearly suffered from a severe psychosis.

Here is Eugene O'Neill's description of the nature of Strindberg's accomplishment (O'Neill also acknowledged Strindberg in his Nobel Prize acceptance speech):

> Strindberg still remains among the most modern of moderns, the greatest interpreter in the theater of the characteristic spiritual conflicts which constitute the drama—the blood—of our lives today. He carried Naturalism to a logical attainment of . . . poignant intensity. . . . Strindberg knew and suffered our struggle years before many of us were born. He expressed it by intensifying the method of his time and by foreshadowing both in content and form the methods to come. All that is enduring in what we loosely call "Expressionism"—all that is artistically valid and sound theatre—can be clearly traced back through Wedekind to Strindberg's *The Dream Play,* [There are] *Crimes and Crimes, The Spook Sonata,* etc.[1]

Clearly, the achievement was quite amazing. Being responsible for the development of one particular artistic style, such as Ludwig van Beethoven with the symphony, Paul Cézanne with postimpressionism, Jackson Pollock and Edgar Allan Poe with abstract expressionism and the detective novel, respectively, is distinction enough. Developing two important styles, therefore, seems monumental. In modern times, only Pablo Picasso, with his explorations into cubism, synthetic cubism, abstract sculpture, collage, primitivism, and his own particular type of abstract painting, has developed multiple artistic styles and forms. Although both Henrik Ibsen and Anton Chekhov are important progenitors of the drama that is written today, Strindberg's naturalism has directly influenced playwrights such as Arthur Miller and Eugene O'Neill; and his expressionism has influenced Tennessee Williams, Sean O'Casey, Elmer Rice, and Pär Lagerkvist as well as theater of the absurd authors such as Eugène Ionesco, living and open theater movements, and indirectly, the work of Luigi Pirandello, Samuel Beckett, and Harold Pinter.

In view of his accomplishment, I was especially intrigued that, following the major production of his great naturalistic plays *The Father* and *Miss Julie*, Strindberg had suffered from a prolonged psychotic period up until right before he began working in the expressionist style. He wrote about this period in an autobiographical piece, *Inferno*,[2] derived from his diaries. There, he describes severe persecutory delusions: that he was being pursued in order to be killed, that he was being shocked by electricity, and that stray events were meant as signs and portents to influence him. He heard voices of people talking about him and experienced visual hallucinations as well. Although there are periods of lucidity and occasional insights in this book, it is overall a disorganized and raving tale of psychotic thinking and belief.

In order to try to understand the relationship between Strindberg's psychosis and his peak creative accomplishments, therefore, I decided first to look closely at the period prior to the onset of his severe decompensation, the period of his writing the great naturalistic plays. Discovering that Strindberg, at the time he wrote *The Father*, had been writing both an autobiographical piece and a nonautobiographical novel, I focused especially on these works. I knew that the autobiographical piece would provide important life information and also, in previous investigations I had done with living writers, I had learned that a piece of nonautobiographical writing—nonautobiographical on the surface, that is—often revealed more about an author's unconscious concerns than did manifest autobiography.

The Father

My study was aided considerably by the fact that quite a large number of Strindberg's works are highly autobiographical. Incidents from his three marriages and direct characterization of himself, his three wives, his in-laws, his children, and his friends are contained in almost all but his historical plays. In addition, he wrote five thinly disguised autobiographical novels that made the events and characters in the plays quite easy to identify.[3]

The writing of the naturalistic play *The Father*[4] paralleled Émile Zola's development of naturalism in the novel. Zola himself hailed the play as great. Many critics today also feel that for sheer power and tragedy, this was Strindberg's outstanding dramatic accomplishment. He composed this play during the same period as two novels, the nonautobiographical *The People of Hemsö*[5] and the autobiographical *The Confessions of a Fool.*[6] Starting first to write the latter piece, Strindberg interrupted this work to write both the play and the other novel. *The Confessions of a Fool* was only completed after the other two works were published.

The themes of the play and the autobiographical piece are virtually the same: both concern his preoccupations in his marriage to his first wife, Siri Von Essen. In the play, the jealous fixation is thinly disguised. The leading characters, the Captain, an eminent scientist, and his wife, Laura, are locked in a virtual death struggle over which of them shall have control over the life of their daughter, Bertha. This culminates when Laura, in order to deprive her husband of his authority, suggests to him that he is not the real father of the girl. When he becomes frantic in response and then morbidly preoccupied about his loss of paternity, she conspires to have him declared insane. First, she convinces a doctor who is boarding in their house that her husband is mad. Then, she effectively convinces his old nursemaid and even manages to enlist her aid in restraining him. At the end, the Captain is put in a straitjacket and, with a helpless burst of fury, he dies on the old nursemaid's lap.

A year after the first appearance of the play, the autobiographical piece *The Confessions of a Fool* was published. Throughout this work, Strindberg states again and again his concerns about the real paternity of the child he and his wife Siri were raising. He writes at length of both his suspicion that Siri had been unfaithful to him and his belief that she was trying to drive him insane. Describing himself as constantly pressing Siri to tell him the truth—just as the Captain presses Laura in the play—he writes that it is better to know the truth, even if terrible, rather than remain perpetually in doubt. In distinction to the events in the play, however, when Siri actually admitted to him that she had on one occasion been unfaithful, he proceeded to divorce her.

Strindberg was intensely preoccupied with the themes of paternity, infidelity, and marriage in both play and autobiographical novel.

The material in the latter describes the marital life circumstances from which the former was conceived, and his preoccupations in the autobiographical work seem at times to be morbidly delusional. An important artistic issue in the play is Strindberg's concern with the issue of existential truth. The Captain's preoccupation with the paternity of the child is cast in the light of a man's inability ever to know the truth of such a matter and, implicitly, the human incapacity to possess ultimate truth of any kind. At the very end, Laura exclaims to her daughter, "My child! My own child!" to which the Pastor says, "Amen."[7] Conveyed is a bitter rendering of a "truth" that only a woman procreates and "owns" a child.

With regard to Strindberg's fantasies, I believe that both works represent the author's attempt to order and control his immediate real experience; the point is to state the truth regardless of its cost or pain. There is, in the play, evidence for the operation of a janusian process that serves both aesthetic purposes and the author's emotional need. A distinct simultaneous antithesis regarding lying and truth emerges from the play's dramatic structure and dialogue. While the Captain rails about his inability to know the truth, it is at the same time fairly obvious that his wife is lying when she tells him that the daughter is not his. It is a ruse to gain control of the girl's future and drive the Captain insane. Aesthetically, this simultaneous antithesis of lying and "truth" regarding paternity heightens the play's focus on issues of abstract truth and is organic to the struggle for power between husband and wife. On an emotional level, I believe it represents Strindberg's ambivalent attempt to convince himself that his wife was tricking him and therefore not unfaithful.

The People of Hemsö

Strindberg wrote *The People of Hemsö* (also translated as *The Natives of Hemsö*) in 1887, the same year that he completed *The Father*. Apparently he did not think too much of his somewhat lightly toned novel, and he told the Danish critic George Brandes that he wrote it for amusement during his free hours. However, this novel has become quite popular in Sweden, and some critics have considered it to be one of the best Swedish novels ever written.

On the surface, the story of this novel is markedly different from both the other works, play and autobiographical novel. It concerns a ne'er-do-well from the agricultural province of Varmland who comes to the Stockholm archipelago (the so-called Swedish skerries) to marry a widowed landowner. The people of these skerries are primarily engaged in seafaring occupations, and a good deal of the story turns about the fact that this ne'er-do-well interloper, named Carlsson, tries to change the ways of these people. In contrast to *The Father* and *The Confessions of a Fool*, this novel contains little or no manifest autobiography. Although Strindberg often vacationed on the Swedish skerries and reportedly loved them a good deal, he did not directly represent any important persons or experiences in his life in this work.

Despite the surface difference from the autobiographical works, I found that the same themes of paternity, marriage, and infidelity are represented in an altered way in this novel of the skerries. I believed that this was potentially quite important because I knew from my research with living authors that works written in sequence or in close proximity in time bear a definite relationship to each other and to the author's ongoing psychological state. This meant that a progression or change of themes, techniques, or characters could be related to a progression or change in the fantasy life of an author at a particular time of his life. In the case of this novel, the change of themes contributed to the aesthetic effect of a rather light-toned novel with nevertheless a tragic moral ending. Such a time-focused approach to unconscious preoccupations and fantasies differs from that of the investigators discussed in the previous chapter who take fictional material literally and, without regard to the context, relate literary themes to psychological factors operating at differing times in the author's life.

As for changes in the paternity theme, then, the ne'er-do-well Carlsson in the novel enters a situation in which he has no claim to paternity whatsoever. He marries a widow with a full-grown son and, in completely unfatherly fashion, he then attempts to deprive the boy of both his rights and his inheritance. With regard to the marital theme, the widow is many years her husband's senior. Carlsson behaves like a young mischievous and irresponsible child to her, and she, in turn, is very protective and solicitous. Essentially, they have a mother-son relationship.

The structure of the paternity and marital themes in this non-autobiographical novel differs from both of the autobiographical pieces. In both of the latter, the male protagonists accuse their wives of depriving them of their paternity. At one point in the play, the Captain says to Laura, "What good's anything now that you have robbed me of my immortality?" In this novel, on the other side of the coin, Carlsson has never been a legitimate father, he bears this relationship in name only, and is a disaster to boot. The marital conflict in the autobiographical works consists of a fight for dominance; both protagonists feel they are striving to maintain their masculine prerogatives in the face of being undermined by their wives. Carlsson, on the other hand, willingly seeks a mother-son relationship in his marriage.

Thematic Analysis

These alterations of the themes of the autobiographical works suggested to me the nature of Strindberg's underlying fantasies during that period of time. With respect to marriage and paternity, Strindberg had met his wife Siri when she was married to her first husband, Baron Von Wrangel. They had an affair, she divorced the baron, and subsequently she married Strindberg. This woman was rather maternal, and it appeared that on a symbolic fantasy level Strindberg had married a person who, like one's own mother, was previously married to someone else. That this was a significant emotional matter for him was supported by psychiatrist Theodore Lidz's excellent study showing that, prior to his marriage, Strindberg's relationship with both Siri and her first husband was very similar to his relationship with his own parents.[8] The mother-son marriage in *The People of Hemsö* seemed, therefore, to represent fulfillment of the author's wish.

During the course of Strindberg's marriage, one child died, and three survived—two females and a male. However, because Strindberg was married to a woman who seemed to have represented his own mother strongly, his children would be emotionally equivalent to siblings. As there is ample evidence in Strindberg's autobiographical writings[9] that he had been intensely jealous of his real siblings throughout his childhood, it seemed fair to assume that he was also jealous and hostile toward his own children. I believed, therefore, that the altered paternity theme in *The People of Hemsö* represented an underlying wish to be an unrelated type of stepfather to them, that is, "a father in name only," as a way of coping with his hostile feelings at that time. If he were not the actual father, he could renounce responsibility for them and, like Carlsson, feel no concern. In this light, the intense accusations that a wife deprives a man of paternity in both the autobiographical play and novel were defensive projections (shifting internal unacceptable feelings outward) of a guilty underlying wish not to be a father.

With regard to the theme of infidelity in *The People of Hemsö*, it is Carlsson, not his wife, who is unfaithful. This episode of infidelity is so important, however, that events in the novel subsequently move to a rapid and decisive close. Suspecting that her husband Carlsson has been unfaithful with a younger woman, the "widow" Flod tramps out into the freezing cold and snow to find them together. As a result, she becomes fatally ill. Shortly afterward, Carlsson himself dies when accidentally getting lost on the ice floes while his wife's coffin is transported over the water.

As with the treatment of the themes of paternity and marriage, the alteration of the infidelity theme in *The People of Hemsö* suggested an underlying fantasy: the intense accusations in the other two works that the wife was unfaithful were Strindberg's projections of his own guilty wishes to be unfaithful to his wife. Indeed, the sequence of events in the novel following Carlsson's act of infidelity suggested the moral diction that such wishes lead to disastrous consequences and must be repudiated and denied. The overall quality of wish fulfillment and denial throughout this novel imparted a somewhat dream-like (including nightmare-like) aesthetic tone.

The Period of Psychotic Decompensation

Armed with these hypotheses regarding Strindberg's unconscious fantasies, wishes, and defensive projections, I studied both his psychosis and his succeeding works to see whether the themes played any role. Although there is a distinctly paranoid quality to *The Confessions of a Fool* as well as to other succeeding writings, both the structure and the content of Strindberg's *Inferno* indicates that he experienced a frank and persistent psychotic decompensation during the year 1894. This followed another marriage, to the writer Frieda Uhl, and the birth of another child, a girl. Strindberg separated from his wife after their child became sick; he gave up writing plays and became fanatically involved in alchemy. He believed he had manufactured iodine and was also certain that he had turned base elements into gold. In the light of my hypothesis regarding Strindberg's hostility toward his children, it was notable that he became frankly psychotic during the period of the illness of his child. Guilt over any hostile feelings toward this, his most recent offspring, could possibly have had some causative effect.

In the plays written subsequent to *The Father*, the themes of marriage (or male-female relationships), infidelity, and false or true paternity continue to be tacitly and explicitly present. In none of these, up until the onset of his psychotic decompensation, are there any further essential changes in the themes. Notably, in none does the theme of hostility to progeny appear in any way. The next plays, *Miss Julie* and *Creditors*, are both naturalistic in style. The former concerns an aristocratic girl who commits suicide after having an affair with her father's valet, and in *Creditors*, there is a conflict between a sensitive artist and his wife and the wife's ex-husband—a theme reminiscent of Strindberg's marriage to Siri Von Essen following her divorce.

After these works and coincident with a gradual sinking into fla-
grant psychosis, Strindberg wrote only one long play, *Keys of Heaven*,
and a series of one-act plays, many of which were experimental but
virtually all of which were primarily trifling or unsuccessful as drama.
Only *The Stronger* (1889), which involves two characters with one only
speaking throughout the play, has been considered worthy of note
from this period. This is the story of a woman's competition and loneliness. *Pariah* (1889) concerns a man who commits murder; *Samum*
(1889) is a strange tale about a supernatural windstorm in Algeria and
a dying soldier; *Keys of Heaven* (1891) portrays a father grieving for his
dead children and who, together with St. Peter, searches for the lost
keys to heaven; *Mother Love* (1891–2) depicts a mother-father conflict
over the legitimacy of their child. The blackmailing of an explorer is
the focus of *Debit and Credit* (1891–2); in *Facing Death*, a father com-
petes with his daughter's suitor; *The First Warning* (1891–2) is a come-
dy about an extramarital affair; and *The Bond* (1892) is a tragedy about
the same theme. *Playing With Fire* (1892) is about several extramarital
affairs.

At the end of 1894, Strindberg was writing no plays at all, and he
wandered through Europe doing alchemy and occasionally painting.
He reported that he was suffering intensely. Believing both that he was
being pursued by the husband of a former lover who was out to kill
him and that enemies who were jealous of his discovery of the secret of
making gold were shocking him with electricity, he sought psychiatric
help at one point and later went to live with his mother-in-law while
his separated wife had gone elsewhere. There, after approximately
four years of frank psychosis and no theatrical writing whatsoever, he
was influenced by his mother-in-law (as well as Honoré de Balzac's
novel *Seraphita*) to look into the religion of Swedenborgianism.
Founded by his countryman Emanuel Swedenborg, this faith asserted
that hell existed in earthly life, an idea that for Strindberg was an
explanation for his suffering. He avidly adopted the religion. Helped
then by this religious conversion with both an emotional focus and a
central idea organizing his thoughts and feelings, Strindberg turned
again to writing drama. He wrote the first two plays of a massive
trilogy entitled *To Damascus*. Highly disorganized in both content and
structure, these plays present a spiritual journey loosely following
Christ's passing through the Stations of the Cross. They also contain
events from Strindberg's unhappy and unsuccessful second marriage
to Frieda Uhl.

Although these plays show some return of Strindberg's skills in
creating dialogue, they are unsuccessful literary works and still evidence the author's psychotic disorganization. His next drama, *Advent:*

A *Miracle Play* (1899), is full of bizarre magical effects. Manifestly presenting the Swedenborgian idea that evil is its own punishment, this play is not as disorganized and incomprehensible as *To Damascus* but continues to show the hand of an unsure and disturbed author.

Resolution of Psychosis and Creative Triumph

With the writing of the very next play, however, entitled [There are] *Crimes and Crimes* (1899), there is evidence of both the resolution of Strindberg's psychosis and the return of his coherence and creativity. Returning to the intense naturalistic style in which he had earlier excelled, Strindberg constructed a plot about a playwright, his mistress from the working class, and their child. Included also is a tellingly meaningful exploration of insanity and the reasons it develops. Strikingly, the hero of the play becomes insane because of guilt over his hostile feelings toward his child—the same type of feeling I had hypothesized! They were Strindberg's tormenting unconscious concerns at the time of writing *The Father* and at the subsequent onset of his psychosis.

[There are] *Crimes and Crimes* is set in France, and in it, the playwright deserts his mistress and child for another woman. Because the child is an obstacle to the happiness of this new relationship, both partners wish it out of the way. Amazingly, the child dies. The father is widely suspected of being the child's murderer, and his playwriting career then falls to pieces. Because he himself believes that his thoughts were responsible for the child's death, the playwright becomes seriously disorganized and finally insane. After much effort from several sources, he is ultimately cleared of suspicion, and then the greatest blow falls: his priest confessor declares to him that he is not innocent. Knowing of his hostile wishes toward the child, the priest points out that he had murdered the child in thought and insists that he must atone for his crime.

It appears, then, that there was a return to effective playwriting and creativity concurrent with Strindberg's explicit recognition of a guilty fantasy or wish that seems to have shattered his own mind. After [There are] *Crimes and Crimes*, he wrote a series of historical plays somewhat like Shakespeare's histories, and these too are in a naturalistic style. In the year 1900, he wrote the play *Easter* and followed it with *The Dance of Death*, the works that ushered in the style of expressionism. Both *Easter* and *The Dance of Death*, together with his later written plays, *A Dream Play* and *The Ghost* [Spook] *Sonata*, are considered to be artistic triumphs on the same scale as *The Father* and *Miss Julie*.

The sequence of events was, I believe, as follows. Struggling with yearnings for care and nurturance at the time he wrote his great play *The Father*, Strindberg also resented his own children as competitors for a maternal type of wife. At the same time, he wished for a liaison with another woman to satisfy passive longings but, as those feelings were unacceptable as well, he defensively projected them onto his wife and accused her of infidelity. In his creative work on *The Father*, he struggled for truth, as every great writer does during the creative process, but seems only to have achieved the glimmerings of insight suggested by the following passage at the end:

> THE CAPTAIN TO THE NURSE: Let me put my head on your lap. Ah, that's warmer! Lean over me so I can feel your breast. Oh how sweet it is to sleep upon a woman's breast, be she mother or mistress! But sweetest of all a mother's.[10]

If this had represented any personal understanding for Strindberg, he was still unable to connect this wish for mothering with his underlying hostility to his children or his accusations about infidelity. Although struggling with paranoid ideas, however, and on the verge of psychotic breakdown, he was still in creative command as evidenced by what appears to be his use of the janusian process as well as other organizing creative processes.

After the writing of *The Father*, his guilt—particularly over hostile and murderous feelings toward his children—was buried deeper and served in part to accelerate his psychotic decompensation. Other factors surely operated as well, but I shall not attempt to trace the complete and highly complicated etiology here. With his marriage to Frieda Uhl, however, and the birth of another child and another potential competitor, his psychosis became full blown, and he turned to alchemy. Although he frequently protests in *Inferno* that he cared for this child of his second marriage, those protests are, I believe, highly unconvincing. At one point, in somewhat garbled fashion, he confessed to having attempted to use witchcraft to make his child ill as a means of effecting a reconciliation with his wife. Later, he stated that his magic backfired, and a child of his first marriage became ill instead. As hostile thoughts toward his children were in this way threatening to come fully into consciousness during this time, his efforts to change base elements into gold may well have symbolically represented his wish to change base feelings such as these into better or purer ones.

Somewhere along the way, he achieved insight, and his psychosis gradually resolved. Some might say that the latter preceded the former and that the adoption of the Swedenborgian religion played an important role. I would not argue with these explanations because I believe they are, in a complicated way, correct as well. But the presentation in the play [There Are] *Crimes and Crimes* of the guilty wish to murder a child—the same wish that very likely precipitated or accelerated his psychotic decompensation—indicates that the return to both health and creativity went hand in hand.

I cannot tell—and in the absence of further information I shall not surmise—whether the writing of the play itself served as the vehicle for Strindberg's achieving insight about his own unconscious denial of paternity and wish to be rid of his child. Nor do I know whether other factors produced the insight and/or resolved his psychotic decompensation. He describes seeing a psychiatrist in the *Inferno*, but this contact resulted in neither insight nor any amelioration of his psychosis. Also, regardless of whether or not the insight actually resolved the psychosis, it is clear that Strindberg had at the very least come to understand something related to his own unconscious processes and represented it on the stage. Insofar as attaining such insight is itself a sign of mental health, the conclusion seems inescapable that the return to the writing of meaningfully coherent drama—the return of creativity—coincided with his returning mental health.

The ensuing period of his life until his death in 1912 was essentially a fertile, creative one. In 1901 he married again, this time to a young actress named Harriet Bosse, and the marriage was essentially peaceful. Notably, even when this marriage also broke up some five years later, Strindberg did not again return to psychosis. During his last years, Strindberg turned primarily to writing prose rather than drama and spent a good deal of time painting—another of his highly developed skills. None of this work shows the disorganization, paranoid preoccupations, or the delusions and hallucinations of the psychotic period of his life.

9 ◆◇ *Homosexuality and Creativity*

In ancient Greece, the blind seer Teiresias was endowed with a great capacity for knowing and perceiving the truth. Only he, of mortal men, could tell King Oedipus the real facts about his kingship and his marriage. Knowing this, that king harassed and threatened him until he finally revealed that Oedipus had killed the previous king, his father, and had married his own mother. Teiresias's enormous gift of inner sight or insight, it was said, was bestowed upon him by the head god Zeus himself to compensate for Zeus's wife Hera having blinded him in a fit of rage.

The story of the blinding was that Zeus had summoned Teiresias to settle an argument between himself and Hera regarding sexual intercourse. Zeus had insisted to his wife that women enjoyed this more than men, and Hera had taken the opposite point of view. Because Teiresias had actually lived his life as both man and woman, he was summoned to Olympus to testify. According to some accounts, Teiresias was a hermaphrodite who possessed both male and female organs at the same time; according to others, he was a male who was turned into a female after having seen two serpents in the act of coupling. Seven years later, he was turned again into a male after seeing the same sight again at the same location. Whatever the version, his experience qualified him as an expert on the apportionment of sexual pleasure between the sexes; and to Hera's fury he gave the following expert testimony:

> If the parts of love-pleasure be counted as ten,
> Thrice three go to women, one only to men.

Females, according to him, enjoyed sexual pleasure nine times more than males. His specific choice of this factor of nine is a rather interesting mystery. What comes to mind is the association with the nine-month gestation of pregnancy, of course, but there is nothing in the mythology which clarifies this. The linkage of blindness and either hermaphroditism or bisexuality[1] with the capacity for inner sight and insight is unequivocal, however. Therefore, paying attention to the lasting wisdom that often comes down to us from the ancients, I shall now consider whether the second condition, bisexuality, or more particularly homosexuality, may also have a link with the type of inner sight that is required for artistic creativity.

Many years ago, when I first started studying creativity, I heard the psychologist Rollo May talk about it, and when he asserted that Ernst Kris, the psychoanalytic theorist, had related creativity to "passive homosexuality," I wanted to point out to him both that he had misunderstood Kris and that there could certainly be no relationship between homosexuality and creativity. I knew that the act of creation called many different and fluctuating aspects of the personality into play and, therefore, no highly organized structural feature of the personality such as homosexuality could possibly account for creativity. I didn't say anything, however, and now, after completing many studies and giving the matter much thought, I'm glad I didn't .

May *was* wrong about Kris (Kris said that inspiration was a passive experience, but not a homosexual passive experience), and I still believe that my basic point about the lack of a necessary relationship between homosexuality and creativity is correct; however, I think it can be said that there may be some important connections between them.

Aeschylus, Sappho, Michelangelo, Leonardo da Vinci, Christopher Marlowe, André Gide, Marcel Proust, Oscar Wilde, Walt Whitman, Hart Crane, and Vaslav Nijinsky were great homosexual artists of the past[2]; and Tennessee Williams, Truman Capote, Edward Albee, Jean Genet, Gertrude Stein, W. H. Auden, Andy Warhol, Carson McCullers, Adrienne Rich, Elizabeth Bishop, Phillip Johnson, Ned Rorem, and Allen Ginsberg have been prominent homosexual artists of modern times. Also, of course, homosexuality was common and widely accepted in ancient Greece, and many artists of that period were actively homosexual or bisexual. There is some reason to believe that Beethoven may have had homosexual tendencies, and the great master Shakespeare himself may have been bisexual; at least, it has been alleged that his great love poems were addressed to a male. Of course, these citations could very easily and correctly be countered by reference to Giotto, Rembrandt, Robert Herrick, Robert Burns,

William Thackeray, Robert Browning, William Wordsworth, Giuseppe Verdi, Franz Liszt, Richard Wagner, Christopher Wren, Auguste Rodin, Paul Gaugin, George Eliot, James Joyce, Lev Nikolayevich Tolstoy, Pablo Picasso, Henri Matisse, and other greats who had unquestionable heterosexual credentials. However, look at the homosexual list again! If Shakespeare himself were homosexual or bisexual, can we insist there is no relationship between that facet of his personality and his wide ranging and universal creations? I think not. I believe there are some definite ways in which homosexuality may contribute and enter into creative production, particularly in the arts.

One such way derives from social factors and culture. Looking at the names and backgrounds of the great homosexual artists I mentioned, it is apparent that they all came to prominence in particular societies and during historical times when marked changes in cultural values were in progress, and intellectual and social freedom was on the rise. Large-scale social change was a factor in ancient Greece and the Renaissance and has surely been one also in modern times. The first period was the time of Sappho and Aeschylus; the second of Michelangelo, Leonardo, Marlowe, and Shakespeare; and the third was the time of the remaining artists on my list. In all three periods of history, there has been a developing emphasis on the importance of the individual and individual responsibility. With the rise of democracy in ancient Greece, the power of authority over the individual was constantly questioned and reassessed. Also, traditional authority relationships between men and women—especially those relationships granting authority to the men—underwent change and scrutiny. Later, during the Renaissance period, concern for individualism vigorously appeared together with a reduction of the power of the Church and civil authority, the rise of capitalism and entrepreneurial initiative, and increased personal mobility and freedom. Again, there was a shift in male-female relationships. In more recent times, beginning toward the later part of the last century, the authority of the Church and of government has once more been widely questioned. People have become increasingly free to move away from their families—they now continually do so in modern American society—and there are increased opportunities for social mobility and upward rise. At the same time, women have attained a great deal more responsibility and freedom. This has meant that women have themselves come to question their traditional family and social roles and, reciprocally, men have raised similar questions about male-female relationships.

In these periods, there has been increased emphasis on the individual rather than on larger units such as fiefdoms, governmental structures, or extended family groups; marital partners rely more on each other because they no longer fit into an existing hierarchy. Traditional apportionments of aggressive functions to the male and more passive or receptive functions to the female are questioned because of the needs of the smaller family unit to carry out a large number of tasks to survive. Furthermore, as women especially move out of confinement to a domicile, they experience new outlets and opportunities and are more interested in change. In recent modern times, of course, the improvement in methods of contraception and the increase in opportunities for child care have released women for participation in new roles and functions as never before.

Under these social circumstances, issues of sexual identity become prominent in the society. I am not saying that the social conditions themselves produce homosexuality—although there may be some causal connection—but rather that in such a cultural climate, the preoccupations of homosexual artists may often be central to the interests of the society. In a complex way, the society supports and is, in turn, led to some extent by these artists. Questions of sexual identity, personal relationships, jealousy, relationship to authority, as well as the individual *vis-à-vis* the society are always of special concern to homosexual persons. Furthermore, with the possible exception of ancient Greek society in which bisexuality and homosexuality were widely accepted, homosexual persons often find themselves discriminated against or excluded and on the outside fringe of their society, a condition social scientists call being "marginal." This marginality (also a factor for Jews, expatriates, disabled people, and, perhaps, younger siblings) seems to have something to do with a person's learning to tolerate ambiguity, project varying points of view, and strike out in new directions—factors that seem to play an important role in creative orientation and ability. As women have also been marginal to society in some sense and their creative achievements have often been unrecognized, the heightened female aggressiveness that is sometimes concomitant with female homosexuality has also been useful to reverse seclusion and secure appropriate social recognition.

Homosexuality seems to have something to do with an interest in and capacity for working with certain types of subject matter in the arts, but it is not a direct cause of creativity. Leading artists such as Tennessee Williams have claimed that homosexuality confers a special type of sensibility and talent in the arts (and assumedly heightened creativity) because "homosexuals had so much to overcome in society."[3] Also, some psychoanalytic theorists have stated that the homosexual person's interest in aesthetics comes from an attempt to overcome and defend against impulses toward soiling or so-called anal interests.[4] On the other side, however, a controlled empirical study has shown that homosexual individuals did not score higher on creativity tests than did heterosexual ones but in fact scored significantly lower. While there must be reservations about this particular study because of the unreliability of some of the particular creativity tests used, there are to date no known statistical bases for assuming that homosexuals are more successfully creative than are heterosexuals.[5]

Beyond the factors of subject matter and themes, it is noteworthy that the performing artistic fields seem to be especially populated with a large number of homosexual or bisexual males, in particular dance, film, and theater. The theater has also seen recently a high concentration of successful homosexual playwrights, namely Tennessee Williams, Edward Albee, William Inge, Terence McNally, and Peter Shaffer. There seem to be several reasons for this—both social and psychological. For one thing, a self-fulfilling prophecy exists. I mean to say that in modern U.S. culture (as well as in other Western societies), interest in the arts is often held to be an effete and feminine type of pursuit. Because male homosexuals are not at all intolerant of so-called feminine behavior, whether or not they themselves display it, they find companionship and gratification in these fields. Also, as male homosexuals are still subject to social disapproval, they often find acceptance in and are attracted to publicly visible artistic fields. There is special gratification for both the makers and performers in the immediate social acceptance derived from performing arts and public display. Also, psychological tendencies to exhibitionism which are frequently found in homosexual males seem to play a role. Opportunities to display one's body in dance and one's voice in theater, particularly on an idealized, perfected level, satisfy both adaptive and exaggerated exhibitionistic needs. Most important perhaps, experience with shifting identity provides advantages for effecting shifting characterizations.

On the other hand, there seems to be no clear connection between female homosexuality and art; for that matter, there is no distinct connection between female homosexuality and any particular occupational field. This does not mean that such connections do not or cannot exist. Both the relative lack of information about female homosexuality in comparison with the male type and the fairly recent uncharted and broad entry of women into occupational fields combine to make such connections, or potential connections, unclear. All of the previously mentioned homosexual women have been successful in literature and, in addition, two other outstanding women writers, Edith Wharton and Virginia Woolf, were very likely bisexual. However, in contrast with males in the performing arts, a reason for the attraction of such women to literature may have been the relative *absence* there of public exposure and display.

Personality matters related to aesthetics broadly underlie some of the social issues. Just as Teiresias was assumedly able to report on the sexual pleasures of both males and females, homosexual persons may well have experiential access to aspects of the inner world of both sexes. Although not hermaphrodites, of course, they do engage in social and sexual practices of the opposite sex, some female homosexuals carrying out characteristically masculine types of aggressive activity roles and males often taking on feminine receptive and passive ones. Because they have inevitably been trained in their own sex's social and sexual orientation as well, no matter how early the homosexuality began, there is some capacity to be on both sides of the gender identity fence, so to speak.

Even though heterosexual persons certainly do at times experience or imagine the inner world and sensations of the opposite sexual role, actual concrete gender role shifting very likely has a more intrinsic effect. I quickly add, however, that it is not really clear what is chicken and what is egg, which factor precedes which in this particular ability to shift identity. It is not clear whether persons become homosexuals in the first place partly because of the drive or ability to shift gender roles, or whether the shifting is an outgrowth of homosexual life itself. In either case, the experience of change of gender roles is very likely, as I said before, connected to an ability to take on and play other roles, particularly theatrical ones, and may also be a factor in other types of artistic creativity. In dance, for example, there seems to be a need for both an orientation to the manipulation of outer space which is associated with male feelings and perceptions as well as an awareness of inner space which is associated with those of females. Ability to depict dual-gender experience in literature, music, and visual art may also be enhanced by homosexual life and orientation. The immortal psychological portraits in drama of female characters such as Blanche Dubois in Williams's *Streetcar Named Desire,* Martha in Albee's *Who's Afraid of Virginia Woolf,* Madge Owens in Inge's *Picnic,* and, if we include Shakespeare, Lady Macbeth in *Macbeth* were surely in part products of the enhanced sensitivity of their authors to female experience. That such sensitivity is not pure appreciation but rather a highly ambivalent regard is evident in the jointly derogatory and sympathetic portrayals in all these cases. There are, moreover, real limitations in all of this, which I shall clarify shortly.

Conflict, as I discussed in Chapter 3, is a prime requisite for the motive to create artistically, and homosexuality is only one of many conflict-ridden conditions responsible. Homosexuality may provide a slight edge over other conditions in that it is close to basic narcissism or self-love and may therefore involve a strong tendency to heightened vigilance or so-called "sensitivity" (not, however, Williams's suffering sensibility). Side by side with ambivalence to the opposite sex, there seems to be a strong motive for males to beautify and idealize other males and the quality of maleness and for females to beautify and idealize other females and femaleness as an indirect way of beautifying the self. Could we not ask whether it was Shakespeare's self-passion that helped him to write great love poems (as claimed) to a real or imagined male like himself rather than to a woman? Or wasn't the idealizing motive of a homosexual artist such as Michelangelo an important factor in the creation of the beautiful male statue of David? Were not the loving hands that formed the marble contours the same that lovingly stroked the bodies of young males?[6] Did not Virginia Woolf's claimed love for women influence her careful telling about the inner world of Mrs. Dalloway? Also, there may be some basis to the idea that the widely noted homosexual focus on mouth pleasure ("orality") has something to do with facility and love for words and therefore a specific capacity for poetry and literature.

Furthermore, let us not fall into the trap of exempting supposedly heterosexual writers from this assessment. Consider the vaunted and highly publicized recent adoption of bisexuality by Norman Mailer. Was his potentiality for such behavior a factor in his creativity in the first place? Norman Mailer had always projected a macho male and stud-like image publicly, and the idea that underlying homosexual tendencies became later activated should not be surprising to any psychologically sophisticated observer. So, too, even that seeming epitome of masculine behavior, Ernest Hemingway, indicated a type of hypersensitivity with regard to homosexuality which suggested that he too might have had strongly repressed latent tendencies. When the critic Max Eastman made a somewhat veiled public reference to such a possibility, Hemingway stormed to Eastman's Scribner Building office, burst in, and punched Eastman in the face—not sufficient, you may say, to prove that he had homosexual tendencies, but certainly, I would insist, the behavior falls in the category of protesting too much and denying one's anxiety-laden wishes. Also, we should not overlook the notorious womanizing of many famous poets and other literary figures. The Don Juan antics of Lord Byron and of Dylan Thomas, for example, might well have been motivated by a need to defend themselves against unconscious homosexual tendencies. Although such latent homosexuality may be more hindrance than advantage with regard to appreciating dual-gender experience, there may be other artistic benefits.

Homosexuality and success are, of course, not found solely in the arts. All other fields of activity and walks of life are replete with successful homosexual men and women, and it would be hard to argue for any special kind of capabilities connected with sexual preference. For example, a fairly large number of homosexual men and women have been noted in sports, particularly tennis, but no distinct connections are apparent. Exact numbers and proportions in particular fields are hard to come by, even though the secrecy surrounding homosexuals has been increasingly reduced in recent years. The number of successful homosexual men and women may actually be publicly exaggerated because they are singled out and noted as both a source of gossip for prejudiced persons and a source of pride for those who are sympathetic and supportive.

On the other side of the coin, homosexuality can and does interfere with the free development of creativity, not just because of social discrimination but also because of difficulties on the level of individual functioning. Although the matter of homosexual disorder is nowadays controversial, to the degree that a person's homosexuality arises from psychopathological processes, lack of choice, and intense rigidifying conflicts, there is impairment in that person's creative process. The impairment ranges from fixation on certain types of subject matter, reduced appreciation for gender differences, false starts, and ongoing inflexibilities and distortions, to overwhelming anxiety and an inability to carry out creative activities at all.

A rarely documented example of an important impairment in the creation of poetry—developing the wrong central image at the start—comes from my research with a noted homosexual poet. It concerns the writing of the specific poem quoted in Chapter 2 and has to do with the wrong use, aesthetically, of the male gender. He and I discussed the problematic effect during our close observation of the ongoing creative process.

He was writing the poem in which a horse and its rider were the central poetic image. In an early version that he showed me, he had introduced the horse with the following lines:

A gentle broken horse
For all he knew it could have been I who first
Broke him, rode him, abandoned him
When I went off to study or to war.

As his goal was to trace a relationship between the rider and his horse, a relationship that would in this poem eventually end in separation and loss, these lines were first designed to provide a meaningful background. They rooted the relationship in a poignant past that was not necessarily factual at all but was really a fantasied possibility for both man and horse. The lines conveyed the sense of symbolic meaning and mysterious earlier ties.

In this version, however, he had described the horse distinctly as a male. Whether for this or some other reason, the lines were not yet working. He left off writing at that point, and, when he returned to the poem the next day, he went through several versions that were still unsatisfactory. Trying to describe an intimate, harmonious feeling of the rider with the horse, he found himself unable to do so. Only after several further attempts the next day did he think of and write lines that produced a breakthrough and allowed him to go ahead. These lines were the following:

> One spring dusk before I went to war
> I found myself for the last time, as things turned out,
> Riding bareback at Shoup's farm north of Woodstock.
> A stillness swarming inward from the first star
> Or outward from the buoyant sorrel mare
> Who moved as if not displeased by my weight on her back.

At this point, he had clearly changed the sex of the horse to female. And with this switch he was then able to write effectively in a version of the very next stanza (quoted earlier) about the feeling of accord between the horse and rider:

> Or outward from the buoyant sorrel mare
> Who moved as if not displeased by the weight upon her.
> Meadows received us, heady with unseen lilac.
> Brief, polyphonic lives abounded everywhere.
> With one accord, we circled the small lake.

The change, therefore, led to or was followed by the creation of an effective poetic image indicating a broad, universal experience of accord and intimacy. Without quoting the rest of the poem, I will assure the reader that this change also was effective for the artwork as a whole.[7] When I asked the poet why he had switched the horse's sex, he said that he had begun to have an erotic feeling about his relationship to the horse while writing the lines, and a change of sex seemed appropriate. He had based the poem on a meeting with a real horse in the desert and, he added, he had not known that horse's sex at the time. With little deliberation, however, he had described the horse as male from the beginning. He had no further speculations about the change but felt strongly that it had improved the poem and his writing of it.

Rather than focusing on his successful breakthrough for the moment, I want to emphasize the presence of constriction and limitation in the early portion of the creative process. Writing about a male horse because of his erotic attachment to males had blocked him in the construction of the image he intended. Although he surely could have written about frank homosexual attachment in this poem, as he had done in others, he intended to describe a more universal experience of intimacy, accord, and loss. That more universal feeling and aesthetic intent were finally achieved by the change of sex from stallion to mare. With this change he had introduced the broader connotation of one's relationship to one's mother because, along with other features of the new lines, the word *mare* is a homonym for the French word *mère*, meaning mother. This jibed with descriptions in the poem of fusion and accord with another being and, for himself, with other broader and deeper meanings.

Many loose ends remain in this story. Looking at the positive side, how was the poet able to overcome the block and move not only more broadly but also to a level that was deeper for him as well? And what does it mean that he changed the sex of the horse when he experienced a conscious erotic feeling toward it? Some of the answers to these questions can be traced to the conflicts he was struggling with during the writing of this poem—his ambivalent erotic attachment to his own mother, for example. Other answers can be traced to his use of the janusian and homospatial processes as described earlier in the construction of these passages—here note specifically the "stillness swarming inward . . . or outward" in the breakthrough version, a janusian formulation of simultaneous opposition or antithesis—because, as I shall clarify in the next chapter, both the janusian and homospatial processes foster the unearthing of unconscious material during the course of the creative process.[8] However, although the limitation and constriction of the creative process were overcome in this case, the main point is that serious blocks due to homosexuality do occur. In many cases, they are considerably more far reaching than in this instance, and in some, they are intractable.

When all is said and done, the creative talent is a highly adaptive one and involves specific and complicated processes of thought. A factor such as homosexuality could never account in any large degree for creative capacity but could only pertain to certain aspects of it. Furthermore, there is no reason to believe that latent homosexuality confers any particular advantages either. Because there is lack of recognition and acknowledgment, there may be even more limitations and restrictions. Telling depictions of both male and female experience, beautiful male and female sculptures, and passionate love sonnets close to Shakespeare's level have been composed in all historical periods by men and women who seem to have been neither overtly nor latently homosexual. Until we can pursue this question with more extensive research, the most meaningful statement about the Teiresian bisexual insight is that homosexuality has something to do with the creativity of certain individuals, but no basic relationship to general creative capacity.

10 ◈ *The Muse in the Bottle*

The following is a description of William Faulkner, the winner of the 1949 Nobel Prize in literature, on a night in August 1937, at the Algonquin Hotel: "He was so drunk that he fell against the steam pipe in the bathroom, burning his back severely. He lay there, face down on the floor, clad only in his shorts, oblivious to the icy November wind blowing through an open window, until anxious friends got the management to open the door and found him. They helped him to bed and summoned a doctor, who treated him for a third-degree burn."[1]

And again, in the autumn of 1951: "At one point he was so drunk that he fell down the stairs at Rowan Oak [his home in Mississippi], banging himself up. Desperate, Estelle [his wife] phoned Saxe Commins [his editor], and he flew down from New York to help. What he found at Rowan Oak shocked him. Faulkner lay on a couch in a stupor, his face covered with bruises and contusions, his body battered and bloated. Commins helped him to bed and began a night-long vigil. As Faulkner pleaded for a drink, tossed and mumbled deliriously, Commins alternately cajoled and threatened him. Since Faulkner couldn't control his bodily functions, Commins had virtually to carry him to the bathroom."[2]

Such are the depths Faulkner went to while drinking. In reacting to this, however, one is tempted to paraphrase Lincoln's famous comment regarding the alcoholism of his general Ulysses S. Grant. When a delegation came to him to demand Grant's dismissal because of his excessive drinking, President Lincoln said, "If I knew what kind of liquor Grant drinks, I would send a bottle or so to some other generals."[3] If we knew what kind of liquor Faulkner drank, we might well be tempted to send barrels of it to many other writers and artists in the world today.

Heavy use of alcohol among highly creative persons, especially writers, is surprisingly frequent. In the United States, five of the eight writers who have won the Nobel Prize in literature have all suffered at some time from severe alcohol abuse and/or dependence, and many writers throughout the world have also had this difficulty.[4] Various lists add or subtract some notable figures depending on the information available, but there is now relative certainty about the alcohol abuse of the following major writers: James Agee, Charles Pierre Baudelaire, Louise Bogan, James Boswell, Truman Capote, John Cheever, Stephen Crane, Theodore Dreiser, William Faulkner, F. Scott Fitzgerald, Lillian Hellman, Ernest Hemingway, Victor Hugo, Samuel Johnson, Ring Lardner, Sinclair Lewis, Jack London, Robert Lowell, Malcolm Lowry, John O'Hara, Eugene O'Neill, Edgar Allan Poe, William Sydney Porter (O. Henry), Edwin Arlington Robinson, John Steinbeck, Dylan Thomas, Tennessee Williams, and Thomas Wolfe. Among painters, Mark Rothko, Arshile Gorky, Jackson Pollock, and Willem de Kooning have been famous alcohol abusers as well.[5] It is a striking list, but I should immediately add, it proves nothing by itself. What I mean is that if we drew up a list of all the great writers throughout history and placed it side by side with this group, we would very likely find that the number of nonalcoholic writers and even of abstainers far, far outnumbers this relatively small assemblage. Indeed, two recent U.S. Nobel laureates, Isaac Bashevis Singer and Saul Bellow, show no indication of alcohol abuse, nor, for that matter, did other greats such as Thomas Mann, Marcel Proust, or William Shakespeare. But that is another story. For the moment, the qualitative information that so many really good writers used alcohol to excess demands explanation and understanding. Questions immediately leap to mind such as whether the alcohol drug itself actually facilitates the creative process or whether—now that genetic factors have been touted as operating in alcoholism—there is some biological propensity connecting creativity with a need to drink. Is there, so to speak, a muse of inspiration in a bottle of gin, whiskey, or vodka? Or, reaching back to a mythical image that for some reason we all hold in our minds, does the storyteller always have a glass of spirits in hand while spinning the tale? These are interesting and to some extent troubling questions because there are many writers who, like Faulkner in the description earlier, have been sacrificed on the altar of this inability to abstain from drinking at some point in their lives. We know that, unlike homosexuality and the factors related to it, the subject matter of alcohol indulgence is not itself of special literary interest because, with the notable exceptions of Jack Kerouac, Jack London, Eugene O'Neill, and Malcolm Lowry, none of the writers mentioned has made any remarkable literary hash from plots regarding alcoholism,[6] nor is the psychology of addiction a very trendy literary or artistic topic.

We can take up first the question of the influence of alcohol on the creative process itself because I have collected data about that. In an assessment of available pertinent biographical and autobiographical material of each of the writers listed, I found that very few did their actual writing, or even their thinking about writing, while under the influence of alcohol.[7] Or, to put it more exactly, their writing was seldom successful when done under the influence of alcohol, and, at various points in their lives, drinking absolutely interfered with their capacity to do any creative work. F. Scott Fitzgerald, denying the reports about his drinking in the newspapers, said, "As a matter of fact I have never written a line of any kind while I was under the glow of so much as a single cocktail."[8] Ring Lardner, in the more pithy style for which he was famous, said: "No one, ever, wrote anything as well after even one drink as he would have done without it."[9] And, in a serious reflective way, the poet Robert Lowell said, "Nothing was written drunk, at least nothing was perfected and finished," and added, "but I have looked forward to whatever one gets from drinking, a stirring and a blurring."[10]

Lowell's afterthought is worthy of some note as it points to some nuances and complications about the relationship between drinking and the creative process. Other authors reputedly have actually used alcohol as the kind of stimulant to inspiration that Lowell indicated. Hemingway, at one point in his life, is said to have awakened regularly at four-thirty in the morning and started to write standing up, "with a pencil in one hand and a drink in the other,"[11] and Fitzgerald also apparently used alcohol as a stimulant later in his life. Short-story writer William Sydney Porter (O. Henry) wryly boasted as follows: "Combining a little orange juice with a little scotch, the author drinks the health of all magazine editors, sharpens his pencil and begins to write. When the oranges are empty and the flask is dry, a saleable piece of fiction is ready for mailing."[12]

Such reports and public statements, as I pointed out earlier on the topic of inspiration, must be taken with large measures of grains of salt. Writers make statements and give out reports such as these to add to what they think should be the writer's public image, and this image factor, as I shall explain in a moment, even plays a role in the motivation to drink in the first place. In reality, the picture is quite mixed in many ways. Although some may indeed use alcohol to stimulate inspiration or, more accurately, to reduce inhibition, by far the majority find it to be an interference. Even Malcolm Lowry, who wrote about alcoholism and drank himself to death, was directly observed to work in the following way: "Lowry drank in order to avoid writing, sobered up in order to write, then drank in order to avoid writing."[13] And Thomas Wolfe, who similarly almost destroyed himself with drink, was also directly observed as follows: "If he was sick or mentally upset or having trouble with his work, he would often use liquor as a kind of cure-all or escape."[14]

Overall, the pattern of alcohol use in all the writers studied was the same as for the ordinary alcohol abuser. By and large, they did not use alcohol while they were actually engaged in writing but tended to drink when they were finished for the day. Early in the course of their illness, they only drank regularly during after-work or evening hours. As the volume of their alcohol consumption increased, they became increasingly uncomfortable, irritable, and anxious during periods of the day when they were not drinking, including times ordinarily set aside for work. Then, in order to sedate themselves, they began to drink during work-allotted hours. This pattern of drinking for sedation and relaxation followed by jitteriness and anxiety when stopping and subsequently drinking again to produce sedation for those effects is typical for any alcoholic ranging from the skid-row derelict to the closet drinker in the executive suite. One possible distinguishing feature for a writer—or for any artist for that matter—is that unlike other kinds of work activity, creative pursuits are often carried out in solitude. Working alone may be a lonely affair, and also the artist can drink without interference or detection from others. This self-enforced loneliness and freedom may enhance the proclivity to drink.

Among the materials that I gathered, here is a fairly typical account given by John O'Hara to the columnist Earl Wilson about heavy drinking in relation to writing. It pertains to the creation of one of his most successful pieces, *Pal Joey:*

> My wife and I were . . . living at . . . 93rd and 5th [New York City]. . . . I had an idea for a story. I said to my wife I'd go to Philadelphia. Hole up in the Hotel Ben Franklin a couple of days, lock myself in, eat on room service. Just work.
>
> But the night before, we went out, and I got stiff.
>
> I got up next morning to start to the station, and I am dying. Now as we got to the Pierre, at 60th Street, I said to the cab, "Stop here." I went in. After a drink or two, I feel what-the-hell. Better take a nap. I check in.
>
> Then began a real beauty. Just getting stiff and passing out. I started

Thursday. By Saturday morning I'd drunk myself sober. I picked up the phone and said, "What time is it?"

The girl says, "Quarter after seven."

I asked her, "A.M. or P.M.?" The girl said, "A.M. and the day is Saturday." They knew me there.

At that point remorse set in. I asked, "What kind of a God-damned heel am I? I must be worse'n anybody in the world." Then I figured, "No, there must be somebody worse than me—but who?" Al Capone, maybe. Then I got it—maybe some nightclub masters of ceremonies I know. . . .

That was my idea. I went to work and wrote a piece about a night-club heel in the form of a letter. I finished the piece by 11 o'clock. I went right home. . . .

The New Yorker bought the story the same day, ordered a dozen more, and then came the play and the movie.

That was the only good thing I ever got out of booze, but mind you, Wilson, I wasn't on a bender at the time I wrote. I was perfectly sober! Have you got that down in your notebook?[15]

O'Hara describes the typical sequence of having to drink the next day after starting the previous night and then continuing into the time of work. Certainly he had been motivated to write a story early in this particular sequence but, except for inducing his guilt, one could not say that the alcohol intake itself facilitated the writing. O'Hara himself makes the point that he could not work while drinking. Even writers who have characteristically used small amounts of alcohol while working have eventually gotten into a pattern of drinking, then guilt, and then abstinence in order to write. William Faulkner is a case in point; later in his life he could not drink at all when writing.

The O'Hara account also illustrates what might be considered a causative—perhaps it would be better to say instigating—factor in writers' and other artists' heavy use of alcohol. In many cultures, especially the modern American one, a certain tough-guy or macho image is associated with heavy drinking and the so-called ability to "hold one's liquor." O'Hara's boasting manner to Wilson along with a later comment which I did not quote by Wilson himself in this same account describing O'Hara as "a pretty good boy with the juice," illustrates such an image. It is not clear what has led to this macho image related to alcohol in this and other cultures, nor is it clear why writers and other artists might be attracted to it. Somehow, an idea of achievement in the face of disability or bravery in the face of danger appears to be involved. For male writers and other artists, there may be a particular need to counter widespread cultural images of effeteness or effeminacy or, in some cases, to deny actual latent homosexual tendencies. Sociologist Robin Room points out that many of the Nobel laureates who were alcohol abusers were born in the late 1880s and 1890s and were part of a rebellious "lost-generation" literary subculture of the time.[16]

Particular ethnic cultural factors may also be involved. Many successful twentieth-century writers in modern times have come from Irish backgrounds, for example, and there is a rather high incidence of alcoholism in that cultural group. Interestingly, drinking and masculinity are especially linked in Irish culture, a social factor some theorists have construed to be an overcompensation against the culturally enforced long period of Irish sons' dependence on their mothers. Several of the twentieth-century writers on the list I gave have Irish backgrounds—John O'Hara, F. Scott Fitzgerald, Malcolm Lowry, Louise Bogan, James Agee, and other heavy drinkers such as James Joyce and Brendan Behan could be included as well. (There is, however, no simple way to connect Louise Bogan to the macho image.)

These social explanations are only a small part of the picture; they do not adequately account for the individual factors in heavy alcohol use among so many highly creative people. They also do not explain how alcohol hinders or facilitates the creative process. To get further into those matters specifically, I shall dwell, for the remainder of this chapter, on the research data I have collected in my work with the author John Cheever.

John Cheever: Creation of a Novel

First, some background: John Cheever wrote more than three hundred short stories and five novels. Known primarily as a modern master of the short-story form, he composed fantasies and satirical social commentary about the people and life of modern suburbia. He won the National Book Award, the Pulitzer Prize, the Howells Medal, and the National Gold Medal and was a member of the National Institute of Arts and Letters. Although he had been nominated for the Nobel Prize in literature several times, this award ultimately escaped him. Despite his reputation as a short-story writer, his novel *Falconer* was recognized as so outstanding that it came close to earning him that highly coveted prize. He received the Pulitzer Prize for his collection of short stories the year after *Falconer* was published because, it is generally acknowledged, of that novel's boost to his reputation.

Born the son of a shoe salesman and the proprietress of a gift shop in Quincy, Massachusetts, Cheever always claimed to be a descendant of an illustrious and legendary New England schoolmaster—a claim that has recently been disputed.[17] He had one sibling, an older brother, and very little formal education. Expelled from Thayer Academy, a prep school, because of poor grades, he never went on to college despite his wide and intense intellectual interests. His first literary success was a short story entitled "Expelled," which he publicly affirmed to be a thinly fictionalized account of his own prep school experience. It wasn't. The boy in the story was expelled for smoking infractions rather than poor academic performance.

The course of Cheever's writing career was quite erratic. Although hailed for his stories and supported comfortably by the income from them, he sought for a more substantial literary reputation by the writing of novels. His first, *The Wapshot Chronicle,* was a wide success, and the second, *The Wapshot Scandal,* was less so. The third, *Bullet Park,* was not at all well received. During the period of his life in which he was writing these novels, Cheever used alcohol to great excess. He also had numerous extramarital affairs, and his marriage to Mary Winternitz was under constant strain. Although his diaries indicate that he also struggled with conscious homosexual impulses throughout this time and had occasional homosexual encounters, he did not engage openly in a homosexual affair until close to the end of his life. As for his alcoholism, he stopped drinking completely before writing, or more accurately, before completing his fourth novel, *Falconer.* My interviews with him took place during the year after *Falconer* was published and are directly pertinent to both his abstinence and his creative achievement.

Cheever struggled with alcoholism for most of his life. How he got started is not clear, but what is clear is that he was exposed to a good deal of drinking by his parents. That his father was an alcoholic and a work failure is fairly well known, but what is not generally known is that his mother also drank excessively despite her more responsible employment history. The father was a failed shoe salesman who was completely supported by his wife, the proprietress of a gift shop as I said earlier. This, however, is how Cheever described his mother's death to me:

> At the age of eighty-two it was discovered that she had diabetes and drank herself to death, quite obviously. I tried to stop her from it but she said, "No." She was fully intending to die, and to die as soon as possible, a very sensible girl. She would have had to have had an amputation; she was quite put out by it. Absolutely pissed at finding out she had diabetes. The last thing she asked for was Old Crow, her dying words. . . . She absolutely loved bourbon. She called the grocer and

ordered a case of bourbon whiskey. Someone called me from Boston and said, "Your mother is drinking herself to death." So I immediately flew down and went to see her. And I said, "You're drinking yourself to death." And she said, "Yes." And I said, "You can't do this . . . you know life's a very splendid mystery, and it isn't in your power to take it." And she said, "You must go to church a great deal." And I said, "Yes." And she said, "High or low?" And I said, "Low." And she said, "Humph, the family was always high." They were practically her last words. . . . Her last request—I moistened her lips, although I was a little embarrassed, with a little bourbon.

Although it was a little hard for me to know whether every part of this story was true, given the ironic pun on the word *high*—that is, alcoholic high or high Episcopal—and Cheever's tendency to tell stories with tongue in cheek, there seems little question that the substance regarding his mother's drinking was valid and that alcohol therefore pervaded his family background. Although we have not yet come to understand all the factors—genetic, dynamic, and educational—connecting parental alcoholism to alcoholism in children, we can say with certainty that in Cheever's case, his background did influence his own severe alcohol abuse. This alcohol abuse intermittently interfered with his work throughout his life until it threatened to kill him three years before our interviews.

The sequence was as follows. In the 1960s, Cheever's reputation was at a very high level. He had been on the cover of *Time* magazine, had won the prestigious Howells Medal, and had a successful movie made from one of his stories. After publishing the unsuccessful *Bullet Park* in 1969, his writing output dwindled markedly, and he drank more and more heavily. Then, in 1973, he suffered a heart attack while mowing his lawn.

Although he vowed never to drink after this heart attack and was told by his doctors that he would die if he did, he soon returned to his old patterns. He went to the University of Iowa Writers' Workshop for a semester, and, together with his teaching activities and a spate of heterosexual affairs, he drank increasingly. Finally, in the autumn of 1974, he accepted an invitation to teach writing at Boston University. He had started the novel that was to become *Falconer*, but his experience in Boston at that point turned out to be, in his own words, "a dreadful mistake." He drank regularly and steadily, and finally required hospitalization to dry out.

From the hospital in Boston he was transferred to the Smithers Alcoholism Rehabilitation Unit of St. Luke's-Roosevelt Hospital in

New York City, where his experiences led to his recovery from alcoholism and complete abstinence from then on. Back to one of our interviews:

> CHEEVER: I have no use for a psychiatrist who assumes he can cure drug addiction or alcoholism. It's truly ridiculous, I think, and it's totally irresponsible.
>
> ROTHENBERG: What made you stop [drinking]?
>
> CHEEVER: Self-confinement to an alcohol and drug rehabilitation place. Hospital room, beds—
>
> ROTHENBERG: How did they help you?
>
> CHEEVER: Made me chill out. They got me away from the bottle. Can't get out—confined for, oh, thirty-three days, something like that.
>
> ROTHENBERG: Oh, it's a cold turkey kind of thing?
>
> CHEEVER: Yeah, it was cold turkey. It was cold turkey in an A.A. branch and the A.A. was right at hand. You were lectured on the A.A. . . .
>
> ROTHENBERG: Just thirty-three days and you never took anything again?
>
> CHEEVER: I still smoke. And if I have to give that up, and I may—if I have more trouble with the spot on my lung, I will go to them. They have a nicotine cure, you sign up for two weeks and here again they beat you over the head with sticks and you cry a lot. . . . Smithers . . . worked for me and a friend of mine, a woman. . . .
>
> It was originally to have been, I think, for sort of upper crusts, terribly expensive. And Medicare or Medicaid, of course, has opened it up for anybody who claims to have an alcoholic problem and you share a room about this big [indicates a small room] with five other men, one bathroom. Some folks may have hallucinations during the course of the incarceration, it's absolutely hell. But it seems to work.
>
> This woman was very wealthy and you might say, a spoiled woman. . . . Truman Capote is, as far as I know, in there now at my insistence. And I think he's been there two weeks, if he's alive. I haven't been in touch with him since I've been on tour. . . .
>
> The letters that I got were tremendously important in getting me through it. It's like the army, or being in a far-away country. Mail, even though your wife mails it over, is really your only—you can't telephone, there's a pay phone, but—

Through this experience, Cheever became a devoted member of Alcoholics Anonymous, attended their meetings regularly, and followed their procedures. In addition to the constant support of the organization, it appeared that, as a religious person throughout his life, he also got some benefit from their spiritual or religious focus.

What other reasons were there for the success of this treatment for Cheever at this point in his life? After all, he was sixty-three years old at the time, had consulted numerous psychiatrists about his problem and, he told me, had previously been very scornful of the Alcoholics Anonymous organization. When I asked him directly about his motivation to stop drinking at that particular point, he stated that he had a heart attack and knew he would die if he continued. Although this certainly may have been a reason at some time, it was inadequate as a real explanation because the heart attack had occurred three years previously and, rather than becoming abstinent, he had actually increased the use of alcohol following his serious brush with death. Confinement, with its care and removal from availability of alcohol, was surely a help, of course, but without motivation confinement alone would have had little effect. No, I found that the real clue to his stopping and the events of that period of his life came from other material in our sessions and pertained to factors in his writing at the time.

The explanation pertains to the novel *Falconer,* the work Cheever completed during the year after he gave up drinking. This novel takes place in the fictional Falconer State Prison and concerns a university professor/drug addict named Farragut who is incarcerated after having murdered his brother. He is subjected to brutalizing treatment by the other inmates, and there is much elaboration of both loving and sadistic homosexual prison relationships. Deeply poignant and meaningful human strivings are also enacted. After having given up his drug addiction in the prison, Farragut escapes by substituting himself in the shroud of a dead cellmate. Totally evading all pursuers, he finds himself finally at an ordinary laundromat and nearby bus stop and, in that banal setting, he experiences a new sense of compassion and freedom. Clearly, it is a tale of resurrection and redemption.

Prior to the interview excerpt that I am about to quote, Cheever and I had been talking about Sing Sing—the prison that was near his home in Ossining—and about some successful teaching experiences he had had with convicts there. Because *Falconer* was set in a prison, I asked the following question:

> ROTHENBERG: The idea for that novel . . . was that a gradual development? Did you have a particular initial idea? Can you remember? Or was the going to Sing Sing part of thinking about the idea of such a novel?
>
> CHEEVER: I had not set the novel in prison until—it's a brother conflict—I had written about the brother conflict, since the beginning. . . . Out of about, what, some three hundred published sto-

ries . . . I think there must be twenty stories about brothers. Brothers or men generally run through my whole work. This is simply another run-through of the scene. But this is the only one in which a murder takes place. In the other stories, one brother hits the other over the head as a rule—or strikes him in some way, or tries in some way to wound him. And very often unsuccessfully. This was the only time— and this was presumably a sum of the experience which is part of my life (as if fiction can bring order to experience). It was emotional in this way.

I've always been close to my brother [Fred].

ROTHENBERG: Is your brother younger or older?

CHEEVER: He was seven years older than I. He died about this time last year.

ROTHENBERG: He was an only brother?

CHEEVER: He was an only brother, yes. We were very close. It was . . . probably, speaking structurally, the broadest and deepest love in my life.

From this discussion and his spontaneous references to his brother Fred it would seem reasonable to assume that Fred was connected in some important way with the creation of *Falconer*. Therefore, it is of interest that, in another interview, he returned to a discussion of his brother in the following way:

CHEEVER: It was the strongest love of my life, certainly the most rewarding. Very strong.

ROTHENBERG: Did you do things together a lot?

CHEEVER: Yes, I adored him. And then, when he went away to college, I didn't see him. He came back and left—I don't know what crossed his mind. I think he saw that I was in trouble; my parents weren't speaking to one another, and he managed to be everything for me. . . . When I was about nineteen, I realized how unnatural this love was and how poignant—

ROTHENBERG: Why do you call it unnatural?

CHEEVER: Um, because it was; it was quite unnatural. And—I mean not homosexual, but we really had very little at that point to give to one another.

At that juncture in the session, Cheever went on to tell me about how, during a period that they lived together in Boston, he and his brother would accompany each other on dates. On one occasion, there was a crisis when a girl wanted to spend time with the brother, but Fred would not leave John's side. Irately, the girlfriend told John that he was ruining Fred's life. Then, Cheever told me, with a flat tone in his voice, he decided to move out of the house the same night. He continued:

> CHEEVER: She was really pissed off.
> ROTHENBERG: Jealous?
> CHEEVER: I'm very grateful to her, actually.
> ROTHENBERG: Why?
> CHEEVER: I think I would have left anyhow. Boston very easily accommodated us as brothers, it's an eccentric society. And we were the Cheever brothers; it would have been dreadful as far as I was concerned.

Here, Cheever was directly indicating his mixed feelings about his brother; staying together, he said, would have been dreadful for him. What has this to do with the novel and with Cheever's alcoholism? It is difficult to pinpoint all of the connections exactly, but consider what the author had to say when I asked him about his experiences with therapy. He had seen three different psychiatrists, none of whom had, he thought, helped him. I asked him why:

> CHEEVER: It's rather hard to say. I don't think I was ever cooperative. My principal concern, as I say, was alcohol. And they would say, "Well, alcohol is simply symptomatic." [However] . . . I was never able to get . . . [name of psychiatrist], I was never able to get either . . . [name of psychiatrist] or . . . [name of another psychiatrist] to go into my brother in depth. I would say, "Look, you know, if there was any problem I would like to discuss it would be my brother." And they would say, "Well, we'll come to that." And then I would say something polite like, "You mean six thousand dollars later we will come to my brother?" And neither . . . [name of psychiatrist] nor . . . [name of other psychiatrist] were terribly interested. And I'd say, "Well I loved him dearly and I've missed him more painfully than I've missed anybody else in my life." They'd say: "Well, we'll go into that later. We'll mind that later." Maybe there wasn't much to say, I don't know.
> ROTHENBERG: You missed him; this is before he died?
> CHEEVER: This love of my brother was mutual. He loved me also very much. We went to Europe together—uh—when I was seventeen, I think. And then he went to Europe when I was eighteen and I was miserable. I was completely miserable without him. More miserable, I think, than I would have been, you know, with the removal of another person in my life.
> ROTHENBERG: Did he marry and have a family of his own?
> CHEEVER: Oh yes, he married, and unfortunately, he married an old girl of mine.

Regardless of whether or not the sessions with the psychiatrists went exactly as Cheever described (I found it hard to believe that two of my colleagues could be as bluntly rejecting of an important topic as he stated),[18] it was clear that he himself felt that he had not been helped to work on a problem that was very important to him. Further, as his own sequence of comments indicates, he connected the problem with his brother directly to his alcoholism.

I shall try to spell out both my answer to the question about why Cheever stopped drinking at the time he did and the connections with his work, specifically with his creativity. First, the writing: Cheever himself stated that he had written several stories about men or brothers, and they had seldom hurt each other seriously. With emphasis, he told me that never did a brother murder a brother. However, in *Bullet Park*, the novel he wrote before his most serious bout with alcoholism, a brutal murder almost does take place. The character Paul Hammer attempts to murder the young son of a man to whom he is inextricably linked, Elliot Nailles. Not only are Hammer and Nailles linked together by name, but their emotions are inextricably intermingled in a manner reminiscent of Cheever's description of his relationship with his brother.

This novel was, as I said, not well received by the public and the critics, and some would say, and have said, that Cheever's ensuing deterioration resulted from that failure. He subsequently went to teach at Boston University and there drank to enormous excess until he was totally unable to function and required hospitalization. Regarding this period, his daughter Susan, in her recent biography of her father, quoted him as saying that the suicide of fellow writer Anne Sexton had upset him terribly, and he could not go on.[19] Sexton taught in the same program as Cheever, and they had been frequent companions up to the time of her death. Upsetting as her suicide must have been, a more important difficulty of this Boston period, I believe, is that Cheever's brother Fred was also living there at that time, and he and Fred saw each other more than they had for many, many years.

My explanation for these events in Cheever's life and work is this: the creative process, as I have described in detail previously,[20] involves a gradual unearthing of unconscious processes. Creative writers, as well as other creative people, use both the janusian and homospatial processes as means of attaining partial insight into their own unconscious contents. To summarize the means by which this comes about: both of these processes operate as templates that reverse the disguising operations of the type of cognition called *primary process*. Primary-process cognition uses particular mechanisms called *condensation* (combining multiple diverse elements), *displacement* (shifting onto something smaller), *equivalence of opposites* (and others) in order to allow the disguised discharge of unconscious material. Because janusian and homospatial processes are conscious, and because they bear a superficial, formal resemblance to the disguising mechanisms of primary process cognition, they serve to reverse and undo the disguise progressively as they are used. They thereby bring unconscious material partially into consciousness and produce partial insight. Make no mistake about it—this is not an eruption of unconscious material into consciousness (nor a "regression in the service of the ego" as described by Ernst Kris, p. 38). A burst of unconscious material does not initiate the creative process, but the unconscious is gradually unearthed in part during the progression. The creative person embarks on an activity leading to discovering and knowing himself or herself in a very fundamental way.

Such an unearthing process is fraught with a good deal of anxiety as it unfolds. Also anxiety and strain arise from carrying out very high-level performance and the especially demanding work of creative accomplishment. There is conscious cognitive strain in the use of unusual logic-defying janusian and homospatial processes. Such leaps of thought are often mentally difficult to employ.

The gradual unearthing of unconscious processes and the progression toward insight are invariably tenuous and may go awry. Because they occur without any real support or help from another person, the unearthing and the progression may both fall far short of the goal. This is not, as I said earlier, a form of therapy, and only partial rather than full insight ever actually occurs. Indeed, even when such a process of inner self-discovery is pursued in the collaborative circumstance of therapy, it may all too easily be diverted or go aground.

I believe that Cheever did go aground on his own in the writing of *Bullet Park*. Intermixed with love for his brother was intense antagonism, jealousy, hostility, and unconscious murderous feelings, and in the writing of that novel, Cheever had come closer than ever before to full unearthing of the latter. Rather than a murder of a brother—or a brother-like figure—however, he depicted the attempted murder of the symbolic brother's young son.[21] I believe, therefore, that at that point he approached recognition of his hidden homicidal emotions toward his brother but could not actually acknowledge them to himself.

The descent into alcoholism during the period in Boston, then, was very likely due to the close association with his brother and the intensification of guilt over his constant but unacknowledged hostile and murderous feelings. With his recovery, there is distinct evidence of some acknowledgment and acceptance of these feelings. As I also declined to do with Strindberg, I cannot here say whether Cheever achieved insight regarding these impulses and wishes directly from improved creative functioning following complete abstinence, whether he achieved it in some other way and then both abstinence and creativity followed, or whether some other sequence was involved. I will insist, however, that his conflict about his feelings toward Fred both intensified his alcoholism and blocked his creativity.

The important facts supporting this conclusion are that Cheever was able to return to work on *Falconer* after he left the Smithers Alcoholism Rehabilitation Unit and that the novel itself portrays an intellectual man who kills his brother. At the beginning of the novel, Farragut has been sentenced to prison because of fratricide. That this represented Cheever's own wish and fantasied punishment was dramatically suggested by the following comments to me about a visit his brother made to him after he had completed *Falconer:* "He [Fred] was . . . seventy. . . . He hurt his hip in a motorcycle spill and went into the hospital for an operation and was discharged as having too weak a heart for the operation. He immediately came here [to see me] and said, 'I think you ought to know that while I was in the hospital I had delirium tremens—this is withdrawal from two glasses of sherry.' And I said, 'Thank you very much for telling me.' And I had completed *Falconer* and I said, 'Oh, I killed you in the book.' And he said, 'Oh, did you? Oh, good.'"

At another time Cheever told me that, when two-thirds through the novel, he developed the idea that Farragut was going to get out of prison successfully. This was early spring, he said, and he actually ran out of his house shouting, "He's out, he's out. He's going to get out." Thus, the events in the novel seem to recapitulate or represent the dynamics of this author's own psychological struggle. Set in a prison, the novel contains a representation of the site of Cheever's recent teaching successes and of his own confinement at Smithers. In describing to me the experience at Smithers, he had explicitly called it an incarceration and indicated that, in all respects, it was like being in a prison. Feeling punished as well as cared for, his guilt about his hostile wishes began to be absolved just as the leading character (drug addict = alcoholic) in the novel experienced punishment and the beginning of absolution for the actual crime of fratricide. The ensuing story of incarceration, eventual freedom, and redemption of this character, then, was driven by Cheever's own struggle with guilt over his murderous wishes toward his brother. His running out of his house shouting about the escape and redemption of Farragut was, I believe, in part a manifestation—temporary or permanent—of his own personal relief and sense of redemption from culpability.

Cheever's creative and alcoholic course was therefore as follows: in his writings, he had returned again and again to the theme of hostility to a brother, and his struggle to unearth and deal with his own unacceptable feelings was one of the dynamics that gave power to his work. When finally the hostility and homicidal feelings toward his brother came close to the surface and threatened to overwhelm him, as they did with the writing of *Bullet Park*, and assumedly also with other events in his life, Cheever turned increasingly to alcohol for sedation and relief. This produced a typical alcoholic vicious cycle in which the physical and psychological effects of using the drug required continuation and increasing amounts to produce desired sedation effects. Finally, he entered into a treatment program that helped him to stop drinking and also to continue the threatening confrontation with his feelings toward his brother in the writing of *Falconer*. The triumphant, more healthy struggle involved in the creative process at that point produced a successful work of art.

Alcohol and Writing

The use of alcohol in this account of Cheever's struggle is, I believe, broadly representative. Most writers do not actually suffer from the same degree of alcohol dependence and abuse that Cheever did, but that is a separate matter that I shall come to more fully in a moment. What does seem to be a cardinal issue, and one that applies to several writers, is the need to use alcohol to cope with the anxiety that is generated by the creative process itself. Because the creative process, when it is successful, inevitably involves the creative person's unearthing unconscious material to some degree, there is always a measure of anxiety. Depending on a writer's stability and proclivities, he or she may cope with such threatening discomfort in various ways. It has long been widely and reliably known that writers and other artists are highly irritable during intense periods of work or for some time afterward. Some writers become depressed, some engage in flamboyant and eccentric behavior, some engage in philandering, some use the other relaxing outlets that the rest of us do, and some drink. Drinking alcohol has a gratifying sedative effect, and given the social reasons that have made it acceptable among writers and other creative people, it may even have become the mode of choice for writers particularly to deal with the anxiety generated by the creative process. The muse may not be in the bottle itself, but the alcohol may be the acceptable way to deal with her glory and threat.

This is not to say that alcohol use and dependence are the inevitable penalties for creative life. Most creative people are like the majority of the population who use alcohol in moderation. In each case the development of alcoholism depends on personality and personal background. In Cheever's instance, I do not have a lot of data about the critical factors entering into his illness. That both parents were alcoholics and that they had a difficult marriage—in which they involved Cheever—as well as Cheever's intensely ambivalent relationship with his brother (and very likely, his father) were all probable causative factors. In cases in which both parents are alcoholics, identification and the need to repeat traumatic experiences of childhood, as well as simple availability and acceptance of alcohol in the house, have effects as important as any postulated genetic factors. We know also that Cheever had a great deal of lifelong conflict about his bisexuality. Such conflicts incorporating problems about homosexuality, passivity, and dependency often have cardinal causative effects in alcoholism. These are, however, general factors that may or may not relate directly to Cheever's creative work.[22]

Factors that do seem to connect Cheever's alcoholism with his writing have some general applicability to alcoholism in other creative people.[23] Living with parents who were frequently in a withdrawn, inebriated state, Cheever as a child felt helpless and unable to communicate with them. His turning to writing served as a way to bring order into a chaotic, disorganized experience and, in a sense, as a way to get his parents to hear him; the writing also became a means of compensating for his own feelings of weakness and loss. His first short-story success turned his expulsion from Thayer Academy for poor grades and failure into an arbitrary expulsion by mindless authorities for smoking a cigarette.

Cheever was loved and preferred by his mother. Although his father was weak and ineffective, Cheever seemed to have identified with him nevertheless in adopting his more severe alcoholism. This identification with the father very likely served as a way of being closer to his mother, a woman who was attracted both to an alcoholic person and to the alcohol drug itself. Over and over again, persons who become alcoholic adopt the patterns of someone loved by their own specially beloved parent, whether it be that parent's own alcoholic father, mother, lover, or spouse. In Cheever's case, identification with his father may, for other reasons, have had something also to do with his motivation to write.

As I have seen in many of my subjects and mentioned briefly in the introductory chapter, creative persons often have a parent who has been tacitly interested in a particular creative field or, in some cases, has tried that field and failed. In such instances, the son—it is most clearly evident in males—lives out the father's unstated wishes and fantasies as well as his overt striving. This is done unconsciously both to gratify the father and make him proud and to beat him out and gain the mother's love. The child perceives that his mother has valued the father's implicit wishes and fantasies, even loved him for them, at some point. In females, the stated and unstated wishes of both parents are complexly involved.

These family dynamics were the operative for Cheever and his father. Despite being an unsuccessful shoe salesman, the elder Cheever kept a personal diary all his life. The writing of such material clearly represented a literary bent and interest, a matter testified by the author/son himself. It was this diary, Cheever told me, that was the inspiration and focus for his successful novel *The Wapshot Chronicle*. He himself had always kept a diary and believed that one of the most successful aspects of his own teaching of creative writing to the inmates at Sing Sing was that he got them to keep diaries as well. Indeed, I personally believe that the latter was not only a brilliant teaching device, but, considering that criminals are particularly loath to keep diaries and incriminate themselves, it was a psychological *tour-de-force*.

With regard to connections between creativity and alcoholism, this parentally derived motivation to create may sometimes coincide with an identification with an alcoholic parent, as it did in Cheever's case. This both loving and competitive identification is then one of the few intrinsic links between creativity and alcoholism and may operate, because of the importance of the creative aspect, to render the alcoholism especially difficult to ameliorate. This was so to some degree for Cheever, and, to come back to my example at the beginning of this chapter, it seems to have been an important factor in the case of Faulkner as well.

Faulkner also had a mother who doted on him and a father who loved cowboy tales and novels. Severely alcoholic himself, the father seems to have died from alcohol's effects. Strikingly, there is reason to believe that Faulkner, like Cheever, was working out ambivalent feelings toward a brother at the time of writing his distinguished novel *Absalom, Absalom,* the novel he himself called "the best novel written by an American."[24] Early in the course of writing this story about antagonism between two brothers, Dean Faulkner, the author's younger brother, died in an airplane crash. Consumed by guilt, according to his own account, because he had introduced Dean to flying in the first place, had encouraged him to enter the flying competition in which he crashed, and had also sold him the plane, Faulkner experienced constant nightmares for several weeks and turned heavily to alcohol. Eventually, however, he resumed his work on the novel, and incorporated a vivid fratricide into the next portion of the story. In writing the fratricide, I believe Faulkner had engaged in a process of unearthing unconscious hostility toward his brother which had undergirded some of his actions and unbearable guilt.

Unlike Cheever, however, Faulkner had long periods of abstinence, or virtual abstinence, during his working life, and it was during
these periods that his great novels were produced. Ultimately defeated
by his alcoholism at the end, however, it is sad to consider how much
more that great writer, and others suffering from such affliction, might
have done.

11 ◆◇ *Eugene O'Neill's Creation of* The Iceman Cometh

*E*ugene O'Neill, it is generally agreed, is America's greatest playwright. At one time, he also had been a fairly severe alcoholic. Therefore, an opportunity afforded me to reconstruct his process of creating one of his most important plays, *The Iceman Cometh,*[1] had special value. In terms of the overall design of the research project on the creative process, the opportunity allowed me to study a work of the past which satisfied the test-of-time criterion of creativity. Although throughout the course of history many works have been hailed as highly creative and great in their day, truly new and valuable achievements should be recognized as such for a long period afterward. With regard to applications to the topic of creativity and alcoholism, here I could study a play with an alcoholism theme by a writer who had himself been alcoholic at a notable point in his creative development. As it turned out, an important result of the particular investigation I performed was my first identification and description of the janusian process. The opportunity to study *The Iceman Cometh* had been provided, as I shall clarify shortly, by the excellent manuscript collection of American writers at the Beinecke Library of Yale University and by the availability and gracious cooperation of Mrs. Carlotta Monterrey O'Neill, the playwright's widow.

Creativity necessarily must stand a test of time. Artistic creations come and go to some extent, and public adulation is fickle. Many of our most hallowed creative giants, such as Mozart and Rembrandt, died ignominious and poor, and many completely forgotten artists, composers, and writers were highly celebrated in their time. In order to take such vagaries into consideration and also to assess another matter of scientific procedure—the possibility that, in my interview studies with living creative people, I was myself influencing the creative process I was observing—I had early on devised a procedure for retrospective study of the creative process in persons of the past. The method was to study successive manuscript versions of specific enduringly successful works in a manner analogous to my focus on manuscript work in progress in my interview studies. To be scientific, specific hypotheses would be developed from such retrospective manuscript studies and then later assessed by means of independently collected data from biographical and other sources. The study of manuscripts of literary works in progress, particularly the successive changes and revisions that appear, provides access to an active dynamic process and, as I hope to show presently, comes as close to a reconstruction of the creative process involved in an artwork of the past as one could probably hope to achieve.

With these considerations in mind, I was pleased to find that many of the original manuscripts of O'Neill's plays had been donated by his widow to Yale University. Not only was every single version—from first to last—of the esteemed *The Iceman Cometh* available for study, but there were also numerous notes and drawings, in O'Neill's own hand, regarding his initial ideas for characters, plot, and the staging of the play. These materials were available for my use as a then member of the Yale faculty and, afterward I was able to arrange for an interview with O'Neill's first wife, Mrs. Kathleen Pitt-Smith, who gave me information about his youth, and then later for an extended series of interviews over a year's time with his third wife and executor, who told me about the period of his life during which *The Iceman Cometh* had been written. To explain the results of all of this, I shall first describe the play, its central symbol of the iceman, and then go into the background of its creation.

The Iceman Cometh

The Iceman Cometh is set in the year 1912 and takes place in a New York saloon and rooming house owned by a character named Harry Hope. In addition to Harry Hope, there are fifteen important characters in the play, all habitués of or actual roomers in the building: nine derelicts, two bartenders, three streetwalkers, and a hardware salesman named Theodore Hickman (nicknamed "Hickey").

The major plot revolves around Hickey. All of the characters wait for his regular arrival to engage in one of his periodical drunks, an event that is eagerly anticipated because he buys everyone drinks, makes jokes, and cheers everyone up. As they wait, they tell both the background of their own current states in life and their hopes for the future. Harry Hope has turned to liquor out of grief for his dead wife, but he intends to return to politics some day. Jimmy Cameron (nick-named "Jimmy Tomorrow"), a one-time Boer War correspondent, has turned to drink because he "found his wife in the hay with a staff officer," but he plans to return to newspaper work eventually. One of the streetwalkers and a bartender intend to get married. A down-and-out Negro hopes to reopen his lost gambling joint. Each has his own story, his own "pipe dream."

Finally, Hickey arrives. Instead of jokes, however, he offers them salvation. To make matters worse, this is not ordinary religious salva-tion but instead an offer to rescue them from their pipe dreams. He pushes each person to face up to his oft-stated and alleged future intention. Reluctantly, and with great suspicion and resentment to-ward Hickey, all do begin to try the things they planned for "tomor-row." It doesn't work at all. After a few faltering steps toward jobs, marriage, or change, they return to the saloon and sink back into alcoholic oblivion. Instead of the peace Hickey had promised them for trying, they are devastated and now collectively find that "the life has gone out of the booze."

Hickey, greatly distressed at this turn of events, then confesses his real reason for having believed they would have peace. Constantly guilty because his wife always forgave him for both his periodical drunks and adulterous affairs, he had finally decided to rid her of what he called her pipe dream: the belief that he, Hickey, would change and be better, tomorrow. To do this, he murdered her and, he said, "gave her peace." Insisting immediately that he did this out of love for her, he recounts the details and inadvertently reveals that, right after killing her, he said something indicating the opposite: speaking aloud to his dead wife, he revealed rage and feelings of hatred for her. Becoming frantic when he realizes what he has revealed, Hickey then tries to deny both the feelings and the actual words; he vehemently insists he must have been crazy at the time. All those in the barroom then imme-diately seize upon this idea as a way of erasing their own painful experience. To insist that Hickey was, and is, crazy means they can return to their drinking and illusions. Detectives who have heard Hickey's confession (tipped off to come to the saloon in advance by Hickey himself) are not so convinced about his mental illness, and they take him off to jail.

A subplot concerns two characters named Don Parritt and Larry Slade. Parritt is a young man, not quite a derelict as yet, who comes to Harry Hope's to find Larry. Both Parritt's mother and Larry had been in the anarchist movement together until Larry became disillusioned and turned to drink. Larry, the "old Foolosopher," now insists to every-one that he is so disillusioned that he constantly yearns only for death. It is clear, however, that he does not really mean this and, like everyone else, is caught up in a pipe dream. Parritt, whose mother is in jail, has come all the way from the West Coast to inform Larry that she was betrayed by someone inside the movement. At first, Parritt's moti-vation for coming to Larry is unclear, but gradually it becomes appar-ent both that Larry actually is Parritt's father and Parritt himself was his mother's betrayer. Like Hickey, this young man tries at first to rationalize his behavior, saying he betrayed her for money alone. Fi-nally, however, he openly confesses that he did it because he hated her. The confessions of Hickey and Parritt are presented together in a dra-matic counterpoint in the last act.

After confessing, Parritt begs Larry to deliver him from guilt. Struggling at first to resist judging him, Larry finally—at the end of the play—despairingly tells Parritt to "get out of life"—to kill himself. Parritt is relieved, goes upstairs to his room, and jumps out of the window to die on the back courtyard of the saloon. The play ends right after the suicide; all, except Larry, are fallen into drunkenness. Larry stares straight ahead—"the only real convert to death Hickey made."

The Iceman Symbol

The title of this play is meaningful and artistically crucial. It highlights the matter of waiting for something or someone to come and points to deeper symbolic meanings pertaining to religion, illusion, and reality. One of these symbolic meanings of the iceman is indicated explicitly in the dialogue. At one point, Larry remarks, "Death was the Iceman Hickey called to his home." O'Neill himself privately indicated a sec-ond meaning to critic Dudley Nichols. He said that the iceman in the title referred to an old bawdy story he knew: a man comes home from work and, on entry into the house, calls upstairs to his wife, "Has the iceman come yet?" There is a moment's pause, and the wife calls back down, "No, but he's breathing hard!"

The curious and now often paraphrased grammatical construc-tion *cometh* points to at least a third meaning as well. Literary critic Cyrus Day first pointed out that this construction evoked the biblical phrase, "Behold, the bridegroom cometh,"[2] from a parable in Matthew 25:5–6 about Christ's coming to the virgins. Day indicated further that a birthday party scene in the play was structured to represent the Last Supper, the twelve habitués of the saloon corresponded to the twelve apostles, the whores represented the three Marys, Hickey was a self-appointed Savior, and Parritt betrayed for money and killed himself, just as did Judas Iscariot. Notably, when Hickey first acknowledges Parritt's presence, he uses the biblical words, "There is a stranger in our midst." Many other religious references in the play also support Day's perceptive analysis. As further corroboration, I have discovered that O'Neill used, and therefore knew, the *bridegroom cometh* quotation in his unfinished manuscript of the play *More Stately Mansions*, which he worked on prior to writing *Iceman*.[3]

The importance of the iceman symbol is indicated throughout. In addition to Larry's statement equating the iceman with death, other specific references to the iceman are interwoven into the dialogue at critical points. Hickey's reputation as a joker is linked early with the fact that he always kids around about having left his wife in the hay with the iceman. Many references are made to the iceman as Hickey's trademark and as a synonym for infidelity as well. After everyone gets angry at Hickey for trying to save them, they turn on him and accuse him tauntingly of having been cuckolded. They tease him by saying that his wife had really slept with the iceman. Then, when Hickey first reveals that his wife was murdered, there is immediate and serious speculation that her infidelity played a part. Also, in the midst of a lengthy exposition of his marital relationship, Hickey suggests that at times he wanted his wife to be unfaithful to him to relieve his own guilt. He says that he kiddingly suggested it to her in the same way that he used to joke about the iceman.

The iceman never appears in the play. In fact, he is never referred to as an actual person and is never described. The only actions attributed to him directly are a coming, and, in an obvious allusion to a future funeral, a walking slowly behind Hickey together with Hickey's wife. The iceman is clearly without substance and exists as a symbol alone.

Now, to the creation of this play—first, the background.

Background of the Play

O'Neill's own alcoholism played an important role in his development as a playwright. Having become deeply addicted to drink in the later part of his adolescence, he gave up an acting career to ship out as an able-bodied seaman on a trip to Buenos Aires. During this trip, his alcoholism worsened, and he returned to New York City to live upstairs from a bar quite like the one in the play. It was also during that period of his life that he developed tuberculosis; he was subsequently required to be confined to the Gaylord Sanatorium for a year. Necessarily sober during his convalescence and confined to relative solitude, contemplation, and inactivity, O'Neill started to write plays for the first time. Prior to that, his creativity was primarily manifest in the writing of poetry and his self-admittedly poor attempts at acting.

Although he did not give up alcohol after leaving the sanatorium, his pattern changed from regular abuse to binge drinking. Psychiatrist Donald Goodwin, writing in the *Journal of the American Medical Association*, has claimed that O'Neill's psychiatric treatment with Dr. Gilbert Hamilton several years later was responsible for his renouncing alcohol completely; Goodwin also proclaimed that Dr. Hamilton deserved his own immortal acclaim for having saved O'Neill's creativity.[4] Although I share the position that O'Neill's reduction of alcohol abuse—which began sometime around the period that he saw Dr. Hamilton—was beneficial to his creativity, I know that no such complete "cure" occurred. Carlotta O'Neill indicated to me that her husband indulged in severe bouts of drinking from time to time up until the end of his life. These bouts invariably interfered with his writing.

After he wrote the play *Days Without End* in 1934, O'Neill worked on a cycle of nine plays about the psychological and spiritual history of an American family. He planned to entitle the cycle *A Tale of Possessors, Self-dispossessed*. Stopping work on the fourth play of his cycle, *More Stately Mansions*, in February 1939, he began *The Iceman Cometh* in June of the same year. Why O'Neill interrupted his work on the cycle to write *The Iceman Cometh* at that particular time is not specifically known. Biographers Arthur and Barbara Gelb state that he was depressed during that period.[5] However, O'Neill's mother was a morphine addict, and he had focused *More Stately Mansions* on an intense relationship between a successful man and his disabled mother. I believe for that reason and for others that I shall go into later that preoccupation with especially difficult feelings toward his own mother was a factor.

The play he turned to, *The Iceman Cometh*, is based on his actual life experience in a New York bar called Jimmy the Priest's which he frequented in 1911 and 1912 as well as a bar called The Hell-Hole which he went to in later years. O'Neill indicated these facts himself on his manuscript outline of the play. He entitled the sheets of that outline "Jimmy the Priest—H. H. play."

The plot is an enlargement of an incident he wrote about in his only published short story, "Tomorrow," which appeared in 1917.[6] Narrated in the first person by a fictional character named Art, "Tomorrow" is primarily concerned with Art's roommate, Jimmy. The narrator, an able-bodied seaman, relates that he has shipped back from Buenos Aires and six months later, is living on nothing but a small allowance in the winter of his "great down-and-outness." Sharing an upstairs room in an "all-night dive" called "Tommy the Priest's," Art and Jimmy while away the days in drink. Jimmy, a former Boer War correspondent, constantly vows that he will give up liquor and will go out and get a newspaper job, "tomorrow." Nobody in the dive takes his vow seriously. Then, to the surprise of all, he finally gathers his courage and does go out. And he lands the job.

After starting work, however, he almost immediately becomes a holier-than-thou preacher against drinking, much to roommate Art's annoyance. This preaching does not last so very long, though, as he soon fails at the job and goes back to alcohol. Shortly after, while drunk and deeply depressed, Jimmy confesses to Art that the reason he had begun drinking in the first place was that he found his wife "in the hay with a staff officer." Saying nothing when he hears this and leaving Jimmy in their room alone, Art flees downstairs to drink with others in the bar. Then, hearing a thud in the backyard, he realizes that Jimmy has jumped out of the back window. "Tomorrow had come," is the sentence that ends the story.

I believe it to be reasonably certain that this short story is based on an actual incident in O'Neill's life. The character Art clearly represents O'Neill himself who, after returning from Buenos Aires, supported himself on a small allowance while living at Jimmy the Priest's. Jimmy's background is the same as that of O'Neill's father's press agent, James Findlater-Bythe (Jimmy Bythe), who committed suicide in 1913 by jumping from a window at Jimmy the Priest's. According to O'Neill's own account, within the same year that Jimmy killed himself, he himself had made a serious suicide attempt.[7] Jimmy's suicide and its associations for O'Neill were apparently lasting and important; he prohibited the reprinting of "Tomorrow" later in his life because, as he said, "of its very personal nature."[8]

There are clear parallels between "Tomorrow" and *The Iceman Cometh*. The idea of a person postponing life plans until a future day is a central theme of the play with its focus on pipe dreams. The character Jimmy Tomorrow has the same Boer War correspondent background as the short-story character Jimmy. Jimmy Tomorrow is referred to as the leader of the "Tomorrow Movement," and he too found his wife in the hay with a staff officer. On the manuscript outline for *The Iceman Cometh*, O'Neill's first title had been *Credit Tomorrow*.

Also, various incidents correspond in play and story. Although Hickey does not preach directly against drinking, as did the character in the story, he does try mightily to save the bums from themselves. Suicide occurs at the end of the play with only a thud heard in the backyard. In both literary works, only one significant person (Larry or Art) knows the meaning of the thud.

Beyond these similarities, other evidence indicates that O'Neill had been thinking of the actual incident on which the story was based when he wrote the play. In his outline for the latter, he had written *Jimmy B.* (Jimmy Bythe) before his description of the character whom he later called *Jimmy Tomorrow;* he had similarly indicated there that other characters in the play were based on real persons who had frequented Jimmy the Priest's bar in 1912. The infidelity issue in "Tomorrow" must surely have been specifically connected with O'Neill's having thought of using the iceman of the infidelity joke in *The Iceman Cometh* title and in the substance of the play.

The Writing of the Play: Study of Revisions

In order to reconstruct the creative process from the manuscripts of the play, I focused on manuscript revisions. More specifically, because of the central aesthetic importance of the iceman symbol, I studied and assessed revisions directly pertaining to it. Manuscript revisions represent a dynamic phenomenon in the writing process; they involve both a perception that a word, a grammatical construct, or a series of words is wrong as well as its reformulation. Assuming that an author always considers the reformulations to be better than the original, these are therefore minute creations, *new* and *better* entities (recall my definition of a creation) developed during the writing process itself. In some cases, the reformulation can represent a rather extensive creation.

Another reason for studying and assessing revisions is that they can reveal an author's unconscious conflicts. Freud's well-established discoveries regarding errors and slips in speech and writing indicate that unconscious conflicts are revealed by any behavior manifesting a discrepancy between an intent and its execution.[9] Because a skilled author usually has specific literary goals in mind as he is writing, a revision involves a failed first execution and therefore potentially reveals unconscious conflict.

It is clear from the wording of the title of the play that O'Neill intended the iceman to be a symbol. From his manuscript notes, I found that he had conceived, or decided on, the *Iceman Cometh* title during the writing of the play's outline. Consequently, his intent regarding the idea of the iceman was formulated prior to writing the play itself, and any failed first execution could reveal specific unconscious conflict. I studied every reference to the iceman symbol in the manuscripts with regard to three questions. (1) Was there any disturbance suggesting anxiety and conflict manifested by persistent revising of

wording and/or substance regarding the iceman? (2) Was any consistent discrepancy between execution and intent revealed in such
revisions? (3) When such a discrepancy existed, what type of conflict
did it indicate, and next, to go to the heart of the issue, what relationship did this conflict have to the *creative* aspect of the revisions and
the *creation* of the iceman symbol?

Results of the Revision Study

O'Neill wrote his first manuscript version in pencil in very small shaky
characters. When he revised, however, it was generally possible to
identify what he had originally written. All later versions were much
easier to read as they were typewritten by Carlotta O'Neill and others.

There was a total of fifty direct references to the iceman (including
pronoun references) throughout the manuscript and six typescript
versions of the play. To my amazement, I found that O'Neill made a
revision in either the manuscript or later typescript versions *in every
single section* containing such references. It was then necessary to test
statistically whether this type of revising indicated a specific and persistent disturbance. So I calculated a ratio of revisions of sentences
referring to the iceman and compared that with the overall ratio of
revising throughout the play. By means of statistical assessment, I
found that O'Neill's tendency to make revisions in sentences containing the word *iceman* was far greater (statistically significant) than his
general level of revising. This suggested that O'Neill either had some
perfectionistic orientation regarding the *iceman idea,* or that there
was a particular unconscious conflict regarding it, or else—knowing
that perfectionism could be related to conflict—that both factors were
operating.

Next, to see whether there was anything about the content of the
revisions in *iceman* sentences that would give some clue to the nature
of the conflict, I compared each first formulation with its reformulation, sentence by sentence. I found that the preponderance of revisions
in these sentences regarded three related themes: (1) the reality of the
iceman; (2) actual infidelity with an iceman; (3) concern about actual
infidelity. This meant that O'Neill, despite his symbolic intention,
tended to construct first formulations that referred to a physically real
and concrete iceman personage and to an actual infidelity. For example, he deleted all of the following first formulations: "He's [the ice-
man] moved in for keeps"; "When you found him [the iceman] in her
bed"; "Was it you caught the Iceman in the arms of your dear [wife]
Evelyn at last, and had to make the best of it and shake hands with

him?" An inescapable conclusion therefore is that O'Neill failed to indicate a symbolic nonconcrete iceman consistently at first, and the effect was achieved through reformulation and revision.

Other revised phrases called attention, either by affirmation or denial, to the concrete reality of the iceman as well as to actual infidelity. Note the following: "Remember the way he always lies about his wife and the Iceman?"; "There was nothing to Hickey's bull about the Iceman"; "yuh mean she really was cheatin' wid de iceman and he caught her?"; "Who cares if she was cheatin' wid de iceman?" Revisions regarding the third theme, concern over actual infidelity, showed frequent inconsistencies in first formulations as well as overemphasis on this concern. O'Neill revised several sentences in which he had initially depicted excessive taunting about infidelity—taunting that would have suggested that infidelity is a reason for a good deal of concern and embarrassment.

My growing conviction about the importance of these particular themes was strongly supported by discovery of a rather dramatically explicit first formulation. O'Neill had Hickey comment about his wife as follows: "I was serious. *I was trying to plant it* [infidelity] *in her mind.* Small chance! She loved me too much. She was too pure and good" [italics mine]. These lines were completely deleted on the typescript.

There seems to have been a consistent disturbance in O'Neill's development of the iceman symbol. He either tended to formulate a real iceman and real infidelity first, or else was ambiguous or inconsistent about the formulation. The high degree of revising and the discrepancies between his intent and initial execution point to internal conflict regarding these themes. Taken together, the themes suggest conflict and preoccupation with infidelity. To those who disagree, asserting that the author revised in this way because he was trying to get an important element exactly right, I say that such an explanation cannot account for either the highly specific type of revising or the consistent nature of the changes. A particular idea may assume conscious aesthetic importance for a writer partly because it has special personal and conflictual meaning.

Evaluation of Hypotheses

After evaluating these data and before arranging to meet with Carlotta O'Neill, I developed some explicit hypotheses. O'Neill's underlying preoccupation with infidelity shown by these revisions could have been due to many different factors. All of the revisions pertained specifically to a woman being unfaithful, and O'Neill, like his character Hickey, may have wished that his wife would relieve him of his guilt about some actual or—unlike Hickey—fantasized infidelity. Possibly he—as I proposed regarding Strindberg—had guilty wishes to be unfaithful himself. Regardless of such specifics, the conflict and anxiety indicated by the persistent revising pointed to deeper problems. My overall knowledge of O'Neill's life indicated to me, as it has to others, that he had serious problems with women.

I met regularly with Carlotta O'Neill over a period of a year. She knew nothing of my findings on the manuscript study, and I made a point of not guiding her toward any particular aspect or period of her husband's life. I asked only for whatever information she cared to give about him, and she gradually became increasingly comfortable and revealed to me more and more about their relationship. She told me how she had provided her husband with many material possessions throughout their marriage, had made many sacrifices for him, and had pampered him a good deal. She gloried in what seemed a child-like side of him and told me many anecdotes indicating that she was very maternal toward him. Stating that she had never previously revealed anything about their sexual life, she told me that she and her husband had only had sexual relations on three occasions during the period of their marriage. Describing the circumstances of each occasion, she told of one in which she pretended to be asleep the entire time. We talked about many factors related to this.

Regarding my hypotheses about O'Neill's preoccupations and conflicts during the writing of *The Iceman Cometh*, Carlotta O'Neill's information meant that there had been no sexual contact between them throughout the period of the creation of the play. Although there is no way of knowing directly from this revelation whether O'Neill was actually concerned with infidelity during that period, it does seem likely that he was either consciously or unconsciously preoccupied with some type of sexual problem.

The Creative Process

With these findings and reconstructions of O'Neill's concerns during the writing of the play, I believe we can gain further understanding of the creative process. However, I want to emphasize first that this case indicates what I have suggested in several places earlier: a study of the completed artwork alone, without access to data such as manuscripts in progress and biographical information regarding the actual writing period, would not be likely to isolate specific findings about the creative process itself—findings such as O'Neill's concurrent absorption with infidelity and/or sexual problems.[10] Indeed, none of the major reviews and critical or psychiatric studies of the play refers to such an issue; only one suggests a related idea that the play's theme is that love is an illusion. Most studies focus on the theatrical presentation of alcoholism and its connection with O'Neill's life history. Although this play surely is about alcoholism, and O'Neill's own alcoholism was involved, the concern about infidelity during the writing process also led me in other directions.

The finding suggested an important and quite specific link between the early "Tomorrow" story, Jimmy Bythe's suicide, and O'Neill's decision to write the play. In "Tomorrow," Jimmy had committed suicide because of remorse over his wife's infidelity. He had confided first in Art—the character representing O'Neill himself—but Art had fallen silent and gone downstairs. Following that, the thud of Jimmy's body resounded in the backyard. Anyone exposed to such an experience would surely feel quite guilty about not having responded to Jimmy and somehow preventing the suicide. Whether this was realistically possible or not, O'Neill himself apparently felt such guilt. Unresolved feelings of responsibility and guilt could then have been directly linked to his conflict about infidelity. If the real Jimmy Bythe had actually wanted his wife to be unfaithful, O'Neill would have felt absolved from blame about the suicide.

Guilt about suicide is depicted concretely in the play through the relationship of Larry and Parritt. Parritt constantly badgers Larry until Larry finally tells him to kill himself. Parritt complies, and Larry becomes the only truly disillusioned person in the play, actively yearning for death. This sequence might well have represented O'Neill's own feelings during the year of Jimmy's suicide; he felt as if he actually told Jimmy to do it and then looked forward to death and punishment.

The plot of the play is dually faceted, concerning both a man who kills his wife and a son who betrays his mother. Although there surely were many factors leading to such a plot construction, both of the facets interconnect with a basic issue often involved in a preoccupation with infidelity: hostility to a wife derived from hostility to a mother. Hickey's feelings toward his wife are highly ambivalent. He convinces himself that he killed her out of love and his desire for her to have peace. Actually, he feels overwhelmingly guilty toward her because she had been quite maternal to him and constantly forgave him for his transgressions. Finally, he reveals his real hostility to her and is taken away to be punished. Not ending at that point, the play continues to a dramatic climax that reveals Parritt's hostility to his mother and ultimate self-punishment. The sequence and structure of the events surely suggest that hostility to one's mother is the greater sin. At the very least, the idea that hostility to a wife and a mother are related is unmistakably shown in the play.

I believe that O'Neill's preoccupation with infidelity including its overtones of hostility to women was related to his own conscious and unconscious hostility to his mother. That his drug-addicted mother was in some way on his mind is suggested by the constant use throughout the play of the term *pipe dreams*—a term that retains the overtones of its derivation from opium smoking. In one place on the manuscript, O'Neill actually wrote the words *dope dreams*—very likely an overt mistake that he immediately deleted. His choice of the themes of alcoholism and the saloon habitués' intractable addiction to drink were determined to some degree by thoughts and feelings about his mother's addiction. The writing of this play was not simply a nostalgic return to the past by a recovered alcoholic, as some critics have alleged, but was more a matter of unearthing and working out of troubling feelings about his mother.

Up to this point, I have focused on the emotional context from which the play arose. Although this serves to emphasize the importance of emotional conflict in determining the content of a work of art, the particular conflicts are not themselves creative. Paying careful attention to the way these conflicts relate to the ideas achieved, however, clarifies the unique thought processes involved in creation.

O'Neill developed the key idea for the play by means of the janusian process. His germinating notion regarding Jimmy Bythe's infidelity consisted of simultaneously opposite or antithetical ideas. In the "Tomorrow" story, his first written formulation, he had depicted Jimmy as committing suicide because of remorse over his wife's infidelity. Clearly, as far as he knew and understood at that time, Jimmy did *not* want his wife to be unfaithful. But in the writing of *The Iceman Cometh* several years later, O'Neill was preoccupied with an opposite feeling—a desire or wish for infidelity. I believe therefore that the sequence of events was the following: intensely concerned with Jimmy's suicide over a period of many years, O'Neill eventually concluded that Jimmy actually had *both* wanted and not wanted his wife to be unfaithful to him. This happened either prior to or during the actual playwriting process, possibly while O'Neill was writing of Jimmy's remorse. Fueled by his own conflict about infidelity, O'Neill consciously formulated the simultaneously opposite and antithetical feelings.

O'Neill's use of the janusian process pervades the creation of this play. The central iceman symbol was constructed by a stepwise accretion of simultaneous contradictions and opposites. In *More Stately Mansions*, the play he worked on before *The Iceman Cometh*, O'Neill had one of the characters say, "When finally the bride or bridegroom cometh, we discover we are kissing death."[11] Hence, early in the development of the *iceman cometh* idea, he had equated Christ's coming, the act promising deliverance and eternal life, with its opposite, the coming of bleak death. At that point, he had also equated a bridegroom with a bride. As I mentioned in Chapter 2, in the later construction of the play itself, he equated the iceman, an adulterer, with Christ, the opponent and antithesis of adultery. In addition, potency, gratification, and sexual relations were the same as annihilation or death. The adulterous iceman representing illicit sexuality is, in a moral sense, quite opposite to the initial symbolic idea of a bridegroom and marriage; and bringing together religion and faith with adultery produces simultaneous oppositions of fidelity and infidelity, of the sacred and the profane. Finally, the words themselves produce oppositional ideas of a banal worldly *iceman* together with the biblical and sublime *cometh*.

Abnormal versus Normal Functioning in the Creative Process

Another clear conclusion from this study is that revision in the creative process is not, as traditional psychoanalytic views allege,[12] exclusively a matter of defensive censorship. O'Neill did not completely revise out the connection between the iceman idea and infidelity. Instead, the total effect of his revising was that the final version *implied* some of the issues about infidelity which were more strongly indicated in first formulations. Because of this, the final work contains subtle implications and is neither a raw confession nor a totally disguised abstraction.

Confessional writing for the purpose of alleviating guilty feelings is not art, and too direct a formulation of forbidden unconscious material creates anxiety and interferes with an audience's appreciation. O'Neill's revision process reveals his extraordinarily sensitive recognition of confessional elements in first formulations which would have hindered the understanding and appreciation of the symbol. This is surely a complex type of sensitivity, but one distinct element appears to be that a creative author like O'Neill deletes out material that he feels or perceives to be closest to his own immediate wishes and motivations. Writing first formulations that express unacceptable wishes and motivations alleviates initial anxiety. Strengthened by this relief as he continues, the writer can return to the material at the revision phase and see how inappropriate or self-indulgent it is. For example, after O'Neill constructed Hickey's obsessed remarks about wanting to plant infidelity in his wife's mind, he very likely experienced or became consciously aware of the intensity of his own wish for infidelity and deleted those remarks as well as other similar formulations.

The janusian process also allows for some let-up of anxiety by its indirect portrayal of some of an author's own disavowed wishes. This is accomplished through a psychological defensive operation termed *negation,*[13] that is, saying something is *not* so sometimes indicates that it is unconsciously present in the person's mind. As a double contradiction is contained in a janusian formulation, defensive negation with respect to the creative thinker's unconscious contents often operates. Not an abnormal type of psychological function, such defensive factors permeate all types of healthy conscious thinking, both creative and noncreative.

Part of the aesthetic appeal of *The Iceman Cometh*—the title and the play as a whole—is its quality of compressing many different conflicting affects and thoughts. The writing of the play also seems to have helped O'Neill work out particular emotional needs. In *More Stately Mansions,* O'Neill had drawn an overly intense relationship between a son and his mother. In this unfinished play, the mother was a highly disturbed person who periodically withdrew completely into her own world and caused her son to feel utterly deserted and abandoned. Surely this represented O'Neill's own experience with his mother's narcotic addiction and her episodic retreat into a morphine-induced realm.

O'Neill's mother continued to be on his mind during the writing of *The Iceman Cometh,* and he ended the play on a calm, accepting note. The habitués of the saloon return to their alcohol and their illusions, but there is a sense of resignation and acceptance of human frailty in distinction to the angry, embittered tone throughout *More Stately Mansions.* That all persons must live with illusions comprises the central aesthetic statement of *The Iceman Cometh,* and this acceptance of pipe dreams (with all its psychological overtones) suggests that O'Neill had begun to forgive his mother for her illusions and her addiction.

The very next play he wrote was his masterpiece, *Long Day's Journey Into Night,* an autobiographical work in which he explicitly portrays a mother's drug addiction on the stage for the first time.[14] It was written, he said in the dedication passage to his wife, "in tears and blood."[15] Part of the power of that play was distinctly derived from the sympathetic and human portrayal of the fictional mother's suffering. I believe that the writing of *The Iceman Cometh* contributed to a progression of his feelings toward his mother between the time of writing *More Stately Mansions* and *Long Day's Journey Into Night* and facilitated that sympathetic portrayal. Here again, as with John Cheever and August Strindberg, it was the working through of emotional difficulties and a progression toward health which contributed to great creative accomplishment. O'Neill's alcoholism provided him only with subject matter from which to construct a meaningful work of art, not with any of the means to do so.

Although O'Neill's progression was a healthy one rather than a symptom of ailing genius, the contribution of such personal struggle to a work's artistic appeal should not be downplayed. For the struggles with the inescapable personal conflicts of life, both conscious and unconscious, with the goal of achieving relief and psychological freedom, are dynamic forces incorporated into great works of art. Such forces are deeply moving to us all.

12 ◆◇ *Creativity and Mental Illness*

The question I have considered throughout this book is not a new one, and misconceptions regarding it will not die easily. Deviant behavior, whether in the form of eccentricity or worse, is not only associated with persons of genius or high-level creativity, but it is frequently expected of them. Creative persons themselves have said or done little to disavow this conception and expectation, and several outstanding ones have even formulated precepts about it. In addition to Plato's statement, cited earlier, that poetic inspiration was a form of divine madness, Aristotle reportedly said, "No great genius was without a mixture of insanity."[1] And the poet John Dryden metrically stated, "Great Wits are sure to Madness near ally'd"[2]; William Shakespeare, it will be remembered, had one of his characters relate poetry to both love and lunacy. On the professional psychiatric side, several psychiatrists at the end of the last century gave a great deal of attention to the question of the connections between genius and mental illness, and the most famous, Cesare Lombroso, wrote a voluminous work in which he connected genius to epilepsy, melancholia, megalomania, alcoholism, moral insanity, syphilitic paresis, and a range of other aberrations which he incorporated under a broader category of degenerative insanity.

Lombroso and others of his time were interested in the physical causes of mental illness as well as what they considered the physical and genetic causes of genius. With the shift in emphasis to psychological factors, which was spurred by Freud and psychoanalysis, the interest in connecting illness to creativity did not abate, but the types of constituents changed. A discipline of diagnostic psychiatric and psychoanalytic writings subsequently developed, particularly in Europe, which has come to be known as pathography. It continues on today. Scores of professionals have searched the artistic works and biographies of great persons and attempted in a manner like the approaches I discussed in Chapter 7 to delineate pathological conflicts and abnormal processes. Additionally, in the United States, not only have many similar types of professional psychoanalytic studies been carried out, but the interest in identifying pathological conflicts and psychodynamics has also been taken up by ordinary biographers. Although use of psychoanalysis in the understanding of biography should not necessarily lead to labels of abnormality, it has proved to do so in the hands of many of these biographers.

This tradition has culminated in the recent wide quoting and citing of two presumably objective studies by Drs. Kay Jamison and Nancy Andreasen. Both of these studies have been consistently discussed in popular as well as professional publications as having proven a connection between affective illness—depression, mania, or both together—and creativity, despite the fact that the first had not been published or reviewed in a scientific journal until quite recently,[3] and the other[4] had a flawed research methodology. The need to believe in a connection between creativity and madness appears to be so strong that affirmations are welcomed and quoted rather uncritically.

Andreasen, who did her study with thirty writers who served during a period of fifteen years on the faculty of the University of Iowa Writers' workshop, reported that 80 percent of these writers experienced some form of affective illness. In arriving at this finding, Andreasen had personally carried out diagnostic interviews with the faculty members at the workshop as well as with a group of what she specified as "matched controls." The latter consisted of persons who were not in the creative arts but were comparable to the writers in age, sex, and education. She reported a statistically significant higher incidence of affective illness in the writers than in the matched control group.

Although, on the surface, this result might seem striking and even impressive, we must strongly hesitate to accept it. For one thing, this investigator had been the sole interviewer of all subjects, and none of the data collected were corroborated by any type of colleague agreements or consensus procedures such as obtaining independent ratings of tape-recorded transcripts of the interviews, publishing the substance of them, or comparing results with independent interviews or diagnostic procedures by other trained observers. Because the investigator clearly knew who in her study were writers and who were controls and was at the same time assessing her own hypotheses, some conscious or unconscious bias inevitably must have operated. Lack of protection against such bias constitutes a serious limitation in research on the incidence of psychiatric illness in human subjects regardless of the interviewer's personal objectivity and professional intent and integrity.

Most problematic, the criteria for creativity and for choosing controls were inexplicit and misleading. The creative group was so designated because the members of it had been on the permanent or visiting faculty of the Iowa Workshop. Andreasen's control group was comprised of a random group of persons described as hospital administrators, businessmen, social workers, lawyers, medical and computer science students rather than comparable persons in some other faculty department, invited lecturers, or even members of the faculty of some other school. In choosing the controls, she did not take into consideration the social and environmental structure of her subjects' work. Also, there was no stated attempt to assess for the purpose of proper matching the success or lack of success of controls or of the workshop group itself. Although, as Andreasen reports, famous writers have been on the permanent and visiting faculty of the Iowa Workshop, that fact gives little indication of whether the particular thirty she studied were actually creative in their fields. The quality of the workshop has been known to vary widely and some of the writers may have been there because they had either never been successful or else were no longer successful and were seeking a refuge—important considerations for assessing depressive illness. Some of the writers in that particular group may have turned to teaching at that point precisely because their depressive symptoms interfered with their writing. Andreasen's particular sample of thirty writer volunteers, in fact, may have contained a high proportion of depressed persons primarily seeking psychiatric evaluation, whereas members of the control group, particularly the hospital personnel and students, may have participated primarily for other motives such as obligation, interest, or pride. However, no assessment of such potentially confounding factors was made. Also, because she collected secondary source information about relatives, an unreliable diagnostic approach,[5] her additional report of a high degree of affective illness among the writers' relatives must be questioned.

Jamison's study reports that 38.3 percent of a mixed group of English writers, visual artists, and biographers at some point had been treated for affective illness. As with the Andreasen investigation, however, little consideration was given to the subjects' reasons for participation. The fault is even more serious here because the only criteria for affective illness used were the subjects' own reports of treatment for that condition. No attempt at independent diagnostic assessment was made. While this constitutes a limit on interpretation of the findings in its own right, it also sheds doubt on whether any kind of representative sample was obtained. Subjects may very well have volunteered for Jamison's study for the same reason that they sought treatment—sophistication, the hope for help, sharing, or further information (N.B., they received no pay for participation, only the promise of published reports). Although Jamison reports that subjects had all been selected on the basis of having received various types of prizes and awards, there is no way of knowing how many similar prizewinners who were not participants in her study did or did not receive psychiatric treatment for affective illness or for any other kind of disorder. In other words, no controlled selection procedure was used. Also, in distinction to the Andreasen study, no attempt at all was made to assess any type of matched "noncreative" controls. Persons who seek treatment may or may not be sicker or less sick than others; they may primarily be better motivated or informed. In addition, as depression and related feelings are far more socially acceptable than other kinds of psychiatric symptoms such as hallucinations, paranoid ideas, or personality difficulties, subjects reporting treatment for depression particularly may actually not be providing accurate or complete diagnostic information.

With regard to the results reported, many different types of disciplines were mixed into the creative sample, but outside of the poet groups, there was a very small number of persons in each category: eight playwrights, five biographers, eight artists, and eight novelists. Because results have been presented in percentages, it has not been readily apparent how many people are actually involved. For instance, Jamison reports that 12.5 percent of the visual artists had been treated for an affective illness, but after calculating the number of persons in that category from the figures given, this percentage represents a total of no more than one person. On the other side of the coin, fourteen of the combined poet and playwright portion of the group had been treated for an affective illness, a number of persons representing approximately 30 percent of the total. As the complete total was an overall 38.3 percent treated, the poet and playwright part of the group accounted for the major portion, if not almost all, of the reported finding. This does not in any way indicate a high degree of affective illness among visual artists. Nor do Jamison's results show a connection between writing in general and affective illness because an additional point is that both novelists and biographers, according to her figures, had a much lower incidence (25 percent or two persons, and 20 percent or one person, respectively) of the condition.[6] In sum, the criteria for selection and hypothesis testing are questionable, and the numbers used are far too small to draw adequate conclusions. Elation and disappointment have long been considered the reward and bane, respectively, of creative effort and achievement. At one point, creativity was considered the *sine qua non* of what Abraham Maslow called "peak experiences,"[7] and assumedly, with such experiences, one could also expect accompanying emotional drops or "valleys." The belief that these fluctuations intrinsically reflect, or result from, illness is conjectural and requires rigorous evidence for support. With respect to creativity in science, I have carried out, with the assistance of an associate, a word-association experiment with U.S. Nobel laureates in the physical sciences, and we found no evidence among them of a depressive response.[8]

Although the conclusions of these two studies cannot be considered valid, their hypotheses do refresh and broaden research regarding creativity and mental illness. Rather than following a more traditional idea of the schizophrenic genius or creator, these studies point toward the affective illness side of the spectrum. Poetic creativity especially has usually been linked with schizophrenia. This is in part because primary process cognition has often been thought to operate prominently in both schizophrenia and the composing of poetry. The primary process mechanism of condensation (combining multiple diverse elements) has been considered the basis of metaphor creation, and the mechanism of displacement (shifting onto something smaller) has been credited with producing various features of poetry ranging from rhyming and alliteration to symbolization. Cited in support of these assumptions are the apparent paranoid schizophrenic illnesses of great poets such as Ezra Pound, Arthur Rimbaud, and William Blake. Although there is certainly no reason for rushing to rediagnose these poets as actually having suffered from manic-depressive psychoses, as some investigators have recently attempted, the emphasis on affective illness turns our attention to mood variations and disorders in writers and other artists and possibly toward less simplistic explanations regarding creativity than the primary process one. As I discussed in Chapter 5, schizophrenic condensations have a long way to go to become poetic metaphors, and I do not believe that displacement is directly responsible for any feature of poetry creation.

To delve further into the matter of connections between creativity and mental illness and also to summarize some of the topics considered in this book, I shall follow an organization I have implicitly used throughout: that is, to make that organization explicit, I shall now look at interrelationships in terms of the components of subject matter created, the person doing the creating, and the creative activity or process. All of these components interact, but each is a separate matter for research, and each is often affected separately by mental illness factors.

The subject matter created is something that is usually quite tangible, but according to some definitions of creativity, it does not need to be. Tangible subject matter includes artwork, scientific theories, experiments and discoveries, inventions, artistic performances, bodies of philosophy, and a whole range of human institutions such as religions and governments. Intangible types of subject matter, frequently connected with creativity in Eastern cultures, are particular states of mind or conditions of mental and physical energy. Also, as I have described in another work,[9] an intangible type of creation is the new and valuable personality structure that is the end product of psychotherapy.

The persons doing the creating are, of course, as diverse as there are fields and outlets for creative activity. They range from the loud and acclaimed to the quiet and inconspicuous. The creative processes they engage in are usually time limited and fluctuating, not comprised of single acts or events and not occurring at all times of life or even steadily throughout a single day. Nor are all of a person's skills, capacities, or personality qualities involved. Preference for a hairstyle, the presence or absence of an athletic skill, or even some obvious mental aberration may have little to do with the process or activity leading to particular types of created products.

Going back to subject matter: in order to understand the value or appeal of an artwork or other type of creation, it is necessary to consider factors in society or culture which may not pertain directly either to the creative process or to the person. Also, many aspects of a work are copies of previous successes rather than being original and new. Neglect of all of these distinctions has unfortunately brought many a creativity study to grief, but I shall not dwell on that further here because I have done so many times before this.[10]

Subject Matter: Types and Times

Depending on the type of subject matter, certain forms of mental or emotional illness may play an influential or even a facilitative role in it. Although poetry may not provide a special edge for the schizophrenic condition, science and other abstract fields may, curiously enough, be a special outlet and allure. In the fields of physics, mathematics, and to some extent chemistry and biology, highly abstract material is often organized into elaborated systems of information and knowledge which attract the interest and activity of persons suffering from schizoid and schizophrenic disorders. Because these disorders involve a good deal of withdrawal from human relationships, together with flattening or deadening of emotional responses, the objectivity and seeming lack of emotionality in scientific subject matter have distinct appeal. Working with scientific material may provide extreme solitude and allow these persons to deny emotions and affect. Also, as thought processes go markedly awry and there is difficulty in maintaining coherence and logic in schizophrenia, immersion in a scientific system can help organize thinking. Intelligence is not lost, and manipulation of a coherent but impersonal symbol system provides a structure that substitutes for chaotic thoughts. Schizophrenic persons often are attracted to highly abstract scientific systems and also to abstract philosophies. As we saw with August Strindberg and Swedenborgianism, they are also attracted to abstract religious systems. Although the particular systems may not always help sustain them, and they may not be able to function well, some highly creative scientists with this disorder have succeeded immeasurably. Examples from my earlier list are Michael Faraday in the field of electromagnetism, Johannes Kepler along with Tycho Brahe in astronomy, and probably Isaac Newton himself. In philosophy, Arthur Schopenhauer and very likely Friedrich Nietzsche, Benedict de Spinoza, and Ralph Waldo Emerson were similarly stricken. Although it is not known in each case how illness facilitated the creativity of these men in the particular disciplines mentioned, intense motivation to work in these highly abstract areas together with sometimes radical deviations from ordinary thought very likely contributed to their ability both to build and break systems. As I have suggested in the case of Strindberg and in other places as well, the lines are thin between janusian and homospatial processes and the primary process type of thinking in psychosis, and the crossover sometimes occurs.

Politics also has been an area in which schizophrenia has sometimes had a creative impact. In the history of ancient times, there are numerous descriptions of leaders who experienced guiding visitations from the gods which were very likely schizophrenic hallucinations. For example, Aeneas, the legendary hero/founder of Rome, is described by Virgil as constantly seeing and hearing gods and receiving their orders. As Aeneas also had paranoid inclinations, the visions and voices were probably his visual and auditory hallucinations that he used to inspire his followers.[11] Hercules, the great but also highly suspicious and paranoid hero, had an episode of madness in which he killed his children. This event led him to undertake his Twelve Labors involving brilliant and inventive exploits and adventures.[12] And Alexander the Great, one of the most imaginative ancient leaders, also reportedly heard guiding voices. Although it is not clear, given the long intervening span of time, whether Joan of Arc's visions were actually visual hallucinations resulting from schizophrenia or from a neurotic illness such as hysteria, they surely dictated her actions and inspired her followers.

As for other types of connections between so-called madness and creativity, I pointed out in Chapter 9 that artistic content was influenced by homosexuality in a manner that was particularly interesting for certain cultures at certain times of history. The subject matter of works by homosexual artists often concerns issues of alienation, gender, and individuality. All of these themes have been especially important in the twentieth century as well as at particular times of change and upheaval in history. Whether homosexual artists are the vanguard who bring these issues to the attention of the societies in which they live and work and thereby foster cultural changes, or whether cultural changes foster homosexuality and homosexual artists is not easy to answer. Very likely, both factors operate and interact in a complex way. To be sure, the themes I mentioned are not exclusively in the province of homosexual artists but are widely found in heterosexual artworks as well. On the other hand, in performing arts such as theater and dance, the body exhibitionism often associated with homosexuality, and in visual art, the loving attention to the physique and body of members of the same sex may enhance aesthetic appreciation and value. Such erotic elements may appeal to the universal same-gender sexual interests, both manifest and latent, of viewers and audiences. Psychiatrist Donald Kaplan contends that sexuality in general is a special preoccupation of homosexual persons and that this same preoccupation accounts for the modern success of so many homosexual playwrights.[13] The plays of Tennessee Williams, Edward Albee, William Inge, and Peter Shaffer are indeed often focused on sexual themes and are highly successful. Many knowledgeable persons would, of course, argue that the plays of successful modern heterosexual playwrights have focused on sex quite fully as well.

Manifest homosexual themes have increasingly appeared in various types of artworks in the last few decades but are still not widely and routinely popular. Homosexual themes or issues related to homosexuality do not seem to contribute directly to scientific subject matter, but that may be because we have not yet learned the intricate relationships between emotional factors and the type of thinking that is done in scientific fields. Emotional and motivational issues other than homosexuality have certainly appeared directly in scientific theories and works. In addition to the examples of emotional reactions by Albert Einstein, Werner Heisenberg, and Erwin Schrödinger which I cited in Chapter 3, Kepler's entire sixteenth-century astronomical theory of the "music [harmony] of the spheres" was explicitly derived from his intense aesthetic and religious feelings.[14] Homosexuality in science may in part be difficult to understand and identify because of a paucity of information due to cultural prohibitions and, until recently, concomitant political security issues.

What about facilitative effects of substance abuse on creativity in modern music? Is there some particular effect of drugs on this type of subject matter? Many, many creative jazz and rock musicians have used narcotics regularly. Because of this and because music is so temporally focused and modern music sometimes quite spontaneous, I tend to believe that the time distortions and the sedative and inhibition-releasing properties of narcotics and alcohol could have some facilitative role. Although no scientific evaluation has yet been made, it would appear that these substances help composer/performers to produce innovative and interesting temporal and rhythmic patterns. Also, as jazz especially involves composition during a performance, the use of sedatives may help in dealing with the intense anxiety of spontaneous creation. As for direct effects on content, certain rock song lyrics concerning the practice of using drugs have aroused interest, if not any lasting aesthetic appeal, among some groups.

With respect to other fields such as literature, substance and alcohol abuse has been a theme in modern works such as Nelson Algren's *Man with the Golden Arm*, William Burroughs's *Naked Lunch*, Malcolm Lowry's *Under the Volcano*, Jack London's *John Barleycorn*, and especially in the writings of Jack Kerouac and other Beat authors. As I discussed in Chapter 10, except for some initial disinhibiting effects, there seems to be no facilitative benefit of alcohol abuse on the literary product, and the same is true for other substances. Also, as I mentioned earlier, there has been little value found for use of LSD, marijuana, or large amounts of alcohol for inspiration or success in the visual arts or in poetry.

Given the diversity of creative subject matter and of cultural interests and tastes, any effects of mental illness can be facilitative in particular societies at particular historical times. In the case of some of the mentally ill immortals I have discussed, the effect spans many cultures and many historical periods because of the person's structural impact on the subject matter of the field, for example, Strindberg on drama and Newton on science. Usually, however, mental illness distorts and destroys the positive value of the product in any area. Although there has been some professional interest in finding consistent value in the artworks of the "insane,"[15] and such exploration can be meaningfully used for therapeutic ends by art therapists, it does not purport to link creative capacity with mental illness. Having now referred to the "insane," I come to the matter of the person doing the creating and the idea of the mad creator.

The Mad Creator

Society and creative people are often antagonistic toward each other. Although society bestows its highest awards on creative efforts, admirers also envy and debunk the very people they prize. On the other side, creative people, because of passionate idealistic devotion to the societies in which they live, often attack and try to change the mores and practices of those societies. Recriminations on both sides abound. It is partly because of this double-sided irritation, I think, that a mythic image has arisen of the highly eccentric, if not deeply disturbed, "mad creator." Every story of alcoholic debauchery, every extended absence, every marital difficulty or excessive public display, and every suicide is focused on as the exemplar and the proof. Mental suffering is considered both the generator and the price of creativity.

For every one of the disturbed creative people I mentioned in the introductory chapter, there are literally manifold numbers of equally creative persons with no demonstrable mental illness such as: writers Dante Alighieri, Jane Austen, Giovanni Boccaccio, Robert Burns, Miguel de Cervantes, Geoffrey Chaucer, Anton Chekhov, Daniel Defoe, John Donne, Alexander Dumas (elder), Henry Fielding, George Eliot (Mary Ann Evans), Thomas Hardy, Robert Herrick, Henrik Ibsen, Thomas Mann, John Milton, Ovid, François Rabelais, Walter Scott, Laurence Sterne, William Thackeray, Anthony Trollope, Émile Zola; artists Pieter Brueghel (younger), El Greco (Doménikos Theotokópoulos), William Hogarth, Henry Moore, Raphael, Pierre Auguste Renoir, Peter Paul Rubens, Augustus Saint-Gaudens, Titian, Jan Vermeer, Anthony Van Dyck, Christopher Wren; composers Johann Sebastian Bach, Johannes Brahms, Claude Debussy, Franz Joseph Haydn, Jean Sibelius, Igor Stravinsky; mathematicians and scientists such as Niels Bohr, Marie Curie, Paul Adrien Maurice Dirac, Edward Jenner, Gottfried Leibniz, Louis Pasteur, Ernest Rutherford; engineers Eli Whitney and James Watt; philosophers and theologians St. Thomas Aquinas, Aristotle, George Hegel, David Hume, Alfred North Whitehead, Charles Sanders Peirce, John Dewey, and Albert Schweitzer. A contemporary list would be somewhat more difficult to compile because all information is not in, but think, for instance, of the numerous Nobel laureates, living and dead, about whom there is really not a whisper of suspicion about mental illness.

Carrying out a definitive statistical assessment of this question would be very complicated, and this is surely why it has never really been attempted. The problem consists of developing clear-cut criteria for defining either (or both) a contemporary and historical list of creative people, as well as stipulating the amount and nature of evidence required to distinguish between mental illness and health among these people. Nevertheless, without deciding who in the general population, and in what proportion, is definitely creative, the degree of mental illness in the group cannot be compared meaningfully with general incidence.

Assessments of creative populations carried out up until now, whether focused on mental illness, genetics, or other matters have often suffered from either over- or underinclusion. Francis Galton's study of genetic patterns of genius, for example, included British persons of accomplishment from a large number of fields including judicial, government, and military[16]; Victor and Mildred Goertzel's studies of persons of eminence covered every American who was in a standard reference work and the subject of at least two biographies (only one, if from outside the United States) in the collection of a particular public library.[17] According to these studies, both noninnovative but successful military commanders and popular celebrities would be classed in the same category of creativeness as Charles Dickens or Saul Bellow. Without disparaging the accomplishment of judges or military commanders, labels of *genius* or *creative* are neither appropriate nor necessary for crediting high or even outstanding achievement. Also, celebrated royalty, sports figures, industrialists, and naturalists who have warranted biographies and inclusion in standard references are surely not, in every case, creative.

On the other side, the high proportion of alcoholism among the eight U.S. Nobel laureates in literature has, as I stated earlier, been cited as evidence for a widespread tendency toward alcoholism among creative writers.[18] Distinguished as they are, this small group cannot be considered to represent the habits, practices, or illnesses of creative writers—even highly creative writers—in the population at large. Beyond the matter of the Nobel laureate group, it is risky as well as unscientific to correlate any particular condition or personality factor with the production of effects without some knowledge or theory of the connecting links. For example, even if we found that a significant number of creative people of all kinds were either shy, or dependent, or else the opposite, exhibitionistic, we would not know whether such factors resulted from creative accomplishment, whether they produced it, or whether there was no important relationship at all. Even finding correlations between such supposedly inborn features as left-handedness or temperament and creative accomplishment would leave us wondering whether some third factor—say, the use of the right hemisphere or frontal lobes of the brain, or the inability to write easily on right hand-oriented desks in school, or exclusion by other children—was responsible for the left-handedness temperament connection, the temperament and creativity connection, or for the left-handedness, temperament, and creativity connection, and so on. Even some of the connections I proposed between homosexuality and creativity are subject to such questions and reservations.

In my own research, one of the few personality factors that has appeared to be both linked to and very highly correlated with creativity is the intense degree of motivation to create, which I mentioned at the beginning of this book. Consistent motivation to create does not result from the experience of highly successful creating, nor is it connected by some third intervening factor. Some exceptions and modifications can be pointed out, such as the motivating encouragement by mentors after successful creating in school or, in adulthood, a motivation to create arising after serendipitous discovery. Also, the finding itself may be considered to be a rather broad one. Nevertheless, it is a consistent link between a personality factor and creativity.

One of the deceptive issues regarding connections between mental illness and creativity is that mental illness is not fixed either in time or in particular effects. No mental illness, even the severest, has a uniform impact on all aspects of human functioning or on all periods or segments of a person's life. Take the important case of schizophrenia. Although persons suffering from schizophrenia may be seriously divorced from reality in many aspects of their lives, the mental skills, motivations, and capacities that enter into creative work may be relatively intact. Even more to the point, at different points in a single day and under different conditions of stress and anxiety, these skills and capacities may flourish or recede. It is, for instance, often asserted that persons with schizophrenia suffer from difficulties with abstract thinking. Classically, as I stated in Chapter 5, they have difficulty interpreting such abstractions as proverbs or aphorisms and understand or respond to them in idiosyncratic concrete ways. Because abstract thinking is a necessary factor in most types of creative activity, this would indeed seem to be a serious difficulty for creative achievement. But no such difficulty necessarily exists because at times when anxiety is lessened, the schizophrenic person frequently shows perfectly adequate abstract understanding. Indeed, as I indicated, highly abstract work may be done in a mathematical or philosophical system.

This tendency to shift levels of functioning in relation to the intensity of anxiety pertains to a psychotic person's contact with reality as well. Extreme loss of contact with reality and withdrawal into an unreal or fantasy world seriously interfere with creative accomplishment, but these experiences fluctuate a great deal during the course of illness. In other types of disorders, such fluctuations also occur. As I stressed in the cases of highly variable alcohol abuse, maintenance of sobriety while engaged in the creative process is the rule. Anxiety in mental illnesses such as personality disorders and neuroses can cause a good deal of disruption at times, but by and large these conditions exist side by side with daily use of creative capacities.

For Emily Dickinson, Eugene O'Neill, August Strindberg, and John Cheever, the picture of mental illness which emerged in these pages differed over the course of their lives; even untreated, the disorder apparently went into remission at various points and, in some cases, was resolved. The effect of mental illness on creativity always differs at different portions of a creative person's life. Alcohol abusers Tennessee Williams, Truman Capote, Sinclair Lewis, and James Agee illustrate this dramatically. All were able to work at times despite their illness, but the use of alcohol got so far out of hand as to interfere totally with their work for very long periods of time. Several writers suffering from serious depression or psychosis have also eventually become unable to write and have committed suicide. Whether the awareness of an inability to work because of illness or the direct effects of the illness itself led to the suicide is difficult to resolve; probably there was a vicious cycle involving both factors together.

The Processes of Creation

The acid test regarding mental illness has to do with the processes directly responsible for creations. If mental illness were to impinge on these processes or, even more pertinent, if these processes had psychopathological roots, we could—with relief or celebration—demand that the question be closed. But the specific creative processes I have described are not psychopathological in origin; they are at the opposite end of the spectrum. Both the janusian and homospatial processes are adaptive and healthy in functions and goals. Oriented toward improving and changing the environment in the best way possible, they go beyond coping, or adjusting, to produce creative effects. Unlike psychopathological processes, which involve rigidity, irrationality, and extreme self-absorption and self-focus, janusian and homospatial processes are flexible and rationally based as well as directed toward other human beings and the environment.

Before going into the psychodynamic structure and function of these processes, I want to reemphasize a point I made in Chapter 3 about how the processes *feel* in the creative thinker's mind; that is, use of either or both involves a great deal of mental and emotional strain. In ordinary thinking based on logic and experience, contradictions must by definition always cancel each other out, and multiple elements surely never can occupy the same space all at once. Hence, defying such definitions and experiences, the creative thinker comes up with unthinkable and unimaginable ideas. Conceiving that an accepted proposition or fact continues to be valid or true and, simultaneously, its opposite or contradiction is also valid or true produces tension and anxiety. Imagine the feelings and thoughts involved in formulating, for the first time, the following ideas within the janusian process: time moves forward and backward simultaneously (Richard Feynman); the sun rises and at the same time does not rise (Ernest Hemingway)[19]; a body moves and is simultaneously stationary (Albert Einstein); and sex and violence are concomitant (Richard Wilbur). Regularly having such ideas and tolerating the accompanying strain require a good deal of mental health and strength. Otherwise, working would be difficult. If one already suffered from intense mental and emotional anxiety, such thoughts might be impossible to pursue.

Using the homospatial process similarly engenders a good deal of mental and emotional tension and anxiety. Although transitory and fleeting, the conception of multiple, discrete elements occupying the same space produces strain. A hand and bandage are mentally superimposed in the same space to create the metaphor "my hand was a bandage to his hurt"[20]; a tarantula and lamp are similarly superimposed for the creation of "the tarantula rays of the lamp spread across the conference room." Stability and rationality are required in order to develop such conceptions into metaphors rather than disturbing images of bandages with actual finger-like appendages or lamps that move like tarantulas. On a more everyday level, anyone can get some idea of the strain involved by trying to bring chairs and tables into the same mental space, or else arms and faces, or colors and smells.

Tension and anxiety are also engendered because of the psychodynamic structure and function of the homospatial and janusian processes. Both are responsible for a progressive unearthing of unconscious material during the course of the creative process—an unearthing that in turn produces anxiety. Despite the discomfort and risk, this progressive uncovering leads to self-revelation, an intrinsic goal of the creative process in diverse types of fields. In art, it is incorporated into the structure of the artwork itself; the artist's dynamic struggle toward knowing himself or herself helps determine such features as suspense, pattern development, and other formal factors. Although in science the drive toward self-revelation is not readily apparent, it is, as I discussed earlier, indicated by creative scientists' remarkable emotional involvement in both the processes of discovery and their outcomes.

Unearthing unconscious material is facilitated by the structure of the creative psychological processes. Both janusian and homospatial processes operate in a manner I have termed the *mirror reversal of dreaming and dream thought.*[21] As I stated in Chapter 10, they function primarily on a conscious level but have superficial aspects resembling the primary process mechanisms that appear especially in dreaming—mechanisms responsible for disguising our frightening and forbidden unconscious mental contents when we dream. When the homospatial and janusian processes operate during creative activity, they reverse these mechanisms—hence the term *mirror reversal of dreaming*—and thereby produce revelation of unconscious contents rather than disguise.

The template operation responsible for the reversal occurs naturally in biological processes, and it is also man-made in industry and artistic fields. An example is the following. An object, say a terra-cotta statue, is covered with a soft malleable material such as paraffin. The paraffin layer then hardens and forms an opposite impression, called a negative, of the statue form. Next, this paraffin negative is filled with another material that forms a larger or harder copy of the original statue—a positive or completed form. Similarly, in genetic transfer, the double-helix structure of DNA operates as a template that allows genetic characteristics of one molecule to be transmitted to another. In the creative process, janusian and homospatial operations function as positive templates that restore unconscious material. Interlocking with, and stripping away disguises, they bring unconscious material into consciousness.

Engaging in the creative process, therefore, produces some degree of psychological insight. However, unconscious processes cannot be fully revealed in this way, and the insight achieved is not of the complete type resulting from the work of psychotherapy. The creative process is not a form of psychotherapy, even though many have talked about it in that manner. The partial insight achieved, however, does represent a meaningful movement toward self-awareness, and the processes that produce such movement must be healthy ones. Because they are reality-oriented, insight-facilitating functions, they are healthy psychological operations.

One reason for the traditional linking of mental illness and creativity is that creative thought processes are unusual in structure. Creative experiences and descriptions of creative breakthroughs sometimes appear, on the surface, to be similar to abnormal ones. The janusian process appears superficially similar to the thinking in opposites or ambivalence of a person suffering from schizophrenia; homospatial images seem to be like what is called autistic thinking as well as, in some ways, visual hallucinations. Because mental illness extensively involves unconscious material and janusian and homospatial processes mirror such material, there are reflections and resemblances. Functionally, however, there are sharp distinctions. For example, psychotic belief that a person can actually jump off a roof and be motionless and survive is markedly different from a knowing, rational conception of simultaneous motion and rest while creating a poem or scientific theory.

In cases I have described, such as those of August Strindberg and Sylvia Plath, some crossing over between psychotic and creative thinking occurred at different periods of time, and only trained literary skills seemed to prevent florid disorganization in the work that was produced. Creative processes may turn into psychotic ones, but seldom does the reverse occur without some prior resolution of illness and reduction of anxiety. All types of mental illness engender anxiety that tends to disrupt creative functioning. Because the creative process involves both cognitive strain and the anxiety produced by the unearthing of unconscious material, any preexisting sources of anxiety dampen and interrupt creative accomplishment.

It is a false and romantic notion that people have to undergo suffering themselves in order to be able to understand the human concerns and sufferings of others. Imagination and creativity consist of special abilities to go beyond one's own experience and history in order to bring forth new ideas and things. While some aspects of art, and even science, may be served by mental illness at times, healthy processes such as the janusian and homospatial ones are used to produce new and valuable creations.

13 ◆◇ Psychotherapy and Creativity

A*s I did* in the beginning, I will tell some stories at the end. Here is the first:

You are a patient at a mental hospital. You have come to this hospital in desperation and fear because of years of suffering and symptoms that command and overwhelm you. Much of the time, you try not to have feelings or even specific thoughts because the things you think, feel, and even see are tormenting to you.

What was that? Was there someone down the corridor complaining that he couldn't stand the odor you gave off when you walked by? In your room, while sitting alone and trying to read John Updike's latest novel, did you hear a voice saying that you aren't worthy enough to live? Putting down the book and cringing in the corner of the room, you wait to hear the voice again. After a while, you get the courage to go out in the hall to look for a nurse who might help you.

Later in the day, still fearful of feelings or thoughts and wondering if that voice will speak again, you go to the shop where your unfinished painting is still in the locker near your usual workspace. The easel is empty and, wondering if working is possible today, you put the painting in place. A thought flashes that your mother would be very angry about the fact that you didn't clean up your room before leaving it to come to the studio. Then, there is a series of thoughts about how little you have done in your life and how impossible it is to get well. Then, you feel nothing at all.

In this state, you go through the motions of putting the painting on the easel, getting the paints ready, and rinsing out and drying the brushes. Then, when you start to work, a familiar thought comes back: this painting will be the one that will get your message to the world. Now, they will see your real greatness, and all the suffering will not have been in vain. Your parents will be sorry for their low opinion of you; all the other patients in the hospital will be in awe of you, and the doctors and nurses will be amazed. Those children in school who teased you years ago in the schoolyard will be really sorry. They will come to you now and ask for favors that are smilingly denied. Your sister will—oh, never mind her now. Fleetingly, you think of telling your therapist later in the day how good you feel.

Later, in the therapist's office, the following occurs:

You, THE PATIENT: I—uh—uh—have been working on this problem in my art. I can't get it out of my mind. I see those shapes—it's a kind of mystical thing—they tell me how it really happened, and how I'm really gonna come out. Sometimes, there's really a burst of understanding. I see all the red and the blood in my painting and it makes me wonder if the world will understand my message—Keep thinking about this all the time, must solve it, *must* solve it. I can't sleep at night.

THERAPIST (softly): You feel the painting will help clarify some message for yourself as well as for the world?

PATIENT: Yes, I feel I'm on the verge of some great realization. If only I could free myself up more; if only I could just get all my thoughts right on that canvas. I know the answer's there and I'll get to it. Sometimes I feel so good when I'm painting I think that I can take off and fly.

THERAPIST (warmly): I guess it would be nice to be Superman, then no one could hurt you.

Somewhat relieved after the therapist's last remark, you find yourself talking about some of the problems that occurred with other patients during the day, and at one point your thoughts flash to your feelings of unbearable fear and loneliness. You do not, however, speak to the therapist about these feelings. You will never be able, you are sure, to talk to anyone about them.

The next day is somewhat similar to the day before. Not having slept well, you are continually preoccupied with that sense of solving a great problem in your painting. If only you could bring it into your mind! Instead, there are only self-recriminations regarding things you said to people the day before and, several times, the voice again says that you aren't worthy to live. During the day, you find yourself going even later to the shop to work on the painting and then accomplishing very little prior to the scheduled therapy session. This time, however, you decide to bring the painting with you—

The session begins in silence. You have propped the painting up next to your chair and are waiting for the therapist to say something about it—he merely sits quietly in his chair and looks at you expectantly. You say nothing for a very long period of time, and some bitterly resentful thoughts about the therapist's silence go rapidly through your mind. Finally, it goes as follows:

YOU, THE PATIENT: I brought—my painting—today.

THERAPIST: Uh-huh.

PATIENT: Do you wanna see it?

THERAPIST: If you like.

PATIENT: I asked you if you wanted to see it. Isn't it important to my therapy?

THERAPIST: If you think so.

PATIENT: Never mind. (You lapse into a long silence again.)

THERAPIST: You're angry now and feel rejected because I don't consider the painting itself more important than you and your thoughts and feelings.

PATIENT: I never know what to do in here. Well, here it is. (You hold up the painting to show the therapist.)

THERAPIST (after studying the painting for several minutes): I see some of the colors and shapes that you have talked about—the large black area here, the red dripping throughout. Tell me, what about the painting moves you?

Unlike the stories I told at the beginning of this book, this one is not mythic. Instead, it illustrates one of the grim realities regarding psychotherapy and creativity. The patient in this story is clearly quite seriously ill; there are descriptions of auditory hallucinations, ideas of reference (reading personal meanings into chance or innocuous events), and delusions of grandeur—and the delusions of grandeur pertain directly to an area of so-called creative work. Because creativity is so highly valued and honored, creative accomplishment is frequently, as here, the subject matter of grandiose ideas. Delusions that one is a great painter, author, musician, or scientist are as common as believing oneself to be Christ, Buddha, or God. This is not to deny that a patient like the one in my story may have actual painting skills, or that such a person could become a good painter or even—as in the relatively rare example of Strindberg in whom delusions of grandeur became reality—a great or outstanding artist. The story should, however, indicate the ways in which particular types of preoccupation with art may arise from emotional illness and also interfere with treatment.

For this hypothetical patient, grandiose ideas about painting function to deny and compensate for feelings of extremely low self-worth. The therapist in the story attempts to point that out with the comment regarding Superman; the grandiose ideas make the patient feel strong and powerful just at the moment of feeling most weak and powerless. There is internal pursuit by images and memories of highly demeaning and critical parents.

Also illustrated here is the caricature of doing productive thinking, or therapeutic problem solving, which sometimes appears together with the focus on creativity or creative activity in severe mental illness. The patient thinks about trying to solve an important creative problem as though that will also solve other serious difficulties. Although creative accomplishment does sometimes help increase one's self-esteem, it falls short of directly improving mental illness. Any of the accounts I have given here about mental illness actually intensifying subsequent to a creative accomplishment serve to emphasize this point.

From the viewpoint of the psychotherapy, this patient may be testing the therapist to see if the latter wants or expects creative accomplishments. Although not included in this story, the patient's interest in painting may have been a product of intense parental pressures to be creative, and there is a need to find out whether the therapist has similar pressuring expectations. This bears on the matter of bringing the painting to the therapy session and requesting the therapist to state whether or not he is interested in seeing it. Why does the therapist not respond to this? Why does he reflect the issue back to the patient rather than saying right out that he wants to see it (or not see it), as some critics of psychotherapists and psychotherapy might say he should? The reason is that, at this point, the therapist does not know what role the patient's painting plays in his illness; specifically, he does not know whether or not showing paintings or other types of accomplishments to parents as a way of getting otherwise withheld approval was a serious problem in the patient's background. Instead, the therapist attempts first to be receptive, then primarily descriptive and focused on the patient's experience. Asking what moves the patient, there is an emphasis on feelings rather than accomplishment.

As I said, although the patient is mentally ill and grandiose about painting, this does not by any means indicate that he cannot become an artist. In a follow-up study, in which I have been recently engaged, of patients hospitalized at the Austen Riggs Center over a twenty-five-year period, we have found that a large number of them continued to follow artistic pursuits begun in the hospital for a long time after they left. Although we cannot yet say how successfully creative all of them are because the study is not completed, a part of the group distinctly appears to be so. On the other hand, pursuit of creative types of activity may be an intrinsic part of the mental illness of particular individuals, as the story here illustrates, and may actually serve as an impediment to therapy. In such cases, a good treatment outcome could well include reducing or giving up artistic work. Psychotherapists who value creative types of activities need especially to keep this in mind because their values and interests must not interfere with the patient's ultimate welfare. Patients who seek treatment because they feel they must become creative in some particular way—whether they suffer as severely as the patient in the story or not—need also to keep in mind that redirection of their interests and goals may be a positive outcome.

Psychotherapy of the Creative Person

Here are a series of other types of "stories"—
Author James Agee, in a letter to Father Flye:

> Psychiatry, and for that matter psychoanalysis still more, interest me intensely; but except for general talk with them—which I would like—I feel reluctant to use either except in really desperate need. I don't yet feel in desperate need, and suspect in fact that I'll pull out of this on my own power. Yet I realize that I have an enormously strong drive, on a universally broad front, toward self-destruction; and that I know little if anything about its sources or control. There is much I might learn and be freed from that causes me and others great pain, frustration and defeat, and I expect that sooner or later I will have to seek their help. But I would somewhere near as soon die (or enter a narcotic world) as undergo full psychoanalysis. I don't trust anyone on earth that much; and I see in every psychoanalyzed face a look of deep spiritual humiliation or defeat; to which I prefer at least a painful degree of spiritual pain and sickness. The look of "I am a man who finally cannot call his soul his own, but yielded it to another."[1]

Arthur Miller, in his autobiography:

> In the early fifties . . . I realized there was something obsessional in my thoughts about my marriage and my work; great swellings of love and hope for my future with Mary [his wife] were followed by a cycle of despairing resentment that I was being endlessly judged, hopelessly condemned. In an attempt to break out, I had begun analysis with Rudolph Loewenstein, a Freudian of great skill, but it was ultimately impossible for me to risk my creativity, which he was wise enough not to pretend to understand, by vacating my own autonomy, however destructive it might continue to be. And so I have never

pretended to a valid estimate of analysis even though it gave me . . . a way of assessing human behavior perhaps more dispassionately than before.[2]

John Updike, to me:

I think psychiatry is a new form of stoicism where psychiatrists insist on people facing up to reality.

John Cheever, to me:

I could never understand how a psychiatrist could treat a writer without reading any of his books. How could he hope to understand the person without knowing what he's written?

All of these, of course, are stories of another kind. I quote them or tell them because they represent a range of positions that creative people who have emotional difficulties often take regarding the idea of entering into psychotherapy. Although none of the specific writers I have quoted was similar to the hospitalized patient I described, Agee and Cheever did suffer from problems that seriously interfered with their creative work. Each of the four stories illustrates one of the concerns that creative people have about the effects of psychotherapy on creativity.

Risk to Creativity

Arthur Miller's concern that therapy (in this case, the specific therapy of psychoanalysis) engendered a risk to his creativity is probably the most common concern among persons with creative skills. In the early days of my own research with creative people, I also wondered about such risks. The question came up right away during preliminary discussions with a research subject about the planned series of investigations because even though it was not therapy, the research called for a careful inspection of thinking and emotional processes which could plausibly interfere with the creative work in progress. First, if mental illness were indeed a factor in creativity—which I did not know at that time—even a research investigation of thoughts and feelings might alleviate the illness enough to interfere with the creative process. Second, the very act of analyzing and understanding might cause undue self-consciousness in the subject or perhaps even disintegration of functions that needed to remain intact.

In these early days, whenever I was asked by a prospective subject about the risk to creativity, I always answered that I thought it was a legitimate concern. Although I did not personally believe that the exploration would become a hindrance, we were embarking on an investigation that had not been carried out previously in that particular way. Therefore, I could not tell for sure. Some of the subjects who accepted the risk continued to feel concern in the early sessions but decided to continue to see how things went.

At the end of the series of sessions—which, as I said, in many cases lasted over a period of years—I invariably asked the subject whether he or she felt that our talks had interfered with progress on the particular work or works we had discussed or on anything planned for the future. Strikingly, in each and every case, I was told that there was *no carryover at all*, deleterious or otherwise. Despite such overt denials, however, I knew definitely that in one case, a highly successful poem had been written on the basis of some material that came out of the discussions. Beyond that, however, other unsuccessful as well as highly successful artworks—one winning the Pulitzer Prize—were completed during the investigation, and I had no clear idea of what role the study had played in either type.

Although it would be misleading to take at face value the stated denials regarding interference or to attempt to apply them directly to the effects of psychotherapy, they do suggest broadly that any disrupting effect of inspection and analysis is far less than might be feared or supposed. None of my subjects interrupted his or her work or developed blocks during the course of our sequence of interviews. As these investigations were not psychotherapy, however, the more pertinent response to the concern is that the processes that are responsible for successful creation are healthy ones. Although the purposes of psychotherapy can go awry, just as any life experience can, psychotherapy overall serves to improve mental health and thereby enhances the functioning of the creative processes.

There are stories of serious difficulties with psychotherapy—Tennessee Williams's several unsuccessful attempts and Anne Sexton's suicide are two examples—but there are no known instances of direct interference with creative production.[3] Furthermore, there are numerous reports of successful psychotherapies of creative people. Although these reports have generally not been published because of confidentiality, numerous clinicians confirm that several prominent writers, artists, musicians, and scientists have been beneficially treated. Some public announcements of direct benefits to creativity have been made by writers such as Eugene O'Neill, Donald Hall, Walker Percy, and William Alfred; a recent biography of Graham Greene proclaims a similar therapeutic result.[4] In my own investigations, such outstanding painters as Jim Dine and Kenneth Noland have told me (and permitted me to state) that they derived a positive effect on their work and a good general outcome from their therapy. Recently, I carried out a correspondence survey of poetry and fiction writers' opinions regarding the connections between creativity and mental illness. One of the respondents, Richard C. Shaner, spontaneously described his personal experience as follows. "I have had depressions and a spastic bowel which were severe enough for me to seek therapy about ten years ago. Fortunately, I found good people, and things progressed quickly because I was used to connecting images, so I can claim with confidence that the spastic bowel is cured and the depressions lightened. My writing also improved, becoming more direct in dealing with emotions." Many other poets and fiction writers also voluntarily testified to improvements as a result of psychotherapy.

Although I once thought there was a legitimate concern about a risk to creativity in embarking on psychotherapy, I no longer think such a threat exists. When emotional difficulties interfere, odds are that psychotherapy will enhance rather than hinder creative capacity and activity.

Concern for Autonomy

James Agee's remarks regarding psychiatry indicate a twofold concern: first, he talks of wanting to pull out of his difficulties on his "own power"; second, he sees treatment as a type of humiliation or capitulation to someone else's domination, and fears not calling "his soul his own."

His first concern involves an important misunderstanding of the nature of psychotherapy. Rather than taking the problem out of the ill person's hands or out of his "own power" as other treatments do, psychotherapy requires the patient to carry out a large portion of the work. This misapprehension often causes people to complain bitterly after they become involved. To some extent, the complaint derives from an underlying dependency that is intrinsically incorporated in all psychological illness and symptoms. Hence, it is important to emphasize that the Agee view is quite misleading because the emphasis on autonomy is such an intrinsic part of psychotherapy. The patient calls the shots in a very definitive way. Not the passive recipient of help, directives, or advice, the patient is always in a position to accept or reject the therapist's comments, interventions, and formulations.

Agee's second concern regarding the loss of "his soul" is a deeper and even more far-reaching matter. I don't know where or in what psychoanalyzed persons he had seen spiritual humiliation or defeat, and I wouldn't argue about specific cases. Everyone who undergoes therapy certainly does not come out improved, and some remain excessively dependent on a therapist or even on psychoanalysis itself as a body of theory. But, contrariwise, the person who really cannot call his (or her, of course) soul his own is one who, like Agee, has a strong drive toward self-destruction and knows "little if anything about its sources or control." It is precisely the enslavement of the emotionally and mentally ill person to forces about which he knows nothing or cannot control—such as the unacknowledged influence of factors from the past upon the present or the continued mindless influence of parental directives upon an adult—which requires therapy. It is expressly the function of psychotherapy to help the patient, creative or not, to free himself from these enslaving forces and in doing so to find and follow his own directives.

The goal, in fact, is to *help* a person come to call his soul his own. Successful treatment results in both the subjective sense and objective condition of personal independence and freedom. Because symptoms are at the same time usually relieved, this result would be sought regardless of any effects on creativity. But the capacity to be independent and free, both emotionally and cognitively, also facilitates the ability to create; for one thing, it allows one to use one's own meaningful types of thinking without concern or fear regarding individuality and any seeming lack of universality. It ensures, in the general case, a lower level of anxiety in work and ordinary living activities. For those specifically so inclined, it facilitates direct engagement in the anxiety-provoking creative process.

James Agee died at the age of thirty-five of a heart attack, but depression and alcoholism had certainly taken their toll and contributed to his early demise. Whether his emotional illness would have been alleviated by effective psychotherapy is impossible to know now. However, the smoke screen of fear of loss of independence that he, and others, have used to avoid getting help for themselves must permanently be dispersed.

My Work Is Me

John Cheever's challenge regarding the therapist's knowledge of the creative person's work brings up the matter of a therapist's sophistication and the place of artworks or other created products in the treatment. Sometimes it is thought that successful therapy with creative persons can only be carried out by therapists who are themselves highly creative or, at the very least, knowledgeable in the person's particular field.[5] Cheever believed that the therapist should actually read his works, and he told me, and others, that he gave autographed copies of his novel *The Wapshot Chronicle* to both psychiatrists whom he saw. In both instances, the therapy failed.[6] Although his expectation that the therapist read his books may not have been a factor in the failures, the issue and its offshoots are nevertheless worth considering.

With regard to the question of whether therapists should be knowledgeable about patients' particular fields of creative activity, the answer, I believe, is a qualified yes. The risk is that knowledgeable therapists could become overly involved and engage in discussions of particular subject matter in an intellectualized and even competitive way. Also, patients can become either unduly impressed or concerned about a therapist's erudition. After all, therapists are not consulted as experts in art or literature or science but as experts in intrapsychic and interpersonal matters. If patients require erudite therapists in order to solve intrapsychic and interpersonal problems, something is amiss. If therapists feel they must have, or display, erudition to help solve such problems, something is even more amiss—these therapists may be primarily attempting to enhance their self-esteem.

On the other hand, if therapists have little knowledge about or appreciation for art or else little sense of the type of thinking that goes into creative work in other fields, they may not be as helpful as possible. There may not be appreciation of particular skills and ways of using words, images, sounds and feelings. There may also be a lack of understanding of the types of unusual thinking used, of the intense level of motivation required, and of the high degrees of anxiety that are sometimes generated by the work itself. Because art, music, and literature are particularly concerned with the same areas of subjective experience as is the psychotherapist, there may be undue competition about expertise unless the therapist appreciates both the accomplishment of art and the nature of the particular patient's work.

As for discussion in therapy sessions of particular artworks or achievements—novels, paintings, musical compositions or scientific theories—this is often a loaded matter. Cheever, for instance, was an extremely verbal and articulate man, and it would hardly seem necessary for a therapist to have read his works in order to learn about his emotional and mental difficulties. In fact, use of a fictionalized account, even if highly autobiographical, is seldom the most effective way of understanding any person's true personality or concerns. Presentation of an artwork to the therapist may be intended to gain appreciation for the patient's productive skills and may thereby be countertherapeutic. The goal of therapy is not for the therapist to value the patient's accomplishments but for the patient to value them himself.

Worse still, this need for appreciation of the artistic work itself may constitute a repetition of a past problematic relationship that may be at the heart of the patient's difficulties. Doing creative work may have been either the major way or else the *only* way for the artist to obtain attention and love when a child; in the parent's eyes, work or production may have been more important than the child himself. Bringing work into therapy may be the artist's way of saying implicitly "my work is me" and testing whether the therapist, like the parents, agrees.

This does not mean that artistic work should never be discussed in therapy. The therapist's invitation to discuss feelings in my example at the beginning of this chapter shows one of the appropriate ways in which it is done. As artworks surely convey meaning and affect, they can be important bases for therapeutic exploration. Yet investment in work and accomplishment is always a particular risk for creative patients and their therapists. It can be carried to the point where therapists feel in awe of their patients' works or reputation and no longer deal appropriately with their particular illnesses. Tennessee Williams, for example, reports that one of his therapists allowed him to bring a bottle of whiskey to the therapy hours in order for him to talk more freely[7]—a highly questionable practice. Also, it appears that Ernest Hemingway was allowed special privileges and was discharged prematurely from the Mayo Clinic because of his reputation and status.[8] Tragically, he committed suicide shortly thereafter.

Work Block

Updike's disclaimer involves the idea of the therapist as a judgmental conscience or enforcer. This idea relates to a fairly common problem for creative people, which sometimes leads them to seek therapy; it has been variously called writer's block, painting block, loss of inspiration, or simply work block. Sometimes, in order to give this psychological problem a euphemistic physical quality, people refer to it as *writer's cramp*—suggesting that the physical act of writing itself has caused insurmountable muscular difficulties. When actual muscle cramping or paralysis of the hands occurs in writers, the cause is usually a so-called hysterical paralysis.

In work block, writers, artists, and composers characteristically find it impossible to start or continue with a creative work. Day after day goes by, and they go into a study or studio but are either unable to work at all or else feel constantly dissatisfied with what they do. Often smoking incessantly and pacing the floor, they finally leave. Escape is sought in critical writing, performing and teaching, or else in vacations, sometimes in sexual affairs and, in more extreme situations, in narcotics and alcohol. Although interference with work activities occurs in all fields, the interruption in creative work has to do with the special nature of the creative process itself. Here, the progressive unearthing of unconscious material that is intrinsic to the creative process may cause difficulties on both a long- and short-term basis. Two examples of long-term interference shown earlier were August Strindberg and John Cheever, both of whose creative activities were disrupted in a complex way by unconscious material that produced intense anxiety until it was eventually incorporated into their works.

On a short-term basis also, creative people—especially the more ambitious ones—become embroiled in their work with anxiety-provoking psychological themes. When the risk of intensification of this anxiety becomes too great, psychological protecting defenses come into operation and prevent the creator from proceeding. This even takes place in a small way on a daily basis in the course of the creative process. I have observed that my research subjects frequently have broken off their work day at a point when the material has gotten uncomfortably anxiety-provoking. After the work break and rest, they were able to return the next day to further creative work and, I observed, further unearthing of unconscious material. In all situations, long term or very short, "work block" occurs either because of the anxiety associated with threatening unconscious material or because of the ineffectiveness of the defenses and other adaptive processes; sometimes both factors operate.

Psychotherapy is helpful for alleviating work blocks of various types. Far from serving as a disapproving conscience or removing the motivation to create, psychotherapy may help complete a process that the creative person has already begun. The creative process involves attainment of partial insights, but these only relieve anxiety in part and may sometimes increase it. Gaining fuller insight and relief with the help of the therapist rekindles creativity. Be assured that motivation for future creative work is not lost through this resolution process; even after psychotherapy is completed and significant internal conflicts are resolved, other conflicts arise and struggles intrinsic to the human condition continue to fuel creative work.

Therapists hopefully never function as work enforcers, but Updike was correct about the reality-oriented nature of psychotherapy. Therapy should help one to give up grandiose and romantic notions about the importance of suffering, hyperindependent self-help, or even retreat into destructive self-indulgence. Not as a denier of instincts and pleasure as suggested by Updike's analogy to stoicism, nor on the other hand the champion of indulgent epicureanism, psychotherapy can facilitate both personal gratification and creative work. While pure gratification of instincts would not be realistic or healthy, effective psychotherapy should not result in loss of the ability to play, to love, or to imagine. The poet H. D. (Hilda Doolittle) said the following about her highly positive treatment experience with Sigmund Freud:

> We touched lightly on some of the more abstruse transcendental problems . . . but we related them to the familiar family-complex. Tendencies of thought and imagination, however, were not cut away, were not pruned even. My imagination wandered at will; my dreams were revealing. . . . Thoughts were things, to be collected, collated, analyzed, shelved or resolved.[9]

Psychotherapy and the Facilitation of Creativity

Finally, here is a creativity story like the one at the start of the book but with a different type of outcome.

> It is the same park in the same big city as you were in before. You are strolling again, and the people around you look the same. This time, however, you have just left your therapist's office and are thinking about what has transpired.
>
> During the last several sessions, you have been talking about your sister and some of the difficulties in your relationship with her. In the session just finished and in the one before, you reported the following dreams.
>
> In one, you descended to the bottom of the ocean and there found yourself in the midst of a large, unfamiliar city. It resembled remembered cities but was not recognizable. As you walked through, nevertheless, it then became unclear to you whether the city was real and even something that existed at all. Next, finding yourself standing in front of a pile of layered earth, you lifted up each layer, and after taking off two or three, you became concerned about having to take responsibility for what you were doing.
>
> In the second dream, a man with a long sword was standing in front of you. Several unidentifiable people were also nearby. Suddenly, the man's sword turned into a sheath of fire, and he started to set three of the nearest people ablaze, all the while saying that it could not hurt them. They burned up.
>
> The therapist asked for your thoughts and associations about these dreams and, for the first, you remembered saying that it reminded you initially of the city where you were brought up. Also, although you frequently had had dreams about descending to the bottom of the ocean and had heard that such dreams represented (laughter) a return to the mother's womb, the descent in this dream seemed differ-

ent in some way. For the second dream, the man seemed to be your father, and a series of incidents came to mind in which your father had hit and abused you while your mother stood by and did nothing. Then, suddenly another thought occurred to you: "Perhaps the man is you," you said to the therapist.

Together, you and the therapist on that afternoon had interpreted the dreams as follows. Both focused on the therapy. In the first, the descent to the bottom of the ocean represented your attempts to go to the bottom of your difficulties. Arriving there, you were afraid—as with the city—that you had come to something false and unreal. Continuing then to try to turn up layer after layer of your unacceptable thoughts and feelings, you had broken off at the point of feeling fearful that you would have to take responsibility for them. The second dream continued the theme. The swordsman/therapist had reassured you that enlightenment and expression of your feelings about the people in your life who were nearest and most important to you would not hurt either them or you. Instead, however, these people ended up burned and completely destroyed. You also reexperienced your mother's lack of intervention with your abusive father, and feared your own feelings of unbearable rage toward her.

Walking by the side of the park and turning these thoughts over, you feel both relieved and slightly uncomfortable, and eventually travel home. In your therapy of the following weeks, you try more than ever to face the fears about mentally destroying both mother and sister by the uncovering of your real feelings toward them.

Over the months to follow, you begin to feel increasingly better. Finding yourself to be more relaxed and better able to get along with women of all types, you also seem to notice more about the physical world around you. When you sit down to work now, or when you walk near the park, you feel a sense of increased energy and freedom.

This is the story of a successful sequence in psychotherapy. Although it does not focus directly on creative activity or creative thoughts, such a sequence should and does result in improved work ability and creative capacity. Knowing this, perhaps we can now close the book on questions of whether mental illness interferes with creativity, whether psychotherapy interferes with creativity, or whether psychotherapy actually facilitates the creative process. But after those questions, my story brings the issue one step further; for beyond the creativity of writers, artists, composers and scientists who have filled these pages, there is the matter of the facilitation of creativity in all the rest of us—the more ordinary persons of everyday life. This is the creativity in the lives of people who quietly go to their work in city buildings or who pursue their sustenance outdoors in fields, mountains, or streams. It is in the lives of people who cook in their kitchens, raise children, participate in sports, run businesses, preach religion, and work in government positions. There is, in other words, the matter of the creativity in everyday life which is also facilitated by psychotherapy.

This type of creativity involves *new and valuable* ways of resolving inner conflicts as well as carrying out everyday activities such as preparing food and wearing clothing. Beyond that, however, the creative principle of everyday life is in the processes of both personal and communal growth. Although individual growth is to some degree automatic in the maturational process, a good deal is motivated and deliberate. We decide to learn, develop our resources and change our personalities and lives; and, as we grow we both automatically and intentionally contribute to social and communal development as well. In fostering personal growth particularly, the psychotherapeutic process promotes creativity.

The process of psychotherapy, as I have attempted to demonstrate in another work[10] and will summarize here, is a mutual creative process involving both patient and therapist. Both collaborate in the process of creation of the patient's personality attributes and structure. In carrying this out, therapists use the specific types of creative processes—janusian, homospatial, and others such as one I have called *articulation*[11]—in order to foster patients' understanding and choice. The end product of the collaboration is a new personality integration,[12] and with it, patients become free of past controlling influences. They also come to accept aspects of their past experience which are consistent with their developing sense of self and identity. Patients become free of the past and at the same time more meaningfully attached to it. They also come to accept and prize connections with other people while they attain a measure of freedom and independence from them. The culmination is a true sense of personal responsibility and freedom consistent with personal growth and gratification.

The best psychotherapy is itself a creative process and one that also functions to enhance creativity of all types. This is true regardless of the degree of mental illness with which the patient begins. In the case of patients caught up in grandiose and self-defeating delusions such as the fictional account at this chapter's beginning, psychotherapy will hopefully lead away from the need for fantasies about great accomplishment and will instead be a guide toward self-acceptance. Another effect may be a more authentic expression of creativity: as psychosis resolves, the patient may become free to function creatively in areas such as interpersonal relationships, work, sports, or eventually even in the arts.

Emotional and mental illness is a decided hindrance to creativity for persons working in artistic, scientific, and other conventionally designated creative fields. It impedes janusian and homospatial processes and other creative operations and functions. For any persons in these fields, including those particular ones who have been accepted by society as outstanding, good psychotherapy should both alleviate any illness and enhance their creativity. The healing effect of psychotherapy consists of facilitating emotional growth, promoting independence, and developing psychological freedom, and all of these factors are intrinsic to creative functioning as well as to mental health. When persons are strongly motivated toward creativity, they will inevitably use the psychotherapeutic process to go beyond ordinary healthy functioning. Overshooting the mark, they even learn a little bit of what it is like to live like the angels.

NOTES

1. A Scientist Looks at Creativity

1. Albert Rothenberg and Bette Greenberg, *The Index of Scientific Writings on Creativity: Creative Men and Women* (Hamden, Conn.: Archon Books, 1974); idem, *The Index of Scientific Writings on Creativity: General, 1566–1974* (Hamden, Conn.: Archon Books, 1976).

2. The overall research design has been described in some detail in Albert Rothenberg, *The Emerging Goddess: The Creative Process in Art, Science, and Other Fields* (Chicago: University of Chicago Press, 1979). Experimental research has been described in the following: Albert Rothenberg, "Word Association and Creativity," *Psychological Reports* 33 (1973): 3–12; idem, "Opposite Responding as a Measure of Creativity," *Psychological Reports* 33 (1973): 15–18; idem, "Psychopathology and Creative Cognition: A Comparison of Hospitalized Patients, Nobel Laureates, and Controls," *Archives of General Psychiatry* 40 (1983): 937–42; idem, "Artistic Creation as Stimulated by Superimposed Versus Combined-Composite Visual Images," *Journal of Personality and Social Psychology* 50 (1986): 370–81; Albert Rothenberg and Robert S. Sobel, "Creation of Literary Metaphors as Stimulated by Superimposed Versus Separated Visual Images," *Journal of Mental Imagery* 4 (1980): 77–91; idem, "Effects of Shortened Exposure Time on the Creation of Literary Metaphors as Stimulated by Superimposed Versus Separated Visual Images," *Perceptual and Motor Skills* 53 (1981): 1007–9; Robert S. Sobel and Albert Rothenberg, "Artistic Creation as Stimulated by Superimposed Versus Separated Visual Images," *Journal of Personality and Social Psychology* 39 (1980): 953–61.

3. Rothenberg, *Emerging Goddess*, 135–206; 268–315.

4. On the importance of motivation in creativity, see also Teresa M. Amabile, *The Social Psychology of Creativity* (New York: Springer-Verlag, 1983).

5. See Albert Rothenberg, "Creativity and the Homospatial Process: Experimental Studies," *Psychiatric Clinics of North America* 2 (1988): 443–59. Specially designed visual stimuli produced creative responses among several groups of writer and artist subjects under controlled experimental conditions.

6. For some recent reviews of creativity and specific types of psychopathology, see Robert A. Prentky, *Creativity and Psychopathology: A Neurocog-*

nitive Perspective (New York: Praeger, 1980); Ruth L. Richards, "Relationships between Creativity and Psychopathology: An Evaluation and Interpretation of the Evidence," *Genetic Psychology Monographs* 103 (1981): 261–326. For an interesting earlier theoretical analysis, see also Lawrence S. Kubie, *Neurotic Distortion of the Creative Process* (Lawrence: University of Kansas Press, 1958).

2. The Creative Process in Art and Science

1. Albert Einstein, "Fundamental Ideas and Methods of Relativity Theory, Presented in Their Development," Einstein Archives, J. P. Morgan Library, New York. The passages quoted here are taken from a subsection entitled by Einstein, "The Fundamental Idea of General Relativity in Its Original Form," trans. Gerald Holton.

2. This story was told to him by his psychoanalyst, Rudolph Loewenstein, M.D.

3. Pulitzer Prize awardee and the designated Poet Laureate of the United States for the year 1988.

4. Joseph Conrad, "Preface to *Nostromo,*" *Nostromo* (London: Dent, 1918), ix.

5. Rudolf Arnheim, *Guernica: The Genesis of a Painting* (Berkeley and Los Angeles: University of California Press, 1962).

6. Henry Moore, interview by Donald Carroll, England; Center for Cassette Studies Tape 29818, Audio Text Cassettes, 8110 Webb Ave., North Hollywood, Calif., 91605.

7. Josef Albers, interview by Brian O'Doherty on National Educational Television, 1962; Center For Cassette Studies Tape 27605, Audio Text Cassettes, 8110 Webb Ave., North Hollywood, Calif., 91605.

8. Leonard Bernstein, *The Unanswered Question* (Cambridge: Harvard University Press, 1976), 41–42.

9. Jung also theorizes about the interchangeability and love of opposites, concepts that differ from the simultaneous opposition in the janusian process described here.

10. Arthur Koestler, *Act of Creation* (New York: Macmillan, 1964).

11. Reprinted by permission. Author's name withheld by request.

12. Henry Moore, "The Sculptor Speaks," *Listener* 18 (1937): 338.

13. See Jacques Hadamard, *The Psychology of Invention in the Mathematical Field* (Princeton: Princeton University Press, 1949), 142–43.

14. Ibid., 81.

15. Henri Poincaré, *Science and Method,* trans. F. Maitland (New York: Dover Press, 1952), 52–53.

16. Eleanor B. Pyle, "Fuller Albright's Inimitable Style," *Harvard Medical Alumni Bulletin* 56 (1982): 46.

3. Inspiration and the Creative Process

1. Ernst Kris, *Psychoanalytic Explorations in Art* (New York: International Universities Press, 1952).

2. See John Livingston Lowes, *The Road to Xanadu* (Boston: Houghton Mifflin, 1927).

3. Phyllis Bartlett, *Poems in Process* (Oxford: Oxford University Press, 1951).

4. This procedure, called "Poet's Own Poem Test," is described in Rothenberg, *Emerging Goddess*, 352–53. It consists of extracting both initially deleted and later added or substituted words from the manuscripts of poems in process and presenting both types (along with neutral "chaff" words) as stimuli to the poet himself or herself in a word association test procedure. Overall results were that poets manifested more anxiety in their responses to later added words from their own poems than they did to initially deleted ones.

5. Einstein, "Fundamental Ideas."

6. Gerald Holton, *Thematic Origins of Scientific Thought* (Cambridge: Harvard University Press, 1973), 133.

4. The Mystique of the Unconscious and Creativity

1. Plato, "Ion," in *The Dialogues*, ed. and trans. Benjamin Jowett (Oxford: Oxford University Press, 1924), 502.

2. Plato, "Phaedrus," in ibid.

3. Eduard von Hartmann, *Philosophie die Unbewussten* (Berlin, 1869).

4. Carl G. Jung, "On the Relation of Analytical Psychology to Poetic Art," in *The Collected Works of C. G. Jung*, ed. Herbert Read *et al.* Bollingen Series 20, no. 15 (Princeton: Princeton University Press, 1966), 84–108.

5. Walter B. Cannon, *The Wisdom of the Body* (New York: W. W. Norton, 1932); Charles S. Sherrington, *The Integrative Action of the Nervous System* (New Haven, Conn.: Yale University Press, 1906).

6. Kris, *Psychoanalytic Explorations.*

5. Psychosis and the Creation of Poetry

1. Poet suicides have included Hart Crane, Sylvia Plath, John Berryman, Randall Jarrell, Delmore Schwartz, and Anne Sexton. Theodore Roethke, Robert Lowell, and Lawrence Ferlinghetti had been repeatedly hospitalized; and Lowell, Berryman, and Schwartz were heavy alcohol abusers.

2. Traditionally, the schizophrenic psychosis, rather than other types such as manic-depressive illness, has been connected with poetry creation, and only schizophrenia will be considered in this chapter. See discussion in Chapter 12 for considerations regarding manic-depressive illness and creativity.

3. Authorship of the writings quoted in this chapter is withheld to preserve confidentiality.

4. Italics in original.

6. Self-destruction and Self-creation

1. William B. Yeats, "Preliminary Poem," in *Collected Works in Verse and Prose*, vol. 2 (London: Chapman and Hall, 1908).

2. Sylvia Plath, "Edge" (1962), in *The Collected Poems* (New York: Harper and Row, 1981) 272–3.

3. Sylvia Plath, "The Fearful" (1962), in *ibid*, 256.

4. Sylvia Plath, "The Detective" (1962), in *ibid*, 208–9.

5. See A. Alvarez, *The Savage God: A Study of Suicide* (New York: Random House, 1972).

7. The Perils of Psychoanalyzing (or Scandalizing) Emily Dickinson

1. Sigmund Freud, "Dostoyevsky and Parricide" (1928), in *The Standard Edition of the Complete Psychological Works of Sigmund Freud*, vol. 15, ed. James Strachey (London: Hogarth Press, 1961), 175–98.

2. John Cody, *After Great Pain: The Inner Life of Emily Dickinson* (Cambridge: Belknap Press, 1971).

3. Ibid., 292–93.

4. Ibid., 142.

5. Emily Dickinson, *The Poems of Emily Dickinson*, ed. Thomas H. Johnson (Cambridge: Belknap Press, 1955), 682.

6. *The Oxford English Dictionary*, vol. 2 (Oxford: Clarendon Press, 1978), 485–6.

7. *Oxford English Dictionary*, vol. 8 (1970), 176.

8. Dickinson, *Poems*, 718.

9. *Noah Webster's An American Dictionary of the English Language*, 1st ed. (Amherst, Mass.: J. S. and C. Adams, 1844).

10. S. P. Rosenbaum, *A Concordance to the Poems of Emily Dickinson* (Ithaca: Cornell University Press, 1964).

11. The poem was constructed at the time of this death, and, even if the poem was not actually sent, the niece's death would certainly have had an important impact on Dickinson. Susan was her closest friend and confidant at that time. Cody suggests that Susan was also a maternal figure for the poet.

12. John E. Walsh, *The Hidden Life of Emily Dickinson* (New York: Simon and Schuster, 1971).

13. Ibid., 108.

8. The Psychosis and Triumph of August Strindberg

1. Eugene G. O'Neill, "Strindberg and Our Theatre," in *O'Neill and His Plays*, ed. Oscar Cargill, N. Bryllion Fagin, and William J. Fisher (New York: New York University Press, 1961), 108–9.

2. August Strindberg, *Inferno, Alone and Other Writings*, ed. and trans. Evert Sprinchorn (Garden City, N.Y.: Doubleday, 1968).

3. Strindberg's complete works in Swedish have been collected into 55 volumes under the title *Samlade Skrifter*, ed. John Landquist (Stockholm, 1912–1919). References to recent English translations can be found in Michael Meyer, *Strindberg: A Biography* (New York: Random House, 1985). Plays cited in this chapter (except *The Father*) may be found in the following English translations: *Strindberg's One-Act Plays*, trans. Arvid Paulson (New York: Washington Square Press, 1969); *Selected Plays/August Strindberg*, ed. and

trans. Evert Sprinchorn (Minneapolis: University of Minnesota Press, 1985); *Plays From the Cynical Life by August Strindberg,* trans. Walter Johnson (Seattle: University of Washington Press, 1983); *Eight Expressionist Plays,* trans. Arvid Paulson (New York: New York University Press, 1972); *Dramas of Testimony by August Strindberg,* trans. Walter Johnson (Seattle: University of Washington Press, 1975).

4. August Strindberg, *The Father* (1887), in *Six Plays of Strindberg,* trans. Elizabeth Sprigge (Garden City, N.Y.: Doubleday Anchor, 1955).

5. August Strindberg, *The People of Hemsö* (1887), trans. E. H. Schubert (London: J. Cape, 1959); also, idem, *The Natives of Hemsö,* trans. Arvid Paulson (New York: Paul E. Erikson, 1965).

6. August Strindberg, *The Confessions of a Fool* (1887), trans. E. Schleussner (Boston: Small, Maynard, 1913).

7. Strindberg, *Father,* 57.

8. Theodore Lidz, "August Strindberg: A Study of the Relationship between His Creativity and Schizophrenia," *International Journal of Psycho-Analysis* 45 (1964): 399–406.

9. August Strindberg, *Son of a Servant* (1886), trans. C. Field (London: Rider and Son, 1913), 142–43.

10. Strindberg, *Father,* 56.

9. Homosexuality and Creativity

1. Of course, hermaphroditism, the possession of both male and female sexual organs, is not the same as homosexuality (at one time there was thought to be a connection through dual gonadal hormones), but the type of experience metaphorized in the Greek myth applies to the discussion of insight and creativity in this chapter. For a discussion of the Teiresian myth and insight in general, see also Samuel Abrams, "Insight: The Teiresian Gift," *Psychoanalytic Study of the Child* 36 (1981): 251–70.

2. For an attempt at extensive documentation of eminent persons of the past who were homosexuals, see Noel I. Garde, *Jonathan to Gide: The Homosexual in History* (New York: Vantage Press, 1964). Although Garde uses somewhat flimsy evidence in many cases, the information he presents provides a good beginning for a more definitive historical study.

3. Tennessee Williams, *Memoirs* (Garden City, N.Y.: Doubleday, 1975), 51.

4. See Janine Chasseguet-Smirgel, *Creativity and Perversion* (New York: W. W. Norton, 1984), 89ff.

5. George Domino, "Homosexuality and Creativity," *Journal of Homosexuality* 2 (1977): 261–67; Williams, *Memoirs.*

6. For a recent psychoanalytic study of Michelangelo's homosexuality, see Jerome Oremland, *Michelangelo's Sistine Ceiling: A Psychoanalytic Study of Creativity* (Madison, Conn.: International Universities Press, 1989).

7. For the full poem, see Rothenberg, *Emerging Goddess,* 16.

8. For the detailed discussion of the use of the janusian and homospatial processes to unearth unconscious material regarding the poet's mother, see ibid., 15ff.

10. The Muse in the Bottle

1. Stephen B. Oates, *William Faulkner: The Man and the Artist* (New York: Harper and Row, 1987), 162.

2. Ibid., 257.

3. Quoted in *Lincoln and the Civil War,* ed. Courtlandt Canby (New York: Dell, 1958), 106, from the original: Benjamin P. Thomas, *Abraham Lincoln* (New York: Knopf, 1952).

4. A high incidence of alcoholism has been reported among Finnish writers (Anja Koski-Jännes, "Alcohol and Literary Creativity: Finnish Experience," *Alkoholipolitiikka* 48 (1983): 263–74). However, it is not clear from this report whether all of the writers tallied were at the same level of creativity.

5. Roe did an extensive study of alcoholism in New York City painters during the 1940s and found widespread alcohol use but only a small incidence of heavy abuse (Anne Roe, "Alcohol and Creative Work," *Quarterly Journal of Studies on Alcohol* 6 (1946): 415–67). Data regarding alcoholism in scientists have generally not been collected.

6. F. Scott Fitzgerald and John Cheever wrote "Babylon Revisited" and "The Sorrows of Gin," respectively, but these were not especially important works. Other works about alcoholism, by both alcoholic and nonalcoholic authors, are "Big Blonde" by Dorothy Parker; *Lost Weekend* by Charles Jackson; *The Victim* by Saul Bellow; and the recent highly successful *Ironweed* by William Kennedy. For more information on this subject, see Thomas B. Gilmore, *Equivocal Spirits: Alcoholism and Drinking in Twentieth-Century Literature* (Chapel Hill: University of North Carolina Press, 1987). For an interesting personal account, see Donald Newlove, *Those Drinking Days* (New York: McGraw-Hill, 1981).

7. Experimental investigations of the influence of alcohol on creative thinking have yielded equivocal results. A study of the influence of different amounts of alcohol on results of the Torrance Tests of Creative Thinking showed little variation and effect, except that individuals who thought they had received alcohol evaluated their own creative performances more highly than those who believed they had not received any (Alan R. Lang, Laurie Verret, and Carolyn Watt, "Drinking and Creativity: Objective and Subjective Effects," *Addictive Behaviors* 9 (1984): 395–99). Experimental studies done in Finland have reported both increase and nonreduction of creativity with the use of alcohol in some instances, but the criteria and measures of creativity are very variable or unclear (Anja Koski-Jännes, "Juoda ja/Vai Luoda?" *Alkoholipolitiikka* 48 (1983): 68–78).

8. André Le Vot, *F. Scott Fitzgerald: A Biography* (Garden City, N.Y.: Doubleday, 1983), 117.

9. Ring Lardner, Jr., *The Lardners: My Family Remembered* (New York: Harper and Row, 1976), 165.

10. Ian Hamilton, *Robert Lowell: A Biography* (New York: Random House, 1983), 389.

11. Jeffrey Meyers, *Hemingway: A Biography* (New York: Harper and Row, 1985), 426

12. Robert H. Davis and Arthur B. Maurice, *The Caliph of Bagdad: Being Arabian Nights. Flashes of the Life, Letters and Work of O. Henry* (New York: D. Appleton, 1931), 361.

13. Douglas Day, *Malcolm Lowry: A Biography* (New York: Oxford University Press, 1973), 30.

14. Elizabeth Nowell, *Thomas Wolfe: A Biography* (Garden City, N.Y.: Doubleday, 1960), 109.

15. Matthew J. Bruccoli, *"An Artist Is His Own Fault." John O'Hara on Writers and Writing* (Carbondale: Southern Illinois University Press, 1977), 181–82.

16. Robin Room, "'A Reverence for Strong Drink': The Lost Generation and the Elevation of Alcohol in American Culture," *Journal of Studies on Alcohol* 45 (1984): 540–46.

17. Scott Donaldson, *John Cheever: A Biography* (New York: Random House, 1988).

18. See the discussion of Cheever's contact with psychiatrists in ibid., 228–30, 249–51.

19. Susan Cheever, *Home Before Dark* (Boston: Houghton Mifflin, 1984), 191.

20. Rothenberg, *Emerging Goddess*, 35ff.

21. Was this also a guilty shifting away from the symbolic brother Nailles and a turning to represent attempted murder of himself as the younger man or younger brother? Or was it a shift from the idea of killing a symbolic father to killing a son—again himself? In light of the way in which he concomitantly turned to a virtual suicidal path in his drinking at that time, these are reasonable speculations.

22. Of course, the conflict over homosexual feelings could have something to do with the content of the writing, as I indicated in the previous chapter. His novel *Falconer* describes many homosexual relationships in the prison and, following the writing of this novel, Cheever himself was able to engage more actively in homosexual relationships.

23. Although the psychodynamics are detailed here in the case of alcoholism in writers, factors of helplessness and inability to communicate with parents, competition and acquiescence with a same-sex parent, and the other general matters very likely also apply to alcoholism in creative visual artists, scientists, and others.

24. Oates, *Faulkner*, 138.

11. Eugene O'Neill's Creation of The Iceman Cometh

1. Eugene G. O'Neill, "The Iceman Cometh," in *The Plays of Eugene O'Neill* (New York: Random House, 1954).

2. Cyrus Day, "The Iceman and the Bridegroom," *Modern Drama* 1 (1958): 3–9.

3. Eugene G. O'Neill, *More Stately Mansions* (New Haven, Conn.: Yale University Press, 1964).

4. Donald W. Goodwin, "The Alcoholism of Eugene O'Neill," *Journal of the American Medical Association* 216 (1971): 99–104.

5. Arthur Gelb and Barbara Gelb, *O'Neill* (New York: Harper and Brothers, 1960).

6. Eugene G. O'Neill, "Tomorrow," *The Seven Arts* 2 (1917): 147–70.

7. Told to his friend George Jean Nathan, O'Neill's statement is quoted in Louis Schaeffer, *O'Neill: Son and Playwright* (Boston: Little Brown, 1968), 211. However, Schaeffer raises doubts about the factual basis of O'Neill's remarks and places O'Neill's suicide attempt at a different time. Gelb and Gelb in *O'Neill* report the O'Neill suicide attempt and the Bythe suicide as occurring in the same year and state that O'Neill and Bythe were roommates, as suggested in "Tomorrow." Whatever the facts of the matter, O'Neill's account in "Tomorrow" seems thinly fictional and points to his intense emotional entanglement with Jimmy and his suicide. His comment on the "Tomorrow" story, quoted by Schaeffer, is as follows: "As a personal record of a section of my life and the memory of a dear personal friend *whose tragic end is there explained,* I hold it in high affection. As writing, it leaves a lot to be desired" (214, italics mine).

8. Ralph Sanborn and Barrett H. Clark, *A Bibliography of the Works of Eugene O'Neill* (New York: Random House, 1931), 15.

9. Sigmund Freud, "The Psychopathology of Everyday Life" (1901), in *The Standard Edition of the Complete Psychological Works of Sigmund Freud*, vol. 6, ed. James Strachey (London: Hogarth Press, 1960).

10. Even the alternative methodologies employed here such as the study of Strindberg's works in sequence and the retrospective interviews of John Cheever were not as focused on the creative process of a specific work.

11. O'Neill, *More Stately Mansions*, 180.

12. I. Roxon-Ropschitz, "The Act of Deleting and Other Findings in Writings of Neurotics," *Psychiatry* 9 (1946): 117–21.

13. Sigmund Freud, "Negation" (1925), in *The Standard Edition of the Complete Psychological Works of Sigmund Freud*, vol. 19, ed. James Strachey (London: Hogarth Press, 1961), 235–42.

14. Eugene G. O'Neill, *Long Day's Journey Into Night* (New Haven, Conn.: Yale University Press, 1955).

15. Ibid., dedication page.

12. Creativity and Mental Illness

1. Quoted by Seneca, *Tranquillity of Mind*, trans. W. B. Langsdorf (New York: G. P. Putnam's Sons, 1900), 90–91.

2. John Dryden, "Absalom and Achitophel," *The Norton Anthology of Poetry,* ed. Alexander W. Allison *et al.* (New York: W. W. Norton, 1983), 360.

3. Kay R. Jamison, "Mood Disorders and Patterns of Creativity in British Writers and Artists," *Psychiatry* 52 (1989): 125–34. Also available in Frederick G. Goodwin and Kay R. Jamison, *Manic Depressive Illness*, in press.

4. Nancy C. Andreasen and Ira D. Glick, "Bipolar Affective Disorder and Creativity: Implications and Clinical Management," *Comprehensive Psychiatry* 29 (1988): 207–17; Nancy C. Andreasen, "Creativity and Mental Illness: Prevalence Rates in Writers and Their First Degree Relatives," *American Journal of Psychiatry* 144 (1987): 1288–92; Nancy C. Andreasen and Arthur Canter, "The

Creative Writer: Psychiatric Symptoms and Family History," *Comprehensive Psychiatry* 15 (1974): 123–31.

5. Andreasen herself, along with associates, has carried out an empirical assessment of the secondary source family history diagnostic method and concluded that it is a lot less reliable than direct interviewing of family members (Nancy Andreasen *et al.*, "The Family History Method Using Diagnostic Criteria: Reliability and Validity," *Archives of General Psychiatry* 34 (1977): 1229–35). For reported differences in results using secondary source methods see also George Winokur, Ming T. Tsuang, and Raymond R. Crowe, "The Iowa 500: Affective Disorder in the Relatives of Manic and Depressed Patients," *American Journal of Psychiatry* 139 (1982): 209–12.

6. Jamison attempts to account for the low rate of treatment among visual artists on the basis of a reluctance to seek verbal help. She also suggests that biographers are a less creative "comparison group" with no history of mood swings or elated states. In the first instance, the matter of anyone's reluctance to seek help is a factor that sheds doubt on the adequacy of Jamison's sampling procedure, as discussed here. Also, there is little evidence that visual artists are, in fact, less frequent users of psychiatric treatment. In the second instance, there is little reason to consider the biographers in her sample any less creative than others (prizes alone being the basis of the selection criteria), and the negative result does not make them a comparison group but rather constitutes a contradictory finding.

7. Abraham H. Maslow, *Religions, Values, and Peak Experiences* (Columbus: Ohio State University Press, 1964).

8. Albert Rothenberg and Paul E. Burkhardt, "Difference in Response Time of Creative Persons and Patients with Depressive and Schizophrenic Disorders," *Psychological Reports* 54 (1984): 711–17.

9. Albert Rothenberg, *The Creative Process of Psychotherapy* (New York: W. W. Norton, 1988).

10. Albert Rothenberg and Carl R. Hausman, *The Creativity Question* (Durham, N.C.: Duke University Press, 1976); Albert Rothenberg, "The Iceman Changeth: Toward an Empirical Approach to Creativity," *Journal of the American Psychoanalytic Association* 17 (1969): 549–607.

11. Virgil, *The Aeneid*, trans. Robert Fitzgerald (New York: Random House, 1983).

12. Robert Graves, *The Greek Myths*, vol. 2 (Harmondsworth, Middlesex: Penguin Books, 1955), 100ff.

13. Donald M. Kaplan, "Homosexuality and American Theater: A Psychoanalytic Comment," *Tulane Drama Review* 9 (1965): 25–55.

14. Isaac Asimov, *Asimov's Biographical Encyclopedia of Science and Technology* (Garden City, N.Y.: Doubleday, 1972), 83–86.

15. See the discussion of art and the mentally ill in R. W. Pickford, "Art and Psychopathology," in *Psychology and the Arts*, ed. David O'Hare (Sussex, N.J.: Harvester Press, 1981).

16. Francis Galton, *Hereditary Genius: An Inquiry into Its Laws and Consequences* (London: Macmillan, 1869).

17. Victor Goertzel and Mildred G. Goertzel, *Cradles of Eminence* (Boston: Little, Brown, 1962).

18. Donald W. Goodwin, *Alcohol and the Writer* (Kansas City, Mo.: Andrews and McMeel, 1988).

19. This conception is involved in the novel title, *The Sun Also Rises*. The use of the word *also* brings to mind simultaneously the opposite idea that the sun sets or else that it does not rise.

20. Adapted from "How long can my hands be a bandage to his hurt?" (Sylvia Plath, "Three Women," in *The Collected Poems*, 185.

21. Rothenberg, *Emerging Goddess*.

13. Psychotherapy and Creativity

1. James Agee, *Letters of James Agee to Father Flye* (New York: George Braziller, 1962), 127.

2. Arthur Miller, *Time Bends: A Life* (New York: Grove Press, 1987), 320.

3. Williams, *Memoirs*.

4. Norman Sherry, *The Life of Graham Greene, Vol. 1: 1904–1939* (New York: Viking Press, 1989).

5. Jungian therapy has sometimes seemed to have particular appeal for artists and writers because such therapy focuses on drawings and mythic themes.

6. See discussion of Cheever's contacts with Drs. Silverberg and Hayes in Donaldson, *John Cheever*, 228–30, 249–51.

7. Williams, *Memoirs*, 207.

8. Mary Hemingway, *How it Was* (New York: Knopf, 1976).

9. H. D. (Hilda Doolittle), *Tribute to Freud* (New York: Pantheon Books, 1956), 18.

11. Albert Rothenberg, "Creativity, Articulation and Psychotherapy," *Journal of the American Academy of Psychoanalysis* 2 (1983): 55–85; see also idem, *Creative Process*.

12. This process should not be confused with those using artistic products as a therapeutic tool such as in art and poetry therapy. These are particular forms of psychotherapy which, when performed well, will also facilitate the patient's self-creation. Using art products or working in an artistic field alone does not necessarily facilitate the type of creativity stipulated here.

INDEX

A.E. *See* Russell, George William
Abrams, Samuel, 185 n.1
Absalom, Absalom (Faulkner), 131
Abstract thinking, 59, 64, 155, 160
Addiction, 116, 145, 147. *See also*
  Substance abuse
Aeneas, 155
Aeschylus, 104–5
Affective illness, 85, 150–53, 161, 173;
  and creativity, studies of, 150–53. *See*
  also Manic-depressive illness
After Great Pain (Cody), 81–91
Agee, James, 115, 119, 161, 169, 170,
  172–73, 190 n.1
Agoraphobia, 85
Albee, Edward, 53, 104, 107, 108, 156
Albers, Josef, 19, 182 n.7
Albright, Fuller, 31
Alcoholics Anonymous, 122–23
Alcoholism: and creative process, influ-
  ence on, 115–32, 137–40, 143–48, 158;
  cultural and ethnic factors in, 118–19;
  as degenerative insanity, 149; genetic
  factors in, 115, 130; and masculine
  image, 118–19; and Nobel laureates,
  115, 159; as topic in literature, 116,
  134–37, 144–45, 157; and visual art-
  ists, 115; and writers, 115, 159, 173;
  and writing, connections with, 129–32,
  148
Alexander, Samuel, 38
Alexander the Great, 155
Alfred, William, 171
Algren, Nelson, 157
Alighieri, Dante, 158
Alvarez, A., 184 n.5
Amabile, Teresa M., 181 n.4
Ambivalence, 95, 109, 130, 163
American Academy of Arts and Letters, 7

American Book Award, 7. *See also*
  National Book Award
Amphetamines, 73
Anderson, Maxwell, 18
Anderson, Quentin (son of Maxwell), 18
Andreasen, Nancy C., 150–53, 188 n.4,
  189 n.5
Antitheses. *See* Opposites
Aquinas, Saint Thomas, 158
Aristotle, 38, 149, 158
Arnheim, Rudolph, 182 n.5
Art, 52–53, 68–70, 75–76, 154, 162, 164
  (*see also under specific types*)
Articulation process, 179
Art therapy, 157, 190 n.12
Asimov, Isaac, 189 n.14
Astrophysics, 28
Athena, Pallas, 3
Auden, W. H., 104
Austen, Jane, 158

Bach, Johann Sebastian, 158
Balzac, Honoré de, 99
Bartlett, Phyllis, 40, 183 n.3
Baudelaire, Charles Pierre, 6, 115
Beat authors, 157
Beckett, Samuel, 53, 93
Beethoven, Ludwig von, 28, 39, 92, 104
Behan, Brendan, 119
Bellow, Saul, 115, 159, 186 n.6
Bergson, Henri-Louis, 38
Bernstein, Leonard, 19, 182 n.8
Berryman, John, 183 n.1
Biography, 80, 90–91, 150, 151–53, 159.
  See also Psychobiography
Bipolar disorder. *See* Manic-depressive
  illness
Bisexuality, 53, 104–7, 109, 113, 130
Bishop, Elizabeth, 104

191

Albert Rothenberg, M.D., has carried out both clinical and experimental research on the creative process for over twenty-five years as Principal Investigator of the project entitled "Studies in the Creative Process." Results of this research have been published in both professional and popular journals and magazines. His books include: *The Emerging Goddess: The Creative Process in Art, Science, and Other Fields* (chosen by *Psychology Today* as a Best Behavioral Science Book of 1979) and *The Creative Process of Psychotherapy.* He currently resides with his wife, Dr. Julia J. Rothenberg, in Stockbridge, Massachusetts, where he is Director of Research at the Austen Riggs Center, and he holds the position of Clinical Professor of Psychiatry at Harvard Medical School (Cambridge Hospital).

Creativity and Madness

Designed by Ann Walston.

Composed by The Composing Room of Michigan, Inc.
in Aster text and display.

Printed by The Maple Press Company
on 50-lb. MV Eggshell Cream,
and bound in Joanna Arrestox and G. S. B. Book Cloth
with James River Papan ESP endsheets.